SIMPLY AIX

SIMPLY AIX 4.3

Second Edition

Casey Cannon, Scott Trent, and Carolyn Jones

Prentice Hall PTR
Upper Saddle River, New Jersey 07458
http://www.phptr.com

Library of Congress Cataloging-in-Publication Data

Cannon, Casey.
    Simply AIX 4.3 / by Casey Cannon, Scott Trent, and Carolyn Jones.
  --2nd ed.
        p.   cm.
    Includes index.
    ISBN 0-13-021344-6 (alk. paper)
    1. AIX (Computer file) 2. Operating systems (Computers)
  I. Trent, Scott. II. Jones, Carolyn. III. Title.
  QA76.76.063C3725 1999
  005.4'469--dc21   99-11803
                                                        CIP

Editorial/Production Supervision: Joan L. McNamara
Acquisitions Editor: Greg Doench
Marketing Manager: Kaylie Smith
Editorial Assistant: Mary Treacy
Cover Design Director: Jerry Votta
Cover Designer: Talar Agasyan
Manufacturing Manager: Alexis R. Heydt
Compositor/Production Services: Pine Tree Composition, Inc.

© 1997, 1999 by Prentice Hall PTR
Prentice-Hall, Inc.
Upper Saddle River, New Jersey 07458

Prentice Hall books are widely used by corporations and government agencies for training, marketing, and resale. The publisher offers discounts on this book when ordered in bulk quantities. For more information, contact:

Corporate Sales Department, Prentice Hall PTR, One Lake Street, Upper Saddle River, NJ 07458
Phone: 800-382-3419; Fax: 201-236-7141; email: corpsales@prenhall.com

Printed in the United States of America
10 9 8 7 6 5 4 3 2

ISBN: 0-13-021344-6

Prentice-Hall International (UK) Limited, *London*
Prentice-Hall of Australia Pty. Limited, *Sydney*
Prentice-Hall Canada Inc., *Toronto*
Prentice-Hall Hispanoamericana, S.A., *Mexico*
Prentice-Hall of India Private Limited, *New Delhi*
Prentice-Hall of Japan, Inc., *Tokyo*
Simon & Schuster Asia Pte. Ltd., *Singapore*
Editora Prentice-Hall do Brasil, Ltda., *Rio de Janeiro*

Trademarks

3Com is a trademark of 3Com Corporation.

AFS is a trademark of Transarc Corporation.

AIX is a trademark of International Business Machines Corporation.

AIX 3278/79 Emulation/6000 is a trademark of International Business Machines Corporation.

AIX/370 is a trademark of International Business Machines Corporation.

AIX/6000 is a trademark of International Business Machines Corporation.

AIX InfoCrafter/6000 is a trademark of International Business Machines Corporation.

AIXwindows is a trademark of International Business Machines Corporation.

AIXwindows Interface Composer/6000 is a trademark of International Business Machines Corporation.

GL is a trademark of Silicon Graphics, Inc.

Gradient is a trademark of Gradient Technologies, Inc.

graPHIGS is a trademark of International Business Machines Corporation.

HP is a trademark of Hewlett-Packard Company.

HP-UX is a trademark of Hewlett-Packard Company.

IBM is a registered trademark of International Business Machines Corporation.

INed is a trademark of INTERACTIVE Systems Corporation.

InfoCrafter is a trademark of International Business Machines Corporation.

InfoExplorer is a trademark of International Business Machines Corporation.

Intel is a trademark of Intel Corporation.

Lotus is a trademark of Lotus Development Corporation.

Macintosh is a trademark of Apple Computer Corp.

Motif is a trademark of Open Software Foundation, Inc.

Motorola is a trademark of Motorola, Inc.

MS-DOS is a trademark of Microsoft Corporation.

NetLS is a trademark of Apollo Computer, Inc.

NetView is a trademark of International Business Machines Corporation.

NetView/6000 is a trademark of International Business Machines Corporation.

NetWare is a trademark of Novell Corporation.

NFS is a trademark of Sun Microsystems, Inc.

Novell is a trademark of Novell Corporation.

OpenDoc is a trademark of Apple Computer Corp.

OpenGL is a trademark of Silicon Graphics, Inc.

Open Software Foundation is a trademark of Open Software Foundation, Inc.

OS/2 is a trademark of International Business Machines Corporation.

OSF is a trademark of Open Software Foundation, Inc.

OSF/Motif is a trademark of Open Software Foundation, Inc.

PostScript is a trademark of Adobe Systems Incorporated.

POWER Architecture is a trademark of International Business Machines Corporation.

PowerOpen is a trademark of International Business Machines Corporation.

PowerPC is a trademark of International Business Machines Corporation.

PowerPC Architecture is a trademark of International Business Machines Corporation.

POWERserver is a trademark of International Business Machines Corporation.

POWERstation is a trademark of International Business Machines Corporation.

PS/2 is a trademark of International Business Machines Corporation.

RISC System/6000 is a trademark of International Business Machines Corporation.

RS/6000 is a trademark of International Business Machines Corporation.

Sun is a trademark of Sun Microsystems, Inc.

Sun OS is a trademark of Sun Microsystems, Inc.

ThinkPad is a trademark of International Business Machines Corporation.

ToolTalk is a trademark of Sun Microsystems, Inc.

Transarc is a trademark of Transarc Corporation.

Ultimedia is a trademark of International Business Machines Corporation.

UNIX is a registered trademark in the United States and other countries, licensed exclusively through X/Open Company Limited.

Windows is a trademark of Microsoft Corporation.

Windows NT is a trademark of Microsoft Corporation.

X11 is a trademark of Massachusetts Institute of Technology.

X.desktop is a trademark of IXI Limited.

X/Open is a trademark of X/Open Company Limited.

X Window System is a trademark of Massachusetts Institute of Technology.

Contents

Preface

AIX 4.3 provides a full multivendor package in terms of scalability, availability, e-business and network computing, security, enhanced systems and network management, better usability, and unmatched serviceability. And that's not just the IBMer in us talking. According to a VARbusiness industry survey of UNIX and NT operating systems, IBM's AIX received top marks in the categories resellers say matter most: reliability, ease of configuration, ease of installation (tied for first), security, technical support, scalability (tied for first), and management capabilities.

Independent software vendors who develop on AIX are also voicing their approval of AIX 4.3's binary compatibility with all previous AIX Version 4 releases. Binary compatibility is a big reason why independent software vendors have already ported over 2000 applications to AIX 4.3.

In addition, IBM's AIX has led the way for UNIX operating systems with a number of firsts, such as being the first operating system in a 64-bit environment to be branded UNIX 98 by the Open Group, the first UNIX operating system in a 64-bit environment to receive E3/F-C2 security certification, and the first server operating system with Virtual Private Network certification.

Who Should Use This Book?

Our goal in writing this book is to help our customers enjoy AIX 4.3 as much as we do! We have written about topics that will be useful to all users, including system administrators, programmers, and end users. Cheat sheets, useful tables, technical tidbits, an easy, fun, plain English, writing style, and pertinent, straightforward information make this book useful to novices as well as the seasoned UNIX user.

Use this book to find out about AIX 4.3; use this book to administer your AIX 4.3 network; use this book to manage your AIX PowerPC. We're not kidding—whether you've tunneled around AIX or have only recently mastered MS-DOS, we'll familiarize you with the basics and amaze you with the functionality of an industrial-strength operating environment.

This book is designed for both new users and more advanced users. A hot pepper icon within chapters indicates that the level of information in the chapter is hot stuff and looks like the following:

The hot pepper icon is used to mark sections that are more advanced. Power users (gurus) may want to read these sections first. New users can become gurus after learning these sections.

How This Book Is Organized

The overview explains the history of AIX, details the information provided in each chapter, and gives you a general introduction to the AIX environment.

Chapter 1, "Customizing Your Environment," shows you how to use the Common Desktop Environment (CDE) tools and launchpad to make yourself feel right at home.

Chapter 2, "Using AIX," teaches you AIX commands, file system structure, shell usage, and additional tricks that will make you a genuine AIX user.

Chapter 3, "I Know Windows/DOS, What's AIX?" compares and contrasts the Windows/DOS and AIX worlds. It gives you the inside information on running Windows on AIX.

Chapter 4, "Editors," gives you an overview and cheat sheets for your favorite AIX editor.

Chapter 5, "Installing AIX," provides easy, fast GUI (graphical menu) tools and instructions for what is often perceived as the most difficult part of a UNIX operating system—getting it up and running.

Chapter 6, "Setting Up Peripherals," tells you how to set up printers, CD-ROM drives, and other devices you'd like to attach to your system.

Chapter 7, "Communicating with the World," describes what you need to know to survive the alphabet soup of AIX-supported communication protocols, including the use of AIX Net Browsers on the Internet.

Chapter 8, "SMIT Happens! Administering AIX," enables you to manage, do simple or complex tasks, and administer your system and/or any other systems on your network using either GUI applications or command line combinations.

Chapter 9, "AIX Speaks Your Language: Internationalization," tells you how to get AIX to speak your language. Look in this chapter for information on how to communicate globally in a different language.

Chapter 10, "All the Help You Need," describes how to use InfoExplorer, the AIX on-line hypertext information library (50,000 pages on-line); AIX developer help available through the Internet; 1-800 numbers and fax sheets; and URL addresses and descriptions for IBM Internet sites.

Chapter 11, Gathering Up the Pieces," wraps up our journey into AIX with information on 64-bit AIX, Year 2000 Issues, performance tools, file system management, the AIX development environment, security, and special tools that help you learn how to resolve common AIX problems, as well as obtain the latest bug fixes from the Internet.

Chapter 12, "Kick Start Your Enterprise," describes the scalable compatible line of RISC systems that can help you develop and maintain a competitive advantage. A server is more than just the sum of its parts and every component is integral to smooth operation. Downtime at any point, whether a result of a power supply failure, a software application failure or scheduled maintenance, can slow down, even shut down, your business. Customers are left waiting, your employees can't perform their jobs, and your business can't keep up. The RS/6000 hardware platform provides a solid foundation for your enterprise, enabling 86,400-second-a-day, 1440-minute-a-day, 24-hour-a-day business system up-time.

Exciting AIX Firsts

AIX 4.3—The first 64-bit operating system certified at the E3/F-C2 level!

The need for security is no longer restricted to governments. With the explosion of Internet technology and e-business, commercial users are now increasingly concerned with security issues and they frequently demand that their systems are certified to be just as secure as the systems used by government and defense.

To meet this requirement, AIX version 4.3 has been re-evaluated and re-certified at the E3/F-C2 security level with a strength of mechanisms "High," according to European Information Technology Security Evaluation Criteria (ITSEC).

It represents a well-defined level of security criteria in the implementation of the security functions and mechanisms of an information technology system. This indicates a high level of security function regardless of the specific requirements of the customer.

AIX is the only UNIX operating system that supports a 64-bit operating environment being evaluated and certified at the E3/F-C2 level.

This evaluation level is achieved through a rigorous inspection of the AIX source code and testing by an independent auditing organization, Industrieanlagen-Betriesgesellschaft (IABG), and certified by the German government authority, Bundesamt fuer Sicherheit Informationstechnik (BSI). BSI is the German certification authority. IBM has been officially awarded the AIX 4.3 E3/F-C2 certificate on May 6, 1998. The certificate is issued in Germany, but as the evaluation was done using internationally accepted standards and on the basis of recognition agreements, it is recognized throughout all Europe and by commercial customers in the United States, Canada, and Australia.

Acknowledgments

We would like to thank our families for putting up with us while we worked on this book night and day. We promise to do more around the house now.

Many thanks to Team AIX for their technical help: Carlos Ayala, Katie Barrett, Raymond Bauer, Davin Bentti, Rick Bowers, Ed Bradford, Gena Brown, Nick Camillone, Faye Dedrick, Doug Woestendiek, Randy Greenberg, Carolyn Greene, Enrique Gomez, Jesse Haug, George Icossipentarhos, Dennis Lee, Tracey Porter, Barbara Rignew, Frank Rojas, Melanie Rose, Jim Shaffer, Marvin Toungate, I-Hsing Tsao, Ed Williams, Becky Wood, and Juan Zalles. Also, Niels Christiansen and John Sullivan deserve thanks for suggesting the title, "Simply AIX."

We are deeply indebted to the folks we worked with at Prentice Hall and the people we worked with at Pine Tree Composition—Greg Doench, Mary Treacy, Joan L. McNamara, Daniel Boilard, and Patty Donovan—for making this book the polished product it is today.

Foreword by Donna Van Fleet, Vice President of AIX Development

We've had a guiding vision that AIX would be a tool to make your work easier—not a tool that makes work for you. To that end, we have designed AIX to be not just easy, but even intuitive for the novice while at the same time, we have preserved the classical UNIX look for sophisticated UNIX-trained users.

It's a tremendous pleasure to welcome you to AIX. It and we are here to make your job easier, even more fun!

Donna

Foreword by Cal Killen, Director of AIX Development, Leader of Team AIX

AIX enables scalability from palmtops to terraflops. It is *the* operating system for UniProcessors, symmetric MultiProcessors, embedded OEM systems, cluster and massively parallel systems. AIX is used in many commercial and technical applications including client, entry, mid-range, and high-end server applications.

AIX has been accepted as the provider of business and mission-critical solutions (including mainframe-centric applications) and the transition to client/server. It leads the industry with exploitation of PowerPC and RS/6000 hardware; high availability servers; software graphics; support of new, emerging devices; integration into PC networks; enterprise management; and the emerging IBM technologies including objects, human-centrics, network centric, interactive broadband services, and parallelism.

AIX has a reputation for quality with our customers. We have achieved ISO 9000 certification and high scores on rigorous internal assessments based on Malcom Baldrige criteria. Our quality program objective is to have ever increasing customer satisfaction. We will continue our evolution to total quality management.

This book will help you get the most from your AIX systems and from your other systems, too, and that will save you time and money. You and your co-workers will learn AIX faster and you will be in a good mood while you're doing it!

Cal

Overview

This book can be used by itself if you don't know anything about AIX or UNIX. It can also be used if you know UNIX but want to also understand the unique features of AIX. This book will focus on the latest and greatest AIX features delivered in AIX Version 4 (and there are lots of them).

Why AIX?

Scalability

AIX runs on high-performance machines which makes it very fast and powerful. This software/hardware combo allows folks to run heavy-duty applications on affordable systems. AIX also runs on non-IBM machines (such as those from Apple, Motorola, and Bull) which gives it a strong future. AIX runs on 32- and 64-bit machines from PCs up to symmetric multiprocessor systems.

AIX is a high quality, IBM-tested operating system. It has been tuned and improved with many performance enhancements. AIX has IBM-backed service and support with goodies like Internet fixes and information as well as personal contact.

AIX speaks many languages! It has multinational support for a variety of languages and locales and characters across the world. AIX can connect in a variety of ways with nearly any machine or software. It supports a long list of different communication protocols (including ipsec and IPV6) and devices. This keeps you connected to your colleagues and the world.

Standards

AIX supports many of the commands and library calls from the old versions of UNIX that have been around since the beginning (such as Berkley and System V), as well as the newer standards such as NIST (National Institute of Standards and

Technology), XTI (X/Open Transport Library Interface), FIPS, XPG4, X/Open, POSIX, UNIX 95, and other standards. Why do you care? If you learn AIX, you can use UNIX just about anywhere and still know what you're doing. You'll also get more applications that run on AIX (standards make programmers' lives much simpler).

Simplicity

IBM has added functions to make AIX much easier for people to use. It's fast and easy to install and administer (unlike typical UNIX systems). AIX teaches you AIX commands as you use graphical interfaces, so you can become a guru as you go. AIX has on-line hypertext (multimedia) documentation so that you can search across many books and get to exactly what you're after.

Solutions

AIX has many applications from IBM and vendors. Related applications and hardware have been grouped into solutions as a one button orderable item that solves the customer's needs.

Style

AIX has the style and personality of UNIX while remaining on the leading edge of technology. AIX has a lot of sizzling software to keep customers up-to-date with the Internet, objects, multimedia, and more.

Why Simply AIX?

You've heard of UNIX. You now have or may want an AIX machine. So, how do you get started? BUY THIS BOOK!!! If you want to learn about and get more out of your AIX system, then you need this book. Even if you use an AIX system only occasionally at school or work, you will want to have this book. We cover topics such as installation and configuration, cool graphic interfaces, and hot tips that improve your productivity as either a user or an administrator. We discuss advanced topics such as how to make your computer do Japanese or other languages.

We've included pullout cheat sheets, useful tables, technical tidbits, hot tips, and fun. This book has it all—from A to Z.

How Did AIX Grow Up?

First of all, what does AIX stand for anyway? It's the Advanced Interactive Executive. You didn't know you were in the executive class, did you?

We needed an operating system that would blow users' socks off with the new processor performance. The AIX operating system didn't originate in someone's garage, but it did have its beginning in a small strip center down the street from the IBM plant in Austin in the early 1980s. There was a project using the beginnings of a RISC processor from research, a compiler that took advantage of it, and a layer of software called the VRM (virtual resource manager) to isolate the software from the hardware.

The project blossomed when it converged with teams from early word processor systems such as the 5520, the DisplayWriter, and the 5280. The commercial UNIX version out in the world at the time was from Interactive Systems Corporation, so that's what we started with. UNIX is very popular because it was and is an "open architecture" which allows flexible applications and system extendability

But when we really started using it we recognized that it was a programmer's heaven, but everyone else would find it . . . complex. In response, a new user interface was written and we added easier system management.

There are also lots of programmers who grew up with UNIX, so we incorporated many UNIX standards so that the same command can be used no matter where you grew up! AIX uses standards from System V, Berkeley, OSF, NIST, and others.

The file system was improved, and the virtual resource manager and virtual memory managers were created. An exciting idea for the time was a virtual terminal, which allowed multiple "screens" on a single display. AIX also included a DOS 3.0 (yes, that was a long time ago!) emulator.

AIX was then enhanced to support almost every protocol customers were using, both IBM protocols like SNA and protocols gaining momentum from universities, such as TCP/IP. We could list them all, but it would fill the page with alphabet soup!

We really worked on improving the quality of the UNIX operating system while keeping its universal appeal. AIX was enhanced to be more reliable and robust for continuous operation so our commercial customers could count on it. The installation and system management were greatly improved. A friendly and powerful on-line publication tool was created to help folks learn the system. AIX went world-wide with messages and menus in many languages.

We have worked on AIX so that it can be the fastest gun in the west! (It was developed in Texas, so it has to be.) The AIX software and compilers work hand in hand with the hardware to optimize the performance of your applications. AIX performance is very important to us!

Then came more standards. There were lots of "UNIXs" floating around and they weren't close enough for an application to simply recompile when moving from one platform to the next, so several standards were developed in the industry that AIX participated in. AIX also brought in commands and libraries that were available, including AT&T's System V and the Berkeley versions of UNIX. Other de facto standards for X Windows, multiple shells, mailers, and postscript printer output format were adopted as well.

AIX Version 4 came up another level in usability and functionality with the Common Desktop, a visual graphics system management tool, symmetric multiprocessing and support for a wide range of hardware systems and I/O adapters.

If you're a history buff, you might enjoy the following articles from the early days of AIX and the RISC family of workstations written by the original architects:

1. *IBM RT Personal Computer Technology*, SA23-1057, 1986.

2. *IBM Tech PC Journal*, Volume 4, Number 12, December 1986, devoted to the RT PC.

3. *The IBM Systems Journal*, Volume 26, Number 4, 1987.

4. *IBM Journal of Research and Development*, Volume 34, Number 1, January 1990.

I'd Like to See How It Ends First!

If you like to read the end of the book first (did the butler do it?), you can use this book from the back, using the index or the chapters that you need first. Or, start from the beginning. The chapters flow so that you can use it right away and get more proficient as you keep on reading. We assume the following:

- You have the CDs or tapes and are ready to install, or you have a pre-installed machine.

- Your hardware is assembled and running.

- You don't have to know anything about AIX.

- You know how to use a mouse and keyboard.

How Do I Find What I Need?

We use an icon in this book to give you a quick perspective of the type of information that is included in a chapter or section. The "hot pepper" icon is HOT STUFF and indicates information that, when mastered, will enhance your standing with AIX wizards and make you an AIX hot shot!

Chapter 1   Customizing Your Environment

Getting Started with the Desktop

CDE, Common Desktop Environment, hides the complexity of AIX—it is designed for end users. The Front Panel (resembles a launch pad) enables any user to sit down and immediately start using the desktop. CDE makes applications easy to use—the Style Manager (located on the Front Panel) enables you to increase or decrease the font size, change fonts, turn off that annoying beep, and enables you to select color combinations and backdrops.

Using the Front Panel

This section explains all the icons on the Front Panel of the common desktop. You can have multiple desktops running at one time—like you have several virtual desks in your office. You can also bring up an editor, a calendar, your mail, and help.

Using Style Manager

This section tells all on customizing the colors, fonts, character sizes, backdrops, keyboard, mouse, that darn BEEP, terminals, and desktop startup.

Using File Manager

The File Manager is great for folks that are still a little queasy about using the command line. Through this application, you can get to your files and directories through a set of menus and action selections. The files are listed right in front of you so that you can pick them out.

Using Application Manager

This section describes how you can bring up applications and add additional applications to the Application Manager—such as multimedia demos, the online publications, tools, printers, and sample programs.

Getting Help

The Help Manager is a super way to learn about the desktop! It gives you the basic skills and allows you to search through the information. On-line help is available for each of the standard applications in CDE. Whether you are using File Manager, Calendar, or Mailer for example, you request and display help topics in the same way. You can also browse help information on your system using the desktop Help Manager.

Chapter 2   Using AIX

Commands—Are These Real Words?

If you want to be a *real* UNIX user, you need to learn some shell commands. This section describes a small subset that will give you the ability to get around the directories, list files and print them, as well as clue you in on more interesting commands like `grep` which searches a set of files for something you're looking for. We'll tell you our favorite commands and demystify some of the acronyms associated with them.

Shells

This section explains what a "shell" is and the differences between those available on AIX so you can pick the best one for you. The shell is very powerful—you can do lots when you put commands together with pipes and redirection! You will also learn about pattern matching and other good guru tricks.

File and User Permissions—What's a Root?

UNIX systems have a security system built into the filesystem. This section explains file permissions, the "root" user, and users and groups.

I'd Rather Call it Sam—Links

If you would rather have your own names for commands and directories instead of the real thing (it's easier to remember), read about aliases.

Paper Dolls—Cutting and Pasting

It's really useful to take a paragraph from the memo from your boss and put it into a memo from you! There are many uses of the cut and paste capability and this section will tell you how to do it.

Where Did My Files Go?

Have you ever lost a file? You know it's in there somewhere, but you can't find it! The directories look like files to you and it's hierarchical so you can't see them all. This section will give you some tricks to find lost files.

Fun Commands

There are a few fun commands that you might like. They're not the CD-ROM multimedia games we play now, they're just some lightweight little programs like fish, blackjack, and tic-tac-toe that can give you a break in the day from your work (but it still looks like you're working!).

Chapter 3   *I Know Windows & DOS, What's AIX?*

OK, Give Me Some Hints!

Many folks know DOS commands but are just learning AIX. This section explains the overall similarities and differences of Windows/DOS and AIX.

Crib Notes: DOS to AIX

This part of the book is a "crib note set" to AIX if you know DOS. It's a list of DOS commands and some parameters translated into the AIX commands and parameters. The whole list is in the book twice, so you can cut the list out and keep it handy but you'll still have a copy in the book.

DOS Functions in AIX

This section describes how you can move files to and from DOS and AIX. It can be real handy to get a list of files on that DOS diskette while you're using AIX. Or you can take that AIX file home to your PC.

Wow! AIX Windows Are Easy, Too!

If you are a Microsoft Windows user, you know the basics about using windows user interfaces. Using AIX CDE Windows will be a snap! You can also run many of the Microsoft Windows applications on AIX with other software, called Wabi and SoftWindows.

SoftWindows Runs Microsoft Windows and App's!

There's a separate product you can install to run Windows 3.11 and Windows applications from your AIX system. That will come in handy if you have some favorites. It could also save you some money if you have invested in a bunch of applications.

AIX Connections Brings Them All Together

This software will allow you to connect NT, OS/2, Macintosh, and other systems to your AIX systems. You'll be able to share files, printers, terminals, and other services.

Chapter 4   Editors

There are lots of different editors available on AIX. This section gives you a how-to that gets you in the file with a few necessary functions (like adding a line, changing the text), and then shows you how to save it and get out. Just a few basics to get you by. There are many good books completely devoted to one editor that we list so you can become an expert. There's also a list of commands that you can cut out of the book and keep handy.

Editor FAQs

This section describes some clever key-strokes you can learn; multiple functions in a few keys, for example, or changing all occurrences of `evrone` to `everyone` in your file. Some of the key-strokes are quite cryptic, but that's what impresses the gurus. Editor FAQs are in the book twice—so you can cut out one list and keep it handy and the other list will still be in the book.

Chapter 5   Installing AIX

How to Get AIX Up and Running

Installing an operating system can be intimidating, so this chapter keeps the instructions simple. AIX is organized into small, installable filesets. You can install only what you need!

All Right! Installation Assistance!

Install Assistant is displayed when you first startup your system. It walks you through the tasks needed to install and configure the system for use. You can also bring up the Installation Assistant by entering `install_assist` on the command line.

Network Installation Manager

You can install AIX using tape or CD-ROM or by using the Network Installation Manager (NIM). NIM is not only an excellent tool for installing multiple machines over a network, it can also be used for software maintenance and machine customizations. Using NIM, you can set up an installation once for machines with identical requirements or customize the specific needs of specific machines.

Chapter 6   Setting Up Peripherals

Using SMIT to Install Devices

Setting up CD-ROM drives and other devices can be frustrating. This section gets you straight to it and gives you the steps to take.

Printers

Printers are a special case because they are so critical to getting work completed. How can you hand in your report when it can't be printed? This section gives you a lot of good printer information, such as setting up the devices, the queues, and the commands available to print. Another essential piece of information is how to fix and get status on the printer queues and processes (there's a daemon back there!). It will explain the mysteries of different file types and how to print them.

Chapter 7   Communicating with the World

Communicating from your system to the outside world is essential in today's work environment. This section describes what you need to know to survive the alphabet soup of communication protocols.

You will learn how to send and receive files and log into someone else's machine. E-mail will be described so that you can pick the mail program that fits your needs the best and you can get up to speed quickly. This section also explains the mysteries behind local and distributed file systems.

We also discuss the power and ease of the Internet Web Browsers that are available for AIX such as the AIX WebExplorer, Netscape, and Mosaic.

Chapter 8   SMIT Happens! Administering AIX

System Management Interface Tool (SMIT)

System administration can be time consuming and complex. The SMIT (Systems Management Interface Tool) application eases that work by providing menus and help screens to allow you to do things like add new users or set up a new printer.

I've Fallen and I Can't Get Up!—The "Running Man" icon is the SMIT indicator of command success or failure. While the command is still processing, an icon at the top of the window will show a man running and running and running . . . If the running man falls down, the command failed. If the running man stops running in place and stands up triumphantly, the command worked!

Distributed System Management (Or Why Just Worry About One Machine When You Can Multitask?!)

The Distributed System Management Interface Tool (DSMIT) adds functionality to SMIT by enabling the SMIT interface to build commands for system management and distribute them to other clients on a network. DSMIT has most of the functionality of the SMIT program, such as fast paths, log files, and flags.

Web-based System Manager

Web-based System Manager enables one to manage AIX systems from anywhere in the Internet/intranet. Web-based System Manager is a comprehensive system management environment that takes advantage of Web technology.

Backup—and Make Restore an Option!

AIX Version 4 provides multiple ways of backing up your systems. If you backup regularly, you'll have the option of restoring files you lose! You can use SMIT or the command line. Backup commands available include `cpio`, `tar`, `pax`, `dd`, `backup`, `restore`, and `mksysb`. SMIT also provides a menu-driven method of backing up and restoring AIX files or the entire `rootvg` volume group. After restoring your files using SMIT, you can use the `fsck` command to check the integrity of the file system after you have restored your files.

Chapter 9   AIX Speaks Your Language: Internationalization

An internationalized and localized computer system should be taken for granted. Messages are displayed in the native language of the user. Date and time formats are familiar and understandable. Lists of sorted data are ordered so that people can find stuff. In other words, the computer works "right" no matter who is using it or in which country he resides.

Why Should I Care About Speaking Your Language?

Well, if you live in the United States, English is your only language, and your customers live in the United States and speak only English, and this will never change, then you probably don't need to care.

But if you don't live in the United States, or if you don't want to use your computer in English, or if your customer wants information processed so that it can be used in another country, then you should care deeply. As an English-speaking person, what would you think if your computer spoke only Japanese?

This becomes an even bigger issue when it comes to selling software and other products overseas.

I'm Convinced! How Do I Get AIX to Speak My Language?

This is the simple part. All you need to do is to make sure that the right parts were installed.

Next, with our help, configuration will be a total snap, and we will have you on the way to editing Japanese files, getting messages in German, reading French, and sending e-mail in Korean!

This Is Interesting! Tell Me More!

Did you know that over 50% of the information technology market is found outside of the United States? Look in this section for tidbits about internationalization, additional sources for more information, and even a couple of interesting anecdotes.

Chapter 10   All the Help You Need

Now that you know your way around AIX some, here's a way to get more info. Get ready to access 50,000 pages of on-line AIX documentation through InfoExplorer, a hypertext information retrieval system. And after you've exhausted the on-line documentation, call 1-800-IBM-FAX to have documents faxed directly to you from a menu including RS/6000, AIX, networking, and SP2 information. We have also provided a list of Internet references to get to AIX information that is currently available on the Net, such as product descriptions, forums, newsgroups, service information, and more! The amount of Internet information is growing by the day, so this list will only get you started.

Chapter 11   Gathering Up the Pieces

64-bit AIX

Learn what 64-bit AIX is, why you should care, what you need to know to run 64-bit programs, administer a 64-bit system, and write 64-bit programs.

AIX and the Year 2000

Learn what the year 2000 issues are, how they affect AIX software and hardware. More importantly, learn what you can do about them.

Performance Tools for System Management

Who doesn't want to know what's going on under the covers? This section describes tools that keep track of memory, disk space usage, processes, and so on.

The AIX Development Environment

Are you curious about what tools and programs AIX provides for programmers? Does AIX have RCS, SCCS? What is CMVC? Can I write C++ programs with AIX? Read on for the answers!

Security and System Management

AIX provides features and tools you can use to ensure that your system is secure. Plus we tell you where the log files are so that you can see what happened on your system over the weekend.

FixDist—How to Get the Latest Bug Fixes from the Internet

Use these fantastic tools to obtain the latest fixes from the Internet, as well as learn how to resolve problems.

Chapter 12   Kick Start Your Enterprise: The RS/6000 System Family

IBM systems account for 105 of the world's fastest computers, ranking first among major vendors on the November 1998 list of the 500 most powerful super-computer sites. The company's increases were even more substantial at the highest end of computing, with 22 RS/6000 SP systems now among the world's 100 most powerful systems, an 83 percent increase.

Whether your enterprise requires one of the world's fastest computers or your needs can be accommodated with slightly less computing power, the RS/6000 hardware line is the information technology answer for scalability, performance, and reliability.

This chapter highlights the features of the RS/6000s available in 4Q98; kick start your enterprise with a hardware choice that enables you to grow your enterprise workloads, response times, and capacity.

Appendix: Handy Command Details

The most frequently used commands are described in this section so you can find exactly what parameter you need when you need it and how to use it. It's not the entire set of commands, but it will get you most of what you need!

The command descriptions are long enough to get details on how to type in the right flags without being overwhelming.

AIX for Busy Managers

Some of you (managers especially) are too busy to learn how to set up your AIX system. If you have the time, do it yourself. If you just won't get to it, don't keep using that old system. You won't be respectable! Here's a way to get your system customized to what you need in your environment. Read this section through completely so you can talk the lingo and then execute the plan.

Here's the plan. First, go buy some really good chocolate chip cookies to share. Then ask your friendly techie guru to help you install and customize your system. You want the latest level of AIX that the office is using, the common desktop environment (CDE), local printers, local networks, DOS compatibility if you need it, local applications added to the CDE application manager, any cool tools the guru uses and likes, CDE customization the guru uses, and e-mail initialized. If you'll have private files stored here (like personnel records), turn off the read/write for group and others. Get access to the on-line publications so you can be self-sufficient.

When the system is ready, ask the guru to demo the system to you so you can see what cool tools they have and see the general usage if you're not used to the windows. Discuss connecting to your e-mail system, especially if you have been using something else before now.

Whew! After that, you'll have to give your guru a raise! Chocolate chip cookies will help and a free lunch wouldn't hurt either!

Read the CDE chapter; it's what you'll need to be functional. CDE is very easy to use, so it will be a breeze! If you're not used to the windowing environment, you'll need to play with window resizing, iconifying, and other actions. Spend a few minutes to see what the help screens are like: indices, searches, hypertext links to more help, and so on, so you'll know where to look when you need information in a hurry. Check out the CDE e-mail program, the file manager, the application manager, the calendar, and printing. They're what you'll use every day.

Keep this book on hand and look up specific sections when you need to perform different tasks. The back sections have a lot of information and references you should browse through also. There's a lot more you can learn.

AIX for System Managers

If you manage AIX systems, you'll want to go straight to the SMIT chapter to install and set up a system. Then read the chapters, "Installing AIX," and, "Setting Up Peripherals," to customize and get printers and devices set up. The chapter, "Gathering Up the Pieces," will give you the tools you need to find out whether the file system is getting full and how it is performing. The chapter, "All the Help You Need," is a wealth of information such as FAQs (frequently asked questions), Internet Web addresses with home pages on IBM, AIX, Talk Radio to exchange information with IBM developers, and other references.

AIX for Novices

If you're a UNIX guru in training, start by reading the Common Desktop Environment—that's the quickest startup. You can get your work done using the CDE text editor, but to be a guru, you need to learn the "vi" editor. It's the de facto standard for editors for UNIX systems. It's very cryptic, so you'll need to practice! There are tables in the "Editors" chapter to show you the different operations available for the editors.

The "Customizing Your Environment" chapter will show you how to change the background to something cool and other stuff to get CDE just like you want.

You'll also want to get on the Internet, so read part of the "Connecting to the World" chapter and the parts of the "All the Help You Need" chapter for the html addresses. There are book references throughout the book if you want to become an expert in a specific area.

You'll need to read the "Using AIX" chapter to get acquainted with the commands, file system, shell, and other systemwide functions. Cut out the "cheatsheet" list of commands and put it next to your computer for reference

AIX for Windows/DOS Users

If you have been using a DOS computer with or without Windows, you should read the chapter specifically written for you, "AIX for Windows/DOS Users." Keep the "cheat sheet" handy and set up aliases to get you up and running rightaway. Read the CDE chapter and use the "Customizing Your Environment." You'll have no trouble using it if you know Windows. Read the "All the Help You Need" chapter to find out about the on-line publications, Internet html addresses, and other very useful references. You'll also need the Editors chapter to learn about changing file contents.

CHAPTER 1

Customizing Your Environment

The Common Desktop Environment (CDE) is a graphical user interface for open systems, jointly developed by IBM, Hewlett-Packard, Sun, and Novell. The desktop was developed to hide the complexities of UNIX and to provide a common user interface for the UNIX environment.

In this chapter we'll highlight how the desktop works and what functions you can perform using the desktop. However, we don't have the space to convey the unlimited functionality the desktop makes available to users, developers, and system administrators. When you're ready to really exploit the desktop, see the Common Desktop Environment documentation available through Addison Wesley.

End user titles include

- *Common Desktop Environment: User's Guide*
- *Common Desktop Environment: Programmer's Overview*
- *Common Desktop Environment: Advanced User's and System Administrator's Guide*

Development environment titles include:

- *Common Desktop Environment: Application Builder's Guide*
- *Common Desktop Environment: Programmer's Guide*
- *Common Desktop Environment: ToolTalk Messaging Guide*
- *Common Desktop Environment: Desktop KornShell User's Guide*
- *Common Desktop Environment: Help System Author's and Programmer's Guide*

- *Common Desktop Environment: Style Guide and Certification Checklist*
- *Common Desktop Environment: Internationalization Programmer's Guide*

Getting Started with the Desktop

CDE hides the complexity of AIX—it is designed for end users. The front panel (resembles a launch pad) enables any user to sit down and immediately start using the desktop. CDE applications look and feel the same—smart applications running on CDE follow the same Motif style and design guidelines. (This means that application menus and window characteristics are similar, enabling you to use the applications without wasting time figuring out how to cut and paste or exit. You complete these types of functions the same way within each application.)

CDE makes applications easy to use—the Style Manager (located on the Front Panel) enables you to increase or decrease the font size, change fonts, and select color combinations and backdrops. With CDE, help is always available.

Upon startup, users can immediately begin using the desktop and applications or can customize the desktop for a more personal configuration. VSM, SMIT, and InfoExplorer can by launched directly from the desktop.

Desktop services, productivity tools, and applications are available through the

- Front Panel
- Style Manager
- File Manager
- Application Manager
- Workspace Objects
- Trash Can
- Mailer

Starting and Ending a Desktop Session

To log into the desktop, enter your login id and password and press Return. Session Manager is started after Login Manager authenticates your login and password. Session Manager provides the ability to manage sessions—to remember the state of your most recent session and return you there the next time you log in. Session Manager saves and restores

- The appearance and behavior settings—for example, fonts, colors, and mouse settings;

- The window applications that were running—for example, your File Manager and Text Editor windows.

To log out, either click the Exit control on the Front Panel, or choose Log Out from the Workspace menu.

When you log out of a regular desktop session, Session Manager saves information about your current session so that it can be restored the next time you log in. Information about non-desktop applications might not be saved.

Ready to Speak Another Language?

1. Choose Language from the Options menu on the login screen.

2. Choose the language group that includes the language you need.

3. Select a language.

4. Log in.

The default language for your system is set by your system administrator. The Options menu enables you to access other languages. Choosing a language in the Options menu sets the LANG environment variable for your session. The default language is restored at the end of the session.

Using the Front Panel

Let's start with the Front Panel, the horizontal window at the bottom of the display as shown in Figure 1–1.

The Front Panel provides direct access to the Style Manager, File Manager, Application Manager, Workspace Objects, Trash Can, Text Editor, Print Manager, Mailer, and Help. The Front Panel continuously displays the time, date, and if you have new mail. Dragging and dropping objects onto the File Manager, Print Manager, Mailer, or Text Editor enables you to copy, print, mail, or edit your files immediately. You can also throw anything away at any time by simply dragging and dropping the object onto the Trash Can. The Front Panel moves with you as you switch workspaces (switch workspaces by selecting the workspace buttons—identified as One, Two, Three, and Four in the Front Panel illustration).

Figure 1–1   Common Desktop Environment Front Panel

Many of the controls in the Front Panel start applications when you click them— for example, the File Manager and Style Manager controls. Some controls are drop zones—for example, the Printer and Trash Can controls. You can drag a file from File Manager or Application Manager to the Printer or Trash Can icons.

Certain icons, such as the clock and busy light, are indicators that tell you something about the state of your system. Other icons have a dual purpose; for example, the Calendar and Mailer icons are both indicators (showing today's date and the arrival of new mail, respectively) and buttons for starting applications.

Subpanels.   If a control in the Main Panel has an arrow button on top of it, then that control has a subpanel. Subpanels always contain

• An Install Icon—use the Install Icon to customize the subpanel;

• A labelled copy of the icon in the Main Panel.

Workspace Switch.   The workspace switch contains the buttons you use to change from one workspace to another. Each workspace occupies the entire display, as though your display has several layers. Workspaces simply multiply the amount of display area available for windows. You can customize your workspaces and label each workspace button accordingly as shown in Figure 1–2.

Using Style Manager

Tired of your backdrop or backdrops? Double-click on Style Manager, select the backdrop icon, select the backdrop you're willing to stare at all day, and select apply. (Note that you can select a unique backdrop for each workspace.)

Is your beep too high, too loud, or just generally annoying? Select the Beep icon, change the volume, tone, or duration of the beep, then click OK.

Figure 1–2   Workspace Switch

Figure 1–3   Style Manager Icon

Can't read your font? Click on the Style Manager Font icon, select a new font, and change your font size, click OK. Isn't this great? The Style Manager icon is located on the right side of the Front Panel (Figure 1–3).

CDE is totally customizable—change your colors, modify the color palette, and/or delete any color palette that is really annoying. You can also modify window behavior by clicking on the Window icon—either select Point In Window To Make Active (makes a window active when the mouse pointer enters it) or select Click In Window to Make Active (makes a window active when the mouse enters it and you click on the left mouse button).

Start Style Manager by clicking on the Style Manager icon located on the Front Panel. Use Style Manager to customize your desktop

- Colors
- Workspace backdrops
- Font size
- Keyboard, mouse, and window behavior

The Style Manager panel is depicted in Figure 1–4.

Figure 1–4   Style Manager Panel

Figure 1–5   File Manager Icon

Using File Manager

File Manager displays the files, folders, and applications on your system as icons. Working with File Manager icons saves you from having to learn complex commands or typing long file names. To open a File Manager view of your home folder, click the File Manager control in the Front Panel. Click on the File Manager icon on the Front Panel (Figure 1–5). Do you see your folders and files?

The File Manager main window as shown in Figure 1–6 is a view of a folder on your system. The folder you are currently viewing is called the current folder.

Ready to use File Manager? Some actions to try include the following:

1.   Move a file to another folder (or directory). Drag and drop the file icon on the new folder icon. Your file is now located in a new directory (and you didn't have to know the AIX mv or cp commands to do this).

2.   Place an icon for a file or folder on the backdrop of your current workspace (remember the workspace switch?). Drag and drop the file or folder icon outside of any window. Note that any changes you make in the file located on your workspace will be reflected in the copy of your file located in the File Manager.

3.   Print a file. Drag and drop the file icon onto the Printer icon. Or, if you have multiple printers, open your Printer subpanel and drop the file on the printer of your choice.

4.   Delete a file. Drag and drop your unwanted file to the Trash Can icon (you can clean up your files and directories without knowing the delete, remove, or erase AIX commands).

You can get help with your files by selecting the file or folder and pressing F1; or by putting the mouse pointer on the object and selecting help from the object's

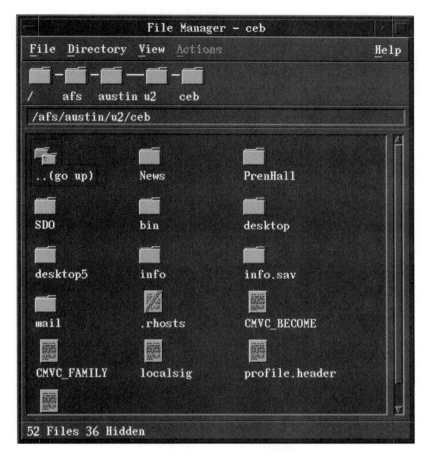

Figure 1–6   My files displayed using File Manager

pop-up window; or by choosing On Item from the Help menu, then clicking on the file or folder's icon.

Once you start piling up lots of files, you might need help tracking them down. File Manager's Find function is just what you need. Select Find from the File Menu, enter the name of the file or folder you want to find, determine where you want the search to start by editing the Search Folder field, and click on Start. Figure 1–7 shows the results after I searched my home directory for a document with the word *network* in the document title.

Figure 1–7   Search Using File Manager Find Option

Using Application Manager

Application Manager provides access to applications you use in your everyday work through action icons. Clicking on action icons starts applications. Action icons are stored in special folders called application groups.

When you click on Application Manager, you'll see the icons for the Desktop_Apps, Desktop_Tools, Information, and System_Admin application groups. The desktop provides these built-in application containers for tools and utilities available with AIX. To run any application within Application Manager, you just double-click on the application icon.

If there are choices within the application, when you double-click on the application icon, the icon will display its contents and you can then choose the specific application function you want to start.

Figure 1–8   Front Panel Control for Application Manager

To open Application Manager, click its Front Panel control (Figure 1–8).

You can place the files, folders, and actions you use frequently on the workspace backdrop as icons (so you don't have to search File Manager or Application Manager for a file, folder, or application). To place an object on the workspace, drag its icon from a File Manager or Application Manager window and drop it directly on the workspace backdrop.

Note that the object you've placed on your workspace is a reference to the actual object, not a copy. Any changes you make to the object will be reflected in the actual object within File Manager or Application Manager.

If you find yourself frequently using a certain application, you can add the application to a Front Panel subpanel. Simply drag the application icon from the Application Manager to the Install Icon control in the Text Editor subpanel.

I frequently use the Edit Resources function (found in the Application Manager System_Admin group as shown in Figure 1–9). So, I installed the Edit Resources icon on the Front Panel Personal Applications subpanel (Figure 1–10).

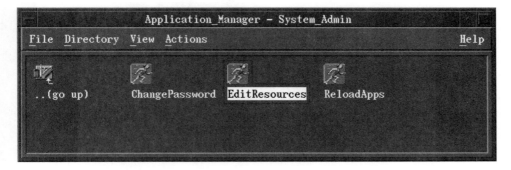

Figure 1–9   Application Manager System_Admin Group

Figure 1–10   Customized Personal Applications Sub-panel

Using the Trash Can

The Trash Can collects the files and folders that you delete. They are not actually removed from the file system until the trash is "emptied." You can only change your mind and *restore* a file you've put in the Trash Can if the Trash Can hasn't been emptied.

Click on the Trash Can icon (Figure 1–11) on the Front Panel to open the Trash Can window. To put an object in the Trash Can follow these steps:

- Choose Put in Trash from the object's pop-up menu (displayed by pressing Shift+F10 or mouse button 3).

- *Or*, select the object's icon, then choose Put in Trash from the selected menu.

- *Or*, drag and drop the object's icon onto the Trash Can control in the Front Panel.

- *Or*, drag an object's icon to the open Trash Can window.

Figure 1–11   Trash Can Icon

To put back a file or folder from the Trash Can drag the object from the Trash Can window to File Manager.

Using Mailer

Mailer is a desktop application that enables you to send, receive, and manage your electronic mail (e-mail) messages. Click on the Mailer icon to bring up the Mailer main window as shown in Figure 1–12.

Once you've started Mailer, you can read, sort, find, delete, file, and send mail. Select a message to read it—the text will be displayed in the Message view area. If the message has any attachments, they'll be displayed in the Attachment list area. Select the Reply button to reply to sender, to reply to sender and all recipients, or to reply to sender or all recipients and include a copy of the message. (Note that the message area only has the Reply to Sender button—the other options are available on the Compose pull-down menu.) Whew! Lots of options.

Select the Compose function from the menu bar to forward a message, save a message as text by choosing Save As Text from the Message menu, or find a mail

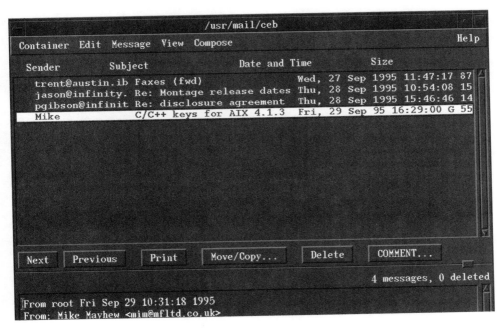

Figure 1–12   Mailer Main Window

message in your overcrowded mailbox by choosing Find from the Message menu. To address, compose, and send a mail message, choose New Message from the Compose menu, enter the recipient's e-mail address, add a subject and cc your friends and family (or anyone else who needs to see the mail). Hit Return and you'll land in the text area. Write your message—edit it using the Compose Edit menu. You can cut, copy, delete, and most importantly, check your spelling. If it's an e-mail to your boss, use the Compose Format menu to align paragraphs, grab templates or add a blind carbon copy to your message (cool function—Add Bcc: enables you to send a copy of a message to someone without those on the To: or Cc: line seeing the additional person's address).

The CDE mailer uses mailboxes to organize mail. You create mailboxes by choosing New from the Mailbox menu, entering the mailbox name and location, and clicking New. The Mailer functionality enables you to file messages in the appropriate mailbox, to drag and drop messages to other mailboxes, and to remove mailboxes.

Using the Text Editor

The Text Editor is useful for creating and editing short documents and files. To start the text editor, click on the Text Editor icon. You create and edit a document in the Text Editor window. You can create a new document or open an existing document. To open an existing document, select Open from the File menu, select the name of the document you want to open, and click OK.

To create and enter text, click in the text window and type following the cursor (I). Use Wrap to Fit to control whether lines are automatically wrapped to fit the width of the window. Move the cursor in a document by using your up and down arrows, your left and right arrows, Home to go to the beginning of the current line, End to go to the end of the current line, Control+End to go to the end of the document, or Control+Home to go to the beginning of the document. To check your spelling, choose Check Spelling from the Edit menu. The Spell dialog box lists misspelled or unrecognized words.

You can insert a text file into your document by positioning the cursor where you want to insert the text file, choosing Include from the File menu, selecting the document you want to insert, and clicking OK.

Using Calendar

Use the CDE calendar to schedule appointments and To Do items, set reminders, make and print appointment and To Do lists, browse other calendars, and schedule group appointments. You can view the calendar by day, week, month, or year.

The Calendar Tool Bar icons include the following:

*   The Appointment Editor (enables you to add, delete, or change meetings or appointments)

*   The To Do Editor (lets you create, modify, update, or set reminders)

*   The Previous view arrow (displays the previous day, week, month, or year)

*   The Today button (brings up the current day, week, month, or year according to your current format)

*   The Next View Arrow (displays your schedule for the next day, week, and/or year)

You can view your calendar using Day View (displays your current calendar format with one day's appointments in the window plus a three-month mini-calendar); using Week View (shows your week's appointments plus a grid of scheduled times); using Month View (shows your month's appointments); or using Year View (shows a calendar of the year, but NOT all of your appointments).

Using dtterm

The CDE default terminal emulator is dtterm. Click on the Terminal icon from either the Front Panel, Application Manager, File Manager, or Window menu to bring up a dtterm. Use the terminal emulator to enter operating system commands, AIX commands, and to copy and paste text. I've put my Terminal icon on the Front Panel so I can access it quickly (shown in Figure 1–13).

Although the desktop provides drag and drop and other user-friendly functionality enabling you to avoid using the command line, those of us who are accustomed to the command line need it around for security reasons (it makes us feel smart when we can remember actual AIX commands).

Figure 1–13   dtterm Icon on my Front Panel

Getting Help

On-line help is available for each of the standard applications in CDE. Whether you are using File Manager, Calendar, or Mailer, for example, you request and display help topics in the same way. You can also browse help information on your system using the desktop Help Manager (shown in Figure 1–14).

Ways you can request Help include the following:

- Press F1—also known as the "help key"—to get context-sensitive help.
- Choose a topic from an application's Help menu.
- Open Help Manager from the Front Panel to browse help on your system.
- Open the Help subpanel to choose help about the desktop or to choose On Item Help.

Press F1—The Help Key

When you have a question, the quickest and easiest way to get help is to press F1. When you press F1, the application you are using displays a help topic most closely related to the component—a window or button for example—that is highlighted. This type of help is called *context-sensitive* because the application determines which help topic is most appropriate.

Using an Application's Help Menu

Most applications have a Help menu that contains commands for requesting different types of help such as an introduction, application tasks, or reference information.

Figure 1–14   Help Manager Subpanel

A typical CDE Help menu includes

- Overview (displays the home topic for the application—the home topic is the first topic of the application's help topic hierarchy)

- Tasks (displays task instructions for most operations performed with the application)

- Reference (displays reference summaries for various components, such as windows and dialog boxes, menus, and application resources)

- On Item (enables you to click an item in any window of an application and view a description of the item)

- Using Help (provides help on using the help windows)

- About *Application* (displays the version and copyright information for the application)

Using Help Manager

Help Manager is a special help volume that lists all the on-line help registered on your system. Clicking the Help Manager control in the Front Panel opens the Help Manager help volume (Figure 1–15).

Click any of the underlined titles to view the corresponding help information. For convenience, you can also find help about the desktop and the Front Panel in the Help subpanel. It also provides On Item help for the Front Panel and its subpanels.

Using Help Windows

The Help System is built into each of the CDE applications (and possibly other applications installed on your system). When you ask for help while using an application, the application displays a help window.

General help windows have a topic tree and a topic display area. The *topic tree* is a list of help topics that you can browse to find help on a subject. When you choose a topic, it is displayed in the lower portion of the help window called the topic display area.

Quick help windows are streamlined help windows. A quick help window has just a topic display area and one or more buttons.

Selecting Help Topics

There are two ways to select a help topic. You can choose a topic from the topic tree. Or, within a help topic, you can select a hyperlink.

The topic tree is an outline of a help volume's major topics. Subtopics are indented under main topics. The current topic, whose contents are displayed in the

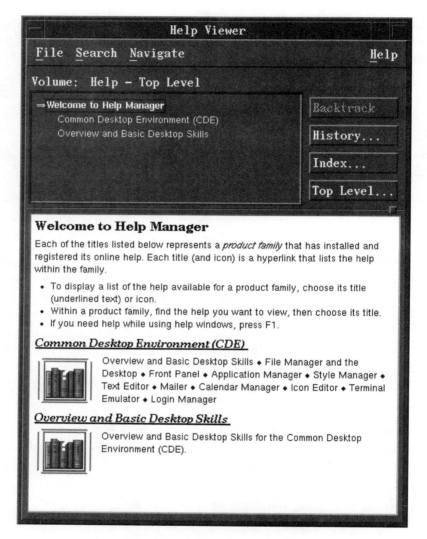

Figure 1–15   Help Manager

topic display area, is marked with an arrow. You can scroll the topic display area to see all your choices or resize the entire help window.

To select a topic follow these steps:

1.   Move the pointer into the topic tree.

2.   Click mouse button 1 on the topic you want to display.

For example, find out more about the File Manager by clicking on Common Desktop Environment and then selecting File Manager Help.

Browsing Help on Your System

You can browse or search all application help volumes registered on your system without having to start each individual application—just start Help Manager from the Front Panel.

To open Help Manager follow these steps:

1. Click the Help Manager control in the Front Panel.

A help window displays a list of help families with on-line help. This is the top level of Help Manager.

2. Scroll the window to find the product group you are interested in and click its title (underlined).

This lists the help volumes available for that product.

3. To open a particular help volume, click its title (underlined text).

4. To get back to the top of the Help topics, click the Top Level button.

To browse File Manager's on-line help follow these steps:

1. Click the Help Manager control.

2. Choose Common Desktop Environment.

3. Scroll the list of help volumes until you see File Manager Help.

4. Click File Manager Help.

File Manager's help is displayed. This is the same help information you would see if you opened File Manager and chose Overview from the Help menu.

Displaying a Man Page

1. Click the Application Manager control in the Front Panel.

2. Double-click the Desktop_Apps icon.

3. Click the Man Page Viewer icon. A dialog box is displayed, prompting you to enter a man page name.

4. Type the name of the command whose man page you want to see and press Return. The man page is displayed in a quick help window.

5. Click Close to dismiss the man page.

CHAPTER
2

Using AIX

Commands—Are These Real Words?

The basic AIX commands (and all UNIX system commands) are, for the most part, very short, cryptic, two-letter command names. Imagine back years ago, when computers had only very slow teletype keyboards and paper "displays." (Some of us aren't imagining, we're remembering!) Imagine also, people who didn't like typing long commands because there was such a long delay between commands and the computer response. If there were any mistakes, the user had to retype the whole thing (especially aggravating for folks that type with only two fingers!).

Also, some UNIX commands came from university students and researchers who weren't bound by usability standards (no rules, merely peer pressure). They could write a very useful, clever command and name it anything—their own initials, for example (awk by Aho, Weinberger, and Kernighan), or an acronym (yacc, Yet Another Compiler-Compiler).

User Configuration—What Environment Am I In?

There are some setup files that create an environment when you log in. These files are executed automatically to give you a customized system. You can use what came in the box, or change it to your special way of working.

The files /etc/profile and /etc/environment are executed for all users of the system and the file .profile in your home directory (a hidden file) is executed when you log into the system (except for C shell users).

Usually these files set environment variables such as "PATH" which lists all the directories you want AIX to look into for the command you type in. It can also set your prompt, default editor, and mail message when new mail is received.

You can add AIX commands in your .profile that you want executed every time you log in (see cron for more information about executing commands automatically at other times of the day or night). My favorite command to put in my .profile file is /usr/games/fortune (this command is in fileset bos.games).

The .dtprofile is used by the common desktop for initial configuration information. The .mh_profile is used by the mail handler, MH, for user customization. The .mwmrc file is used by the motif window manager.

By convention the .kshrc file is executed by the Korn shell when you log in (the line export ENV=$HOME/.kshrc must be in your .profile file). Alias definitions are usually stored in the .kshrc file. The .login and .cshrc files in your home directory are executed by the C shell.

A file named /etc/motd (Message Of The Day) is displayed when users log into the system. It doesn't really set anything up but it shows up during your login. You can use this message for daily reminders. If multiple people share the system, it can be used to announce system changes, or more importantly, birthdays!

Shells

UNIX systems offer a shell around the system that allows you to execute commands and write programs with those commands. No compiler is needed. The shell interprets the logic.

Over the years, several shell versions have evolved and AIX provides the ones our customers want. The shells available in AIX systems are the Bourne shell, the C shell, the Korn shell, variations on these shells, the Restricted shell, and the Trusted shell.

The first shell, the Bourne shell (/usr/bin/bsh), was created by Steven Bourne at Bell Labs. The Bourne shell is a popular shell to use when writing "shell scripts", or text files that use shell programming constructs to carry out some task.

The C shell (/usr/bin/csh) was created by Bill Joy at the University of California at Berkeley. It uses a format similar to the C programming language. It lets you recall and employ previously used commands, define and use aliases, and do job control. The phrase "job control" here is not related to empowerment, but rather the ability to suspend currently running programs, resume them, and/or move them to/from the background/foreground.

The Korn shell (/usr/bin/ksh and /usr/bin/sh) was developed by David Korn at AT&T Bell Labs. Although it is based on the Bourne shell, it also draws upon functionality found in the C shell, and thus supports recalled commands, aliases, and job control.

The Restricted shell (`/usr/bin/Rsh`) is based on the Bourne shell and prevents users from changing directories, changing the PATH and SHELL environment variables, executing programs not specified in the current PATH, modifying or viewing any files not in the current directory, and redirecting output. This may sound pretty restrictive, but to be truly restricted, the system administrator should ensure that the user does not have access to any program such as `vi` in the PATH that could be used to overcome these limitations.

The Trusted shell (`/usr/bin/tsh`) is based on the Korn shell and gives the user a slightly restricted environment intended to protect from `trojan horses` (a user modified command that masquerades as a real command), computer viruses, and other undesirables. The Trusted shell does not read in user profile files such as `.profile`, but rather only reads the `/etc/tsh_profile` file. It will not support user function and alias definitions or command history, and uses several additional built-in commands (`logout`, `shell`, and `su`) to ensure that the intended command is executed. This book does not go into detail about computer security. That's a whole book in itself!

The Bourne shell was the default for AIX Version 3 and the Korn shell is the Version 4 default. That is, on AIX Version 3, `/usr/bin/sh` and `/usr/bin/bsh` are the same, and on AIX Version 4, `/usr/bin/sh` and `/usr/bin/ksh` are the same. The Korn shell has always been recommended as the default login shell on AIX. It was made the default system shell in AIX Version 4 since the AIX Version is standards compliant (XPG4 and POSIX).

There are several important shell concepts that all users should be familiar with. These include environment variables, aliases, I/O redirection, command history, file globbing, and regular expressions. Each of the shells supports programming constructs which allow users to quickly write powerful "shell scripts" which enable automation of nearly anything you can do on the command line. One of the great things about shell programming is that you can edit the shell program and run it without the compiling step; that makes it much faster. However, we will not cover shell programming here. If you are interested in that, or just want to know more about shells, you may wish to check out one of the following books:

1. Morris Bolsky and David Korn, *The New Korn Shell Command and Programming Language,* New Jersey: Prentice-Hall, 1995.

2. Daniel Gilly, *Unix in a Nutshell,* Sebastopol, CA: O'Reilly & Associates, 1992.

3. Bill Rosenblatt, *Learning the Korn Shell,* Sebastopol, CA: O'Reilly & Associates, 1994.

4. Stephan Kochan and Patrick Wood, *Unix Shell Programming,* New Jersey: Hayden Books, 1985.

5.   Gary Anderson, *The Unix C Shell Field Guide,* New Jersey: Prentice-Hall, 1986.

6.   Martin Arick, *Unix C Shell Desk Reference,* QED Technical Publishing Group, 1992.

Environment Variables

The environment is the system "sky" all around you when you're using a UNIX system. There are all kinds of things floating around out there (some you see, some you don't) that affect the way the system acts. There are predefined environment variables that contain information your applications may want to use. You can create variables for your own purposes.

Although each shell supports environment variables, they each tend to have a different method to change them. To set environment variable FOO to AIX, on Bourne shell or Korn shell, type FOO=AIX; export FOO. When using the C shell, type setenv FOO AIX. You can change environment variables at the command line, and the change will be effective until you log off. If you want to permanently change your environment then you will have to edit the appropriate configuration file (.profile for the Korn shell and Bourne shell, and .login for the C shell). To view a single environment variable such as FOO, type echo $FOO. If you want to see all of your environment variables, then type env and you will see something like this:

```
MANPATH=/afs/austin/common/usr/man
LANG=En_US
LOGIN=carolynj
NLSPATH=/usr/lib/nls/msg/%L/%N:/usr/lib/nls/msg/%L/%N.cat
VISUAL=vi
PATH=/usr/bin:/etc:/usr/sbin:/usr/ucb:/usr/bin/X11:/sbin:.
HISTFILE=.sh_history
LOGNAME=carolynj
MAIL=/usr/spool/mail/carolynj
LOCPATH=/usr/lib/nls/loc
USER=carolynj
SHELL=/bin/ksh
HOME=/afs/austin/u/carolynj
CMVC_FAMILY=aix
TERM=dtterm
MAILMSG=[YOU HAVE NEW MAIL]
```

```
PWD=/afs/austin/u/carolynj
TZ=CST6CDT
```

Generally environment variables serve to communicate configuration information to either the shell or other system programs. Other environment variables convey information from the shell to the user or other programs. Some of the common environment variables that are supported in all shells include:

- **HOME**   This environment variable refers to your home directory. This is the most frequently used variable.

- **LANG**   This environment variable refers to the current locale. If you set this environment variable to 'C' you will get the best performance. By setting it to other locales, you can make your system support a variety of national languages.

- **MANPATH**   This environment variable specifies a list of paths to search for when looking for man (manual publications) pages with the man command.

- **NLSPATH**   This environment variable specifies where files of translated messages called "message catalogs" can be found.

- **PATH**   This environment variable specifies which directories the shell should check and in what order when looking for a command that you type in.

- **LOCPATH**   This environment variable specifies which directories the system should check when looking for the locale specified by the LANG environment variable.

- **USER**   The shell sets this to your user ID.

- **SHELL**   This environment variable specifies which shell you want to use when executing a shell from another program.

- **TERM**   This variable specifies your terminal type (aixterm, dtterm, xterm, and vt100, are popular values depending on what you use).

- **TZ**   This variable specifies your time zone, along with some interesting information such as whether or not your computer should follow daylight savings time, and so on.

Aliases

Many command line users like to set up aliases for long or complex commands to save typing (or they may have a bad memory). This is especially helpful while a person is learning or if they are used to different commands that map into AIX commands. Frequently typed commands are good candidates.

If you type the `alias` command it will show you all your current aliases:

```
ls='/usr/bin/ls -F'
stop='kill -STOP'
suspend='kill -STOP $$'
myfiles='ls /u/home/trent'
```

To create an alias `ls` that replaces the `ls` command with a customized option, type `alias ls='ls -F'` on the Korn shell. To do the same on the C shell type `alias ls 'ls -F'`. (Notice that the C shell does not like the equal sign.) Bourne shell does not support aliases.

I/O Redirection and Piping

Once you get used to redirection and piping, it will be your favorite and frequent sequence of commands. There is no limit to the number of combinations of commands you can put together to get something done. It's easy and quick.

In its simplest form, I/O redirection can be used to prevent output from a command from going to the screen, and instead send it to a file. Likewise, many commands will take input from a file if it is specified with I/O redirection.

For example, you can redirect *output* from the `ls` command to a file like this:

```
$ ls
Mail a.out hello.c todo
$ ls > output
$ cat output
Mail
a.out
hello.c
output
todo
```

You can also redirect *input* to a command such as `cat`. (I know this is sort of trivial, since the `cat` command will take input from a file anyway!)

```
$ cat < hello.c
main()
{
printf("Hello world\n");
}
$
```

More interesting is the ability to "pipe" the output from one UNIX command to another UNIX command. For example, suppose you have a command that generates a lot of output, such as the `ls -al` command on a large directory. You can pipe its output to other commands that process it. For instance, you could count the number of lines to get an idea of how many files are in the directory with the wc -l command like this:

```
$ ls -al /usr/bin | wc -l
    647
```

Now we know that there are 647 files in the directory /usr/bin.

Piping from one command to another, and maybe another after that, saves you disk space. You don't have to save the output from each command, just the final output.

Command History

Wouldn't you like to reuse the command you just typed, instead of retyping the whole thing? Or would you like to see a list of the commands you just executed to see how you got into a mess? You'll learn how in this section.

Since command history is not supported on the Bourne shell, we will describe how it works on the Korn shell and the C shell. By default the Korn shell keeps track of the last 128 commands. You can see the last 15 of them by simply typing history. You can then execute a specific command again by typing r followed by the number of that command, or you could type r l to rerun the last command that started with the letter l. You can also just use r by itself to rerun the last command:

```
$ history
1          ls
2          vi hello.c
3          echo Hi Mom!
4          history
$ r 3
echo Hi Mom!
Hi Mom!
$ r l
ls
a          b          file
```

To use command history with the C shell, you will need to ensure that you are using AIX Version 4.1.4 or later, and that the following two commands are in your .cshrc file:

```
set savehist=100
set history=100
```

Then, similar to the Korn shell, you can list recent commands with the history command, and can rerun commands by using the exclamation point (!) character. To repeat the previous command, use ! !:

```
$ history
1       ls
2       vi hello.c
3       echo Hi Mom!
4       history
$ ! 3
Hi Mom!
$ ! 1
a       b       file
$ !!
a       b       file
```

You can recall a recent command, edit it, and then execute the modified command. To do this, you'll have to learn the vi editor (see Chapter 4, Editors) if you don't already know it. You really need to learn vi for many reasons, but I'll give that pep talk later. To set up the ability to edit the recalled commands, type:

```
set -o vi
```

Press <Esc> k to recall the last command, then keep pressing the "k" key to get the commands before that until you get to the one you want. Then use the vi editor commands to change the command. Then press Enter and execute it.

File Globbing Goes Wild!

File "globbing" is the technical UNIX way to refer to the use of wild cards in filenames to specify a group of files. This can also be called "Pattern Matching Notation for Files", but I think that "globbing" sounds more interesting. Most users are familiar with the use of "a*" to refer to all files in the current directory that start with the letter "a". Wherever you can type a file name in a UNIX command, you can generally use file globbing.

This section looks scary because of all the special characters, but don't be intimidated. Read through it and pick out a couple things to try and use. You'll be surprised how useful it will be!

File globbing consists of the use of a number of metacharacters that can be used as a form of shorthand to match other characters and files. There are only three main kinds of file globbing characters. The simplest type of file globbing is the question mark (?), which will match ANY single character. The question mark (?)

will match "a" or "q" or "z" or "w" or any other single character. Typing `ls ?` would list all single character files in the current directory.

The asterisk (*) will match any number of characters including NO characters. Some examples are listed here:

- `*`   matches all files.
- `*a*`   matches any file that has an "a" in it somewhere.
- `a*`   matches any file that starts with an "a".
- `*a`   matches any file that ends with an "a".
- `a*a`   matches any file that starts and ends with a different "a", including "abracadabra", and "aa", however it will not match "a", since each "a" in the pattern has to match to a unique "a" in the file name.

The most interesting (and complicated) type of file globbing is the bracket expression. Like the question mark, it only matches a single character. There are three main types of bracket expressions. A simple bracket expression like `[abc]` will match a single "a" or a single "b" or a single "c", but nothing else. Bracket expressions can also contain ranges; `[a-z]` will match any single lower case character in the En_US locale. This form of bracket expression should actually be avoided since the characters in the range from "a" to "z" will depend on the locale and code set being used. Rather, the preferred way to use a bracket expression to match something like "all lowercase letters" is to use a "character class expression," such as `[[:lower:]]`, which will match any single lowercase character no matter what locale is being used. The following character classes are available for use in bracket expressions in all locales:

- `[[:alnum:]]`   Match a single alpha-numeric character.
- `[[:alpha:]]`   Match a single alphabetic character.
- `[[:blank:]]`   Match a single blank character (space or tab).
- `[[:cntrl:]]`   Match a single control character.
- `[[:digit:]]`   Match a single numeric character.
- `[[:graph:]]`   Match a single graph character (all printable characters minus the space character).
- `[[:lower:]]`   Match a single lowercase character.
- `[[:print:]]`   Match a single printable character (including space).
- `[[:punct:]]`   Match a single punctuation character.
- `[[:space:]]`   Match a single white space character.

- `[[:upper:]]`   Match a single uppercase character.
- `[[:xdigit:]]`   Match a single hexadecimal numeric character.

One nifty feature of bracket expressions is the ability to specify a "nonmatching list" in which the first character in the bracket expression is the exclamation point (!). When this happens, the bracket expression will match any character that is NOT inside the brackets. For example, `[!abc]` will NOT match "a", "b", or "c", but will match "d", "e", "f", and so on. If the exclamation point is not the first character in the expression then it loses its special meaning. For example, `[a!b]` will match "a", "!", or "b". Bracket expressions can also match collating symbols and equivalence classes.

Of course, all three of these types of expressions can be combined to form complex and useful patterns. You could use an expression such as `version1.[abc]*.c` to make a list of all files that start with `version1.a` or `version1.b` or `version1.c` and end in `.c`. Or if you want to see a file that is called either `bob` or `Bob` or `8ob`, you could use the pattern `?ob`. These few constructs allow for a wide variety of file-matching possibilities.

Here are a couple of down-to-earth examples of how I use file globbing:

- `rm *.tmp`   (remove temporary files in directory)
- `cc *.c`   (compile all c programs in directory)
- `cat prog[123]?.c`   (`cat` certain c programs)
- `ls [adt]*`   (look at all files or directories starting in a, d, or t)

What do you do if you want to actually use one of these special characters in a file name? You can use metacharacters such as *?[] in file names by simply quoting the file name with either single or double quotes. For example, `cat '*'` would `cat` a file called '*' rather than `cat` all files in the directory.

Regular Expressions

Regular expressions are related to, but have significant differences from, file globbing. There are two types of regular expressions: Basic Regular Expressions (BRE) and Extended Regular Expressions (ERE). For the most part, simple BREs will work on programs expecting EREs for input. The type of regular expression a program expects depends on the program. For example, `grep` expects a BRE as the matching pattern, and `egrep` expects an ERE as the matching pattern. Although we will cover all major features of regular expressions, we will not detail every nuance. The best source for more information is either IEEE's POSIX or X/Open's XPG4 standards documents. Other useful sources include InfoExplorer and the O'Reilly book, *Sed & awk*.

- BRE Wildcard Metacharacter (.)

In a BRE, the period matches any single character. It is similar to the question mark in file globbing.

- BRE Interval Metacharacter (*)

The asterisk matches zero or more occurrences of the previous element. So "a*" will match one or more "a"s. If you wish to make an expression that will match anything, then ".*" is the correct expression rather than "*".

- BRE Beginning of Line Anchor Metacharacter (^)

The circumflex will match the beginning of a line if it occurs as the first character in the pattern. However, it matches itself if it is not the first character in the pattern. (Circumflex has other meanings within bracket expressions.) The command `grep ^a` will match all lines that start with the letter "a", and `grep a^` will match all lines that contain the string "a^". Use of the circumflex to match the beginning of a line is referred to as anchoring, since it anchors the pattern to the beginning of the line.

- BRE End of Line Anchor Metacharacter ($)

The dollar sign will match the end of a line if it occurs as the last character in the pattern. However, it matches itself if it is not the last character in the pattern. The string `grep a$` will match all lines that end with the letter "a", and `grep $a` will match all lines that contain the string "$a". Use of the dollar sign to match the end of a line is referred to as anchoring, since it anchors the pattern to the end of the line.

The $ and ^ metacharacters can be combined to match an entire line. For instance, the pattern "^apple$", will match only a line that contains only the string "apple", and "^$" will match only empty lines.

- BRE Subexpressions

Any valid BRE can be enclosed in escaped parenthesis to form a subexpression. For example, "\(apple\)" will match the string "apple", as will the pattern "\(app\)\(le\)", as will the pattern "\(a\(ppl\)e\)".

- BRE Backreferences

It is possible to repeat a subexpression with the metacharacter string "\#", where # is a digit between 1 and 9. The string "\1" refers to the first started subexpression, "\2" refers to the second started subexpression, and so on. The pattern "\(apple\)\1" will match the string "appleapple".

- BRE Duplication

Any character, metacharacter, or subexpression can be duplicated a specified number of times. The construct "\{m\}" will match exactly m occurrences of the preceding character, metacharacter, or subexpression, "\{m,\}" will match m or more occurrences, and "\{m,n\}" will match between m and n occurrences inclusive. Examples, "a\{3\}" will match "aaa", "a\{3,\}" will match "aaa", and "aaaaa", but not "aa", "a\{2,3\}" will only match either "aa" or "aaa". Additionally, ".\{3\}" will match any three characters, and "\(apple\)\{2\}" will match "appleapple".

- BRE Bracket Expressions

Similar to file globbing, BREs support bracket expressions that match a single character. Bracket expressions can contain a list of characters to match (for example, "[abc]" still matches either "a" or "b" or "c"), a range expression (for example, "[a–c]" will match "a" or "b" or "c" in the En_US locale), and character class expressions such as "[[:upper:]]" match any single uppercase character. Like file globbing, bracket expressions can also match collating symbols and equivalence classes. Unlike file globbing "nonmatching lists" are specified by using a circumflex as the first character in a bracket expression, rather than the exclamation point. For example "[^abc]" will NOT match "a", "b", or "c", but it will match "d", "e", "f", and so on. If the circumflex is not the first character in the expression, then it loses its special meaning. For example "[a^b]" will match "a", "^", or "b".

- BRE Bracket Expressions

As with file globbing, these expressions and characters can be combined to arbitrary complexity. For example "[abc]\{2,3\}\([[:upper:]]\)\1..foo$" will match a string that has two or three characters from the set "abc", followed by any uppercase character repeated twice, followed by any two characters, followed by the string "foo" that must be at the end of the line.

That pretty much wraps up a simple introduction of Basic Regular Expressions. Extended Regular Expressions provide for several more features than BREs, and in some cases provide for a cleaner pattern, since parenthesis and braces are not escaped as in BREs. I will describe the main differences between BREs and EREs here.

- ERE Subexpressions vs. BRE Subexpressions

With EREs you do not need to precede parenthesis with backslashes. So the BRE "\(abc\)" should be written as "(abc)" as an ERE.

- ERE Brace Range Intervals vs. BRE Brace Range Intervals

As with subexpressions, with EREs you do not need to precede braces with backslashes. So the BRE "a\{5\}" should be written as "a{5}" as an ERE.

- ERE Anchoring with ^ and $ vs. BRE Anchoring with ^ and $

The main difference in anchoring between ERE and BRE is how the meta-characters ^ and $ are treated if they're not at the beginning and end (respectively) of the pattern. With BREs they lose their special meaning and get treated as the characters themselves, however with EREs they are assumed to retain their special anchor meaning. So an ERE like this "a$b" will try to match an "a" at the end of a line, followed by a "b" on the next line. However, most programs that do regular expression matching look at data line by line, and thus this particular line spanning pattern would never match anything.

- New ERE Interval Metacharacter (+)

The new + metacharacter matches one or more occurrences of the previous element. For example, the pattern "a+" will match one or more occurrences of the letter "a". The "+" character is equivalent to the ERE expression "{1,}" or the BRE expression "\{1,\}".

- New ERE Interval Metacharacter (?)

The new ? metacharacter matches zero or one occurrences of the previous element. For example, the pattern "a?" will match zero or one occurrences of the letter "a". The "?" character is equivalent to the ERE expression "{0,1}" or the BRE expression "\{0,1\}."

- New ERE Alternation Metacharacter (|).

The new | metacharacter allows the matching of either the element that precedes it or the element that follows it. For example "a | b | c" will match either "a" or "b" or "c". Of course, this particular example is equivalent to the simpler pattern "[abc]". Alternation can also be used on subexpressions or longer patterns, for example, "apple | orange" will match either "apple" or "orange".

- ERE Backreferences

EREs do not support backreferences such as "\(a\)\1" as used in BREs.

File and User Permissions—What's a Root?

The word "root" in AIX (and all UNIX systems), means two things: the root user is the superuser and the root directory is the top of the directory tree.

Root User.   Users have a name in the system. You define your user environment, home directory, and user login name. The system comes with one predefined user, the root. The root user has a password also. The root user can read and write into any directory. (See the file attributes section for more information.) The system is usually protected so that only the root user can change system operating characteristics. To change from your user ID to the root, use the

su (superuser) command. To go back to your user ID from the root, press
<Ctrl> d. If you can't remember which ID you are currently using, type
whoami.

Root Directory.   The top of the file system at "/" is known as the root directory.
If you picture a tree upside down, it looks like the file system structure with the
"/" as the tree root. Although some system files are at the root, user files should
not be stored at the root directory. This tree is a family tree. The directory above
your current directory is the "parent" directory. The directories below are child
directories. This analogy is also used for process hierarchy. Commands
(processes) that invoke another command are "parent" processes with child
processes.

User Authorities

There are 3 entities concerning file permission authority:

- owner
- group
- other

Each file has an owner, the creator of the file. Each user belongs to one or more
groups that are defined in the system. The system comes with some predefined
groups, such as "staff" and "system". The designation of "other" allows anyone
the specified access to the files.

Each directory and file have permissions set individually for the file owner, specified group, and other:

- read
- write
- execute

The read permission allows users to look at the contents of a file. Write permission allows modification and deletion of a file, and execution permission allows a program file to execute.

There are additional special bits for advanced users:

- set user id
- set group id
- sticky bit

When a file has the "set user id" attribute, it executes as the owner of the file regardless of who actually typed the command. The "set group id" attribute is sim-

ilar, but for the group instead of the user. The "sticky bit" attribute changes the way the link permission acts; only the owner of the file can delete it. (Traditionally, the sticky bit was used to request that a program stick around in memory after being accessed.)

To view the permissions on a file, go to the Desktop File Manager, click a file, elect `selected`, and `change permissions`, then you will see something like Figure 2–1.

To view the permissions from the command line, type `ls -l` and you'll see something like this:

```
ls -l
total 33
-rw-r--r--    1 carolynj system    3212 Aug 28 21:15 chapt5
-rw-r--r--    1 carolynj system    1773 Aug 28 21:02 chapt6b
-rw-r--r--    1 carolynj system    5337 Aug 20 15:01 chapt8
-rw-r--r--    1 carolynj system    5337 Aug 28 21:02 chapt8b
```

The files all have read and write (`rw`) permission for the owner, carolynj. The middle set of three characters (`r--`) define the read permission of the group "system". The last set of three characters (`r--`) allow read permission for others.

To change the permissions on a file, use the desktop file manager or the `chmod` command. The `umask` command sets the default for newly created files. The `chown` command changes ownership of a file (only the root user can do this).

Figure 2–1   CDE File Manager—Permissions Screen

Process Control—Do I Have Daemons Running?

Each command is at least one process while it is executing. Some processes run in the background where they are invisible to the user. Others run in the foreground where you can see them running. Some processes run forever; they are called "daemons". OK, UNIX can't spell "demon" right, but you can get the idea!

Here is a quick list of actions you can perform on processes:

ps	Process Status
kill	Terminate the process
&	Use "&" after a command to execute it in the background
<Ctrl> z	Pause a command (system is waiting on you)
bg	Put the command in the BackGround
fg	Put the command in the ForeGround

To get a list of the processes running in the system, use the ps process status command. If you run ps without any parameters, you'll get a list of the processes running for just you, in that terminal, for example:

```
> ps
    PID TTY    TIME CMD
 10868 pts/0 0:00 ksh
 11640 pts/0 0:00 ps
```

You can get a very long list of all the processes running in the foreground and background for all users by running ps -a (process status for all). The list is too long to show here and will depend on your system setup. The ps -1 will show the long status:

```
> ps -1
    F S UID PID PPID C PRI NI ADDR SZ WCHAN TTY TIME CMD
200001 A 0 10868 8772 1 60 20 c9e 152      pts/0 0:00 ksh
200001 A 0 11644 10868 9 64 20 857 148      pts/0 0:00 ps
```

There's a lot of information in this read out that you won't usually need, but it's there if you do. I usually use ps or ps -e | pg to find the process ID, especially the processes that run in the background.

You can kill processes with the kill command. You'll need the process identifier (PID). You'll need this command if you have a runaway command you wish you hadn't started. If you execute kill <pid>, the system will ask the process to die nicely. If it refuses, you'll have to use stronger measures! The kill -9 <pid> command kills the process without giving it a chance to clean up before its end. Use kill -9 as a last resort.

Advanced users can explore the system resource controller (SRC), which provides commands and library calls to start, stop, and get status on processes. AIX uses the SRC to start many of the daemons at boot time. The actions taken by the system when it first starts up is partially defined by the file /etc/rc, other /etc/rc* files, and /etc/inittab.

I'd Rather Call it Sam—Links

You may have a file that belongs in more than one directory. But it is too much trouble (and it would take up more disk space) to copy it over every time you change the file.

Use a symbolic link and the system will give you one file with multiple names or directory paths. Link from the real file to the link, for example:

```
ln -s memo jan.memo
ln -s memo /u/guest/memo
```

Now there will be three names for one file which all appear and act like three different files in different places. But there is only one real file. How can you tell if the file is unique, or a link?

```
$ ls -l
lrwxrwxrwx 1 carolynj system 4 Aug 28 21:35 jan.memo->memo
-rw-r--r--   1 carolynj system 0 Aug 28 21:34 memo
```

The linked file shows up with an arrow pointing to the real file.

Paper Dolls—Cutting and Pasting

Cutting and pasting is a function that is very useful and easy. You can cut text to and from files or onto the command line itself.

Let's say you are looking at a memo your boss sent you and you would like to take part of it and put it into a different memo. There are several methods you could use. It's as easy as 1, 2, 3:

1. Bring up your favorite editor for the new memo.
2. Cut: Use the mouse to highlight the parts of your boss's memo that you want (just hold down the left mouse button while moving it across the text).
3. Paste: Move your mouse pointer over to the new memo and click with the middle mouse button (or both mouse buttons, if you have only two).

Now you can quote your boss in your new memo, you can add your own text, save the file, print it, whatever.

If you're not a great typist, cutting commands and long file names will save a lot of aggravation. Here's an example:

```
$pwd
/afs/austin/projects/framebook/chapt5
```

Now cut the path name using the left mouse button. Type part of the command you want to execute, paste, type the rest:

```
ln -s <paste-it> <type-the-rest>
```

Where Did My Files Go?

Some users get lost and confused by the hierarchical file structure. There are a lot of system files and directories that come with the system, all nested within each other.

Here is a snapshot of many of the AIX directories that come in the system:

`/bin, /usr/bin, /sbin`	Binary commands
`/lpp, /usr/lpp`	Licensed program product applications
`/etc`	System configuration files
`/home, /u`	User directories (linked directories)
`/dev, /cdrom`	Device system information
`/lib, /usr/lib`	Libraries for program linkage
`/tmp`	Temporary files stored here

If you name your directories in a simple organized manner, it helps. Usually boring file names are better than too much creativity. Use a descriptive name for the contents of the file. I wouldn't use `Hawaii` for the file name of my financial report. Keep track mentally of where you are, or change your command prompt to show what directory you are currently in.

If you use the Korn shell, you can add this to your `.profile` file:

```
export PS1=' $PWD: '
```

The desktop file manager always shows the directory path of where you are (see the chapter on CDE, the Common Desktop Environment).

If you type in `cd` on the command line with nothing else, you will go to your "HOME" directory. This is the directory where your files are stored by default. The path is usually `/home` followed by your login name. There is a "HOME" environment variable stored in your profile (the `.profile` file in your home directory) which tells the system the name of your home.

If you lose track of where you put a file, you can search for it in a couple of ways:

- Using the desktop file manager, select `File` then `Find`

- Using a command, type `find <starting point> -name <filename> -print`

  For example: `find /home/sue -name memo -print`
- This command lists all files and directories under the home directory recursively.

  `ls -R $HOME | more`

Fun Commands

The following commands are all shipped with AIX in the `bos.games` fileset:

`/usr/games/arithmetic`	Quizzes you on simple arithmetic
`/usr/games/back`	The game of backgammon
`/usr/games/bj`	The game of blackjack
`/usr/games/craps`	The game of craps
`/usr/games/fish`	The game of go fish
`/usr/games/fortune`	Displays amusing statements
`/usr/games/hangman`	The game of hangman
`/usr/games/moo`	Guess four-digit number
`/usr/games/number`	Displays numbers you type in English
`/usr/games/quiz`	Quizzes you on a variety of subjects
`/usr/games/ttt`	Tic-Tac-Toe
`/usr/games/wump`	Find the Wumpus!!!!

Well, obviously, you didn't purchase your computer to run these programs. But they can lighten up your day for awhile.

AIX Commands

Now we get into the commands that you can use to get work done from the command line. Commands are very flexible and powerful! The list that follows is printed in the book twice so that you can cut out one of the pages and put it next to your computer or in a handy place, as a cheatsheet.

You can get your work done using the desktop functions, but there is a lot more you can do from the command line. If you want to be more of a guru, learn some commands. We grouped similar commands together and capitalized letters in the description that make up the command to help you remember. We also added some of our favorite command combinations that may come in handy!

Commands have two parts: the action and the parameters. UNIX systems care about upper and lowercase. If you type CP, it's not the same as cp, theoretically there could be two separate commands. Parameters are usually prefaced by a dash "-" and are one character long. In the example that follows, the parameters are shown in brackets "[ ]". Some commands require file names or other user specified information, such as the cp command to copy from the infile to the out-file.

```
cp [-p -r -]... infile [indir] outfile [outdir]
```

Directory Commands

- `mkdir`   MaKe a new DIRectory
- `cd`   Change to new Directory
- `pwd`   Print Working Directory (where am I?)
- `rmdir`   ReMove DIRectory
- `mvdir`   MoVe DIRectory under different directory or rename
- `ls, li`   LiSt, LIst the files in a directory
- `.`   Abbreviation for the current directory
- `..`   Abbreviation for the parent directory
- `df`   Disk Free space status
- `whereis`   Show directories WHERE command IS stored

File Commands

- `cp`   CoPy a file
- `mv`   MoVe a file to a different directory or rename it
- `rm`   ReMove a file
- `ln`   LiNk a filename to another file
- `cat`   Show file contents, conCATenate a file
- `pg`   Show contents of a file, one PaGe at a time
- `more`   Show MORE file contents
- `enq`   ENQueue a file to print
- `chmod`   CHange read/write/execute MODe of file
- `cmp`   CoMPare binary files
- `diff`   Show DIFFerence in text files
- `grep`   Search for text in a file
- `join`   JOIN two files based on first column
- `sort`   SORT contents of a file

Backup Commands

- `compress`   COMPRESS files to take up less backup space
- `uncompress`   UNCOMPRESS the compressed file
- `cpio`   CoPy Input / Output
- `tar`   Tape ARchiver
- `pax`   Portable Archive interchange(X)
- `dd`   Device to Device copy
- `backup`   BACKUP files (use with restore command)
- `restore`   RESTORE files from backup format
- `mksysb`   MAKe SYStem Backup for rootvg volume group

Miscellaneous Commands

- `crontab`   Set commands to run at a specified time/date (CRONological TABle)
- `clear`   CLEAR the screen
- `lpstat`   Check Line Printer STATus
- `date`   Current DATE and time
- `hostname`   Local system HOST NAME
- `whoami`   Current login name
- `su`   Change to another user login (Default Super User)
- `wall message`   Broadcast a message to all logged-on users (Warn ALL)
- `banner "text"`   Screen BANNER for text

Help Commands

- `<cmd> -?`   List parameters for command
- `<cmd> -help`   Short help for command
- `man <cmd>`   On-line MANual pages for command
- `info`   INFOrmation from the on-line help
- `learn`   Lessons for a subject or command

Handy Commands

- `ls -lRs`   Long, recursive sorted file list (sorted by modification date)

- `echo "text" > file`   Create a file with one line in it
- `echo "End" >> file`   Puts a final line on the file
- `ls | more`   List files and pause at each page
- `sed "s/|/ /g" file`   Change all pipe symbols to blanks
- `aixterm -fn Rom22 &` Use very big font for command line
- `sort file | uniq | more` Show unique sorted list
- `mail user@location < file` Send a file as mail
- `enscript -q -p - -r -f Courier8` Print with small font, landscape (to postscript printer)
- `fgrep <string> file | cut -c1-80 > newfile` Filter out lines without the string, cut all but columns 1-80, put in `newfile`

- `tee <file> <cmd>`   Write command output to two places, standard out (typically the screen) and a file

- `wc -l file`   Count number of lines in file
- `du | sort -rn | pg`   Disk usage sorted for largest first
- `sdiff file1|file2`   Compare two files side by side
- `for i in *.txt; do lpr $i; done` Print all files in current directory that end in `.txt`.
- `find . -print |xargs grep pattern` Find all files that contain pattern in the current directory hierarchy

Directory Commands

* `mkdir`   MaKe a new DIRectory
* `cd`   Change to new Directory
* `pwd`   Print Working Directory (where am I?)
* `rmdir`   Remove Directory
* `mvdir`   MoVe DIRectory under different directory or rename
* `ls, li`   LIst, LiSt the files in a directory
* `.`   Abbreviation for the current directory
* `..`   Abbreviation for the parent directory
* `df`   Disk Free space status
* `whereis`   Show directories WHERE command IS stored

File Commands

* `cp`   CoPy a file
* `mv`   MoVe a file to a different directory or rename it
* `rm`   ReMove a file
* `ln`   LiNk a filename to another file
* `cat`   Show file contents, conCATenate a file
* `pg`   Show contents of a file, one PaGe at a time
* `more`   Show MORE file contents
* `enq`   ENQueue a file to print
* `chmod`   CHange read/write/execute MODe of file
* `cmp`   CoMPare binary files
* `diff`   Show DIFFerence in text files
* `grep`   Search for text in a file
* `join`   JOIN two files based on first column
* `sort`   SORT contents of a file

Backup Commands

* `compress`   COMPRESS files to take up less backup space
* `uncompress`   UNCOMPRESS the compressed file
* `cpio`   CoPy Input / Output
* `tar`   Tape ARchiver
* `pax`   Portable Archive interchange(X)
* `dd`   Device to Device copy
* `backup`   BACKUP files (use with restore command)
* `restore`   RESTORE files from backup format
* `mksysb`   MAKe SYStem Backup for rootvg volume group

Miscellaneous Commands

- `crontab`   Set commands to run at a specified time/date (CRONological TABle)
- `clear`   CLEAR the screen
- `lpstat`   Check Line Printer STATus
- `date`   Current DATE and time
- `hostname`   Local system HOST NAME
- `whoami`   Current login name
- `su`   Change to another user login (Default Super User)
- `wall message`   Broadcast a message to all logged-on users (Warn ALL)
- `banner "text"`   Screen BANNER for text

Help Commands

- `<cmd> -?`   List parameters for command
- `<cmd> -help`   Short help for command
- `man <cmd>`   On-line MANual pages for command
- `info`   INFOrmation from the on-line help
- `learn`   Lessons for a subject or command

Handy Commands

- `ls -lRs`   Long, recursive sorted file list (sorted by modification date)

     `echo "text" > file`   Create a file with one line in it
- `echo "End" >> file`   Puts a final line on the file
- `ls | more`   List files and pause at each page
- `sed "s/|/ /g" file`   Change all pipe symbols to blanks
- `aixterm -fn Rom22 &`   Use very big font for command line
- `sort file | uniq | more`   Show unique sorted list
- `mail user@location < file`   Send a file as mail
- `enscript -q -p - -r -f Courier8 <file>`   Print with small font, landscape (to a postscript printer)
- `fgrep <string> file | cut -c1-80 > newfile`   Filter out lines without the string, cut all but columns 1-80, put in `newfile`
- `tee <file> <cmd>`   Write command output to two places, standard out (typically the screen) and a file
- `wc -l file`   Count number of lines in file
- `du | sort -rn | pg`   Disk usage sorted for largest first
- `sdiff file1|file2`   Compare two files side by side
- `for i in *.txt; do lpr $i; done`   Print all files in current directory that end in `.txt`.
- `find . -print |xargs grep pattern`   Find all files that contain pattern in the current directory hierarchy

AIX Command Details

You'll need details on some of the AIX commands. We've included some of the commonly used commands, but not all the commands, because there are so many. See the appendix for more details. There are whole reference books for all the commands and libraries that you can get if you're a real guru, guru wanna-be, or writing your own programs.

This list of reference books will get you started:

RISC System/6000 Technology

Elements of AIX Security

Printing for Fun and Profit Under AIX

AIX Performance Monitoring and Tuning Guide

AIXtra Magazine

AIXpert Magazine

Life with Unix, Ressler Libes

The Design of the Unix Operating System, Back, Prentice-Hall

Unix in a Nutshell, Billy, O'Reilly & Associates

Unix Power Tools, Peek, Loukides, O'Reilly

POSIX Programmer's Guide, Lewine

Practical C Programming, Oualline

Using C on the UNIX System, Curry

UNIX for FORTRAN Programmers, Loukides

Software Portability with imake, DuBois

AIX Operating System Technical Reference

CHAPTER 3

I Know Windows/DOS, What's AIX?

OK, Give Me Some Hints

The windows user interfaces of AIX and DOS have many similarities. You'll be able to use AIX windows (CDE) very easily. The crib notes for DOS to AIX commands will help you get productive in quick order. You will also need to use the Appendix to see which parameters to use. This section includes info on other DOS functions available in AIX to use DOS diskettes, windows applications, and share remote files between DOS and AIX systems.

Hey, DOS Windows and AIX Windows Are Easy!

If you are used to Windows on DOS systems, you won't have any trouble with the AIX Common Desktop Environment (CDE). The borders on each of the two windows are quite similar and they act a lot alike. The following is a list of similarities and differences:

- Both windows have an icon on the top left to act on the whole window. It includes these commands:

  ```
  Restore

  Move

  Size

  Minimize

  Maximize

  Close
  ```

- DOS Windows 3.11 (before Windows 95) has a "Switch-To" option, where CDE has an "Occupy Work Space" option, and Windows 95 has a task bar which can be hidden (auto hide).

- Both have a title on the window top which you can select with the mouse (hold down the left button) and move the whole window around.

- Both allow you to resize the window using the mouse (put the mouse cursor on the window border edge, press and hold down the left button, and re-size.)

- Both have an icon on the top right corner to Maximize the window (make the window fill the whole screen). They each have a different button indicator—DOS Windows 3.11 has a down arrow where AIX CDE has a box. When the CDE icon is "pressed in" the window is maximized. Windows 95 has an icon representing a single sheet of paper for Maximize and it changes to several tiled sheets of paper when the window is not maximized.

- Next to the Maximize icon is the Minimize icon. This will hide the window and present only a small icon in its place. AIX and Windows 3.11 have you double click on the small icon to bring it back to its previous form and Windows 95 requires a single click in the taskbar.

- You can have lots of windows open at the same time on the screen. Both let you click on the window title to bring it to the front. All the applications in all those windows can run at the same time with AIX.

Crib Notes: DOS to AIX

A quick reference may be your best friend while you are learning AIX. The following table is a list of the basic commands that you will use all the time. We put the crib sheet in this book twice so that you can cut one out and put it next to your computer for easy access.

BASICS

DOS	AIX	Description
COPY <from> <to>	cp <from> <to>	File copy
DIR	ls	Directory listing
MD and MKDIR	mkdir	Make a new directory
MOVE <from> <to>	mv <from> <to>	File move
DELETE and ERASE	rm, del	Delete/Remove
TYPE <file> | more	pg <file> or cat <file> | more	Show file contents
|	|	Pipe output to another command
>	>	Redirect output
<	<	Redirect input
PRINT <file>	enq <file> or lpr<file>	Print/Enqueue file
/ <flag>	- <flag>	Command flags
CD \ and CHDIR	cd /	Change directory (note the difference in the slash)
RENAME <from><to>	mv <from> <to>	Rename a file
CLS	clear	Clear screen
CONFIG.SYS, AUTOEXEC.BAT	/etc/rc, /etc/inittab, .profile (in user directories)	System and user configuration scripts

	MORE COMMANDS	
DOS	**AIX**	**Description**
MSBACKUP COPY and XCOPY RESTORE DISKCOPY REPLACE	backup tar cp cpio dd	File backups
FDISK	smit, smitty	Modify disk partitioning
ATTRIB	chmod	Change file read/write access
FC /B <file1> <file2>	cmp <file1> <file2>	Compare binary files
FC /L <file1> <file2>	diff <file1> <file2>	Compare text files
PKZIP/PKUNZIP	compress, uncompress, zcat	Compress files
VER	oslevel	Show system version
DELTREE	rm -r	Erase entire directory and subdirectories
FIND	grep, fgrep, egrep	Find character string in files
FORMAT	format	Format a disk
DOSHELP HELP F1 function key <cmd> /?	man <cmd> <cmd> -? <cmd> -help	Help information

BASICS

DOS	AIX	Description
COPY <from> <to>	cp <from> <to>	File copy
DIR	ls	Directory listing
MD and MKDIR	mkdir	Make a new directory
MOVE <from> <to>	mv <from> <to>	File move
DELETE and ERASE	rm, del	Delete/Remove
TYPE <file> | more	pg <file> or cat <file> | more	Show file contents
|	|	Pipe output to another command
>	>	Redirect output
<	<	Redirect input
PRINT <file>	enq <file> or lpr<file>	Print/Enqueue file
/ <flag>	- <flag>	Command flags
CD \ and CHDIR	cd /	Change directory (note the difference in the slash)
RENAME <from><to>	mv <from> <to>	Rename a file
CLS	clear	Clear screen
CONFIG.SYS, AUTOEXEC.BAT	/etc/rc, /etc/inittab, .profile (in user directories)	System and user configuration scripts

MORE COMMANDS

DOS	AIX	Description
MSBACKUP COPY and XCOPY RESTORE DISKCOPY REPLACE	backup tar cp cpio dd	File backups
FDISK	smit, smitty	Modify disk partitioning
ATTRIB	chmod	Change file read/write access
FC /B <file1> <file2>	cmp <file1> <file2>	Compare binary files
FC /L <file1> <file2>	diff <file1> <file2>	Compare text files
PKZIP/PKUNZIP	compress, uncompress, zcat	Compress files
VER	oslevel	Show system version
DELTREE	rm -r	Erase entire directory and subdirectories
FIND	grep, fgrep, egrep	Find character string in files
FORMAT	format	Format a disk
DOSHELP HELP F1 function key <cmd> /?	man <cmd> <cmd> -? <cmd> -help	Help information

File Names

DOS file names are restricted to one to eight characters but AIX file names can have up to 256 characters! DOS file names ignore upper and lowercase; AIX uses upper, lower, and mixed case as different file names. DOS displays everything as uppercase on the command line; AIX displays mixed case as it is used.

DOS file names allow characters, numbers, and special characters except the following:

```
*  ?  =  +  |  {  }  ;  /  <  >  ,  "
```

AIX file names allow ALL characters, numbers, and special characters except the slash. However certain characters such as the following should be quoted or escaped:

```
*  ?  |  {  }  ;  /  <  >  ,  "  !  (  )  #  &
```

So, think of the possibilities with AIX! You could have a file named `Great_Proposal_1.1_with_Illustrations`. But don't get too crazy, you'll have to type this long file name a lot and your fingers will get tired! Also, your coworkers will gripe at you for long, mixed case, and special character file names. But if you use graphical point and click interfaces and don't usually type file names, use whatever file names are the most useful.

Wildcards

DOS uses wildcards for each part (name and extension) of a file name. For example `dir a*.*` will list

```
abc.bat
arrival.exe
```

You have to tell DOS about both parts of a file name. AIX looks at the file name as a series of characters. For example `ls a*` will list all files starting with "a". You have a lot of flexibility to list just what you are looking for. For example `ls aug*9*95` will list

```
august_090795
august_090895
august_090995
aug.9.9.95
```

AIX will also list files at the current directory and subdirectories: `ls -R` will list all the files at the current directory and all the files below it. The DOS command `DIR /S` accomplishes the same result in DOS.

DOS allows you to copy all the files in the current directory by typing

```
COPY *.* <directory>
```

DOS copies subdirectories with the XCOPY command. In AIX, you can copy the current files, subdirectory structures, and subdirectory files by typing

```
cp -r <from-directory> <to-directory> (-r is for recursive)
```

In DOS, DELETE *.* doesn't erase all subdirectories, but the DELTREE will (including the hidden files). In AIX, type rm -r to delete all subdirectories and files.

Be careful! If you get confused about where you are in your directory structure, you could do a lot of damage!

In DOS, if you use the DELETE *.* command, DOS will ask, "Are you sure?" In AIX (typical for UNIX systems), it won't warn you! Power users would get irritated with a bunch of warnings! You can, however, use the del command and it will ask first before deleting.

File Attributes

Files have certain characteristics that you can change, such as being writable or not. You can change the default characteristics that come with the creation of a file. AIX will check the current permissions (attributes) on the file to see if you are allowed to change it.

DOS files have the following attributes:

- read only
- read write
- archived
- not archived
- hidden
- system

AIX files have these attributes for the file owner, group, and other categories:

- read
- write
- execute
- sticky

Additional attributes of an AIX file are the owner and group(s) that read/write/execute permissions apply to. To change these, use the chown and `chgrp` commands (see the section on users, groups, and root for more information).

To list hidden files you need to use additional parameters:

In DOS type: "DIR /A:H" (attributes hidden)

In AIX type: "ls -a" (a is for all).

Hidden DOS files are not copied, moved, or erased with wildcards (`DELETE *.*`) until you take off the hidden attribute. In AIX, a file is hidden when the first character is a period (.). Even if you accidently name a file .sam it will be a hidden file! If you want to change it to be visible, just change the file name. AIX is similar to DOS in its treatment of hidden files with copy, move, or remove operations as they aren't copied, moved, or removed with wildcards. If you type the file name in AIX, all operations work as if the files were not hidden. In DOS, the hidden attribute must be removed before anything can be done with the file.

Other attributes of files are the date and time of its last modification. The operating systems take care of this information for you, but you can change it yourself by entering the AIX command `touch <file>` and it will now have the current day and time.

The DOS copy will preserve the original date and time on the newly copied file. AIX will put the date and time that the copy operation was performed on the new file, unless you use the `-p` option to preserve the original date and time.

Directories

Both DOS and AIX have hierarchical directory systems. The thing you'll notice the most is that DOS and AIX (all UNIX systems) use different symbols for the directory separators. DOS uses " \ " and AIX uses " / ". DOS uses " / " for command parameters where AIX uses " - ". AIX puts commands in standard directories: /bin, /usr/bin, /etc . DOS allows the user to install the DOS commands in any directory.

DOS Functions in AIX

AIX allows you to put a diskette with DOS files into an AIX drive to read and write the files into and out of AIX. Use these commands to exchange files between DOS and AIX:

- `dosdir`
- `dosread`
- `doswrite`
- `dosformat`

The AIX `dosdir` command lists DOS files from AIX. The `dosread` command reads a DOS file in and makes a copy into an AIX file system format. The `doswrite` command copies an AIX file onto a DOS formatted disk in DOS file format. The `dosformat` command formats a floppy disk for use as a DOS diskette.

If you intend to take an AIX file to a DOS system with a command such as `doswrite`, you may need to replace the tabs with the appropriate number of spaces with the `untab` command.

DOS text files use a two-character line termination sequence (^M^J) which is `<linefeed, carriage-return>`, or, in C terminology, `\015\012`. AIX uses only "`\012`" to terminate a line. This means that text files may need to be cleaned up a little after transfer unless you use the `-a` option. These DOS compatibility functions must be selected during install; they are not on the system by default.

SoftWindows Runs Microsoft Windows and Spreadsheets!

There's a separate product you can install to run Windows 3.11 or Windows95 and Windows applications from your AIX system called "Soft Windows." This will come in handy if you have some favorites. It could also save you some money if you have invested in a bunch of applications!

SoftWindows is separately ordered and installed. Since the system will be running two operating systems at the same time, it might need more memory. Be sure to check. Bring up an AIX window from the Common Desktop Environment (CDE) or use the AIX command line and type `swin` to run SoftWindows (see Figure 3–1) or `swin95` to run SoftWindows95. You can use your Windows and MS-DOS applications as well as customize it to come up the way you want. You can run your spreadsheets, word processors, databases, graphics packages or, ugh, do your taxes!

SoftWindows is compatible with most Windows and MS-DOS applications, which makes it easy to use. These programs can be run as is with SoftWindows. All Microsoft Windows functions, including control panels, the program manager, help, the file manager, and the print manager, are available.

You can cut and paste between windows and between them and AIX windows. DOS commands may be used. Object linking and embedding (OLE) and dynamic data exchange (DDE) are supported between Windows applications, which gives leading edge applications more power.

SoftWindows works with Novell NetWare, LAN Server, LAN Manager, Windows NT, and Banyan VINES. It has full TCP/IP networking support and sup-

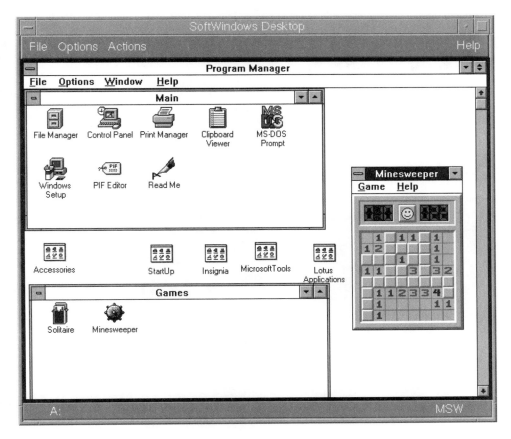

Figure 3–1   SoftWindows AIX Running MS-Windows 3.11

port for LAN WorkPlace for MS-DOS, too. Now you're connected! There is also an on-line user's guide and administrator's guide from the help system within SoftWindows.

AIX Connections Brings Them All Together

Read the Connectivity chapter and the AIX Connections section to find out more about how to get your different PC's hooked together to share files and printers.

The beauty of AIX Connections is that you can connect a DOS system to an AIX system and use the AIX system to store the DOS user files. Both systems can access the files, the DOS system uses DOS or Windows to see the files and the AIX system uses AIX and CDE to access the same files.

CHAPTER
4

Editors

I n this chapter we will explain how to use vi, Emacs, CDE text editor, and INed, the most popular editors available on AIX. When you have finished reading this chapter, you will know the fundamental differences among the editors and you will have acquired survival skills in each. All of these programs are text editors, which means that they create and modify text files. That is all that they do. Unlike modern word processors and desktop publishing programs, text editors do not allow you to do things like change fonts, incorporate graphics, bold or italic characters, and so on. Text editors are, however, very useful tools for editing system files, programs, and simple data files. In fact, since they are all screen-based editors, they are considerably easier to use than their predecessors, line-based editors.

You might want to try each editor if you haven't settled into a favorite. Bring it up and see how it looks and acts. Each editor has its forte. The CDE editor is very easy to use; it has pulldown menus and help. The INed editor uses the PF keys and has excellent block operations. The vi editor is very fast—you can get in, change what you want, and save the file in seconds. The Emacs editor is very powerful and integrates a variety of functions.

vi

If you want to learn only one editor, and want to be able to edit on any UNIX platform out there, vi is for you. The vi editor (rhymes with "bye" or pronounced by spelling it out (V-I)), is the most widely available UNIX editor. (It is even available in public domain form on other platforms such as DOS.) The name vi comes from the first two characters in the word "visual". As the name implies, vi was written to be a visual screen editor, as opposed to a line-based editor.

You may have to talk yourself into learning vi because it is a little intimidating with the key combinations. It's really not that hard—you've learned a lot more complex things than this! You need to be able to use vi because it is available on all UNIX systems. When you become a vi user, you will be an official UNIX user and you will be respected by the techies. One other reason to learn vi is for the shell command line editing; you'll use vi key combinations to edit retrieved commands. If you are a command user, this is a must. Give it a whirl!

A concept that would be good to keep in mind is that for the most part the text you are editing with vi is in "volatile" memory until saved. This means that if you make a mistake and want to revert to the previous saved version of a document you are editing, you can do so by quitting without saving your changes. On the other hand, it also means that if the power goes out during an editing session you may lose your changes. However, see the FAQ section at the end of this chapter for a nifty way around this.

Installing and Invoking vi

vi is installed on every AIX machine by default. You do not have to do anything special to get vi.

An important thing to keep in mind when using vi is that it has two main modes; a command mode in which you can enter commands and move the cursor around the screen and document, and an input mode in which you can type new text.

To start editing a new document, simply type

```
vi
```

You will see a blank screen (well, not quite blank, vi will show a bunch of lines that each contain a single tilde (~) to indicate the end of the document).

Adding Lines

When you first start vi, it is in the command mode. The easiest command is probably i, which switches you into the input mode. Enter the following text, using the i command:

```
i        <do not press return>
```

Notice nothing appears to have changed on the screen. However, vi is now in the insert mode, and characters that you type will be added to the document at the cursor position. Try typing the following (remember to press the return key after each line):

```
The quick brown fox
jumps over the
lazy dog.
```

Now lets switch back to the command mode by simple pressing the escape key:

```
<esc>
```

Saving a File

Saving a file in vi is pretty simple. To save a file called `testfile`, type the following (from the command mode):

```
:w testfile
```

If `testfile` already exists and needs to be replaced, then you may need to type this:

```
:w! testfile
```

When you do this, you should see a status line on the bottom of the screen that tells you the name of the file you wrote, along with the number of lines and characters in this file.

Loading a File

To load a file from vi, type the following in the command mode:

```
:e testfile
```

Quitting vi

There are a couple of ways to exit vi. All of them require you to be in the command mode, so if you're not sure which mode you are in, pressing escape a couple of times should ensure that you are in the command mode. The recommended method to exit vi is to simply type ZZ. The advantage of this command is that it will automatically save the file for you. If you need to exit without saving your changes then enter

```
:q!
```

Invoking vi and Editing an Old File

Let's try editing the message of the day file that is displayed each time a user logs on. If you are root you can actually change this file, otherwise you will only be able to get practice using vi. Type the following:

```
vi /etc/motd
```

You should now see the message of the day file displayed on your screen, with a status line at the bottom that tells you the name of the file, as well as the number of lines and characters that are in this file. This status line will change when you type other commands.

Moving the Cursor

The ability to move the cursor is fairly critical, so spend some time experimenting with the following basic cursor movement commands:

j	Moves the cursor one line down
k	Moves the cursor one line up
h	Moves the cursor one character left
l	Moves the cursor one character right
^F	(Control-F) Jump forward one page
^B	(Control-B) Jump backward one page

Hint: These commands must be done from the command mode, so press the escape key if you have to. Notice that the j, k, h, and l keys are right next to each other on the keyboard and are in a natural position. That will make it easier to remember which keys do what.

Editing Text

Here are the basic editing commands that you will need to know. To edit, ensure that you are in the command mode. Use the cursor movement commands above, and place the cursor where you want to change text. Then use one of the following basic editing commands:

i	Insert text starting at the cursor. This puts vi into the input mode. Press escape when done.
x	Delete the character the cursor is on.
dd	Delete the line the cursor is on.

Additional vi Tricks

You can precede commands with a number to cause that command to occur that number of times. For example 57j will move down exactly 57 lines. Likewise, you can delete 10 characters at the cursor by typing 10x.

If you would like to know for sure when you are in the input mode you can type :set showmode from the command mode. This will display the text "INPUT

MODE" on the status line whenever you are in the input mode. If you type `:set noshowmode` vi will not show the mode you are in.

If you would like to see line numbers displayed for the document you are editing, type `:set number` from the command mode. To hide line numbers type `:set nonumber`.

If you do programming and want to verify that parenthesis, braces, or brackets balance, or if you would like to see which character they match, then place the cursor on one of these characters and press the percent key (%). Then vi will jump to the matching symbol if one exists.

To jump to the first line in the file, type `:1` from the command mode. To jump to the last line in the file, type `:$` from the command mode. To jump to the fifty-seventh line in the file, type `:57` from the command mode.

Emacs

Although Emacs can be called a text editor, it is an incredibly powerful editing environment, from which you can do literally anything you can think of. In addition to editing normal text files, it has special commands and macros to facilitate editing a variety of types of text files ranging from different programming languages, to `nroff` files, to outlines, to ASCII art, and so on. It also has built-in modes to compile programs, read and send mail, manipulate files, read net news, and execute shells and other programs. If this isn't enough, Emacs is expandable, since you can write and incorporate lisp functions into your Emacs environment.

Although there are several flavors of Emacs, we will describe GNU Emacs, which we will only briefly introduce since there are several fine books dedicated to the subject.

Installing Emacs

Use anonymous FTP to get the file `/u2/emacs/GETTING.GNU.SOFTWARE` from `prep.ai.mit.edu`. (See the chapter on Internet for more information on using anonymous FTP.) Once you get this file, follow the instructions in it to obtain the software. After you have acquired it, unless you are able to find a binary executable for the AIX operating system, you may need to compile it before you can use it.

Using Emacs

Emacs supports a large number of buffers, each of which can be used for a different task, such as editing various documents, reading e-mail, and so on. It is possible to switch between buffers, as well as define multiple text windows in a single screen. This ability to break a single window or screen into several smaller ones, made Emacs a very attractive editing environment in the days before X-Windows and graphical window based computing environments. Currently, many potential Emacs users find Emacs's complexity somewhat daunting.

In this section, text such as C-x means press Control-X. Something like M-x (Meta-x) means press the escape key, then press the x key.

Although text you enter appears directly in the main window, commands and their arguments are generally displayed in the "echo area" at the bottom of the screen. If you should need to abort a command sequence before it is done, type C-g (Control-G)

Invoking Emacs

Emacs can be invoked by typing in the name emacs, optionally followed by a file name to edit:

```
emacs
```

or

```
emacs filename
```

Adding Lines

After invoking emacs, you are automatically in a text editing buffer that you can use to enter text. You could go right ahead and type the following text (press return at the end of each line):

```
The quick brown fox
jumps over the
lazy dog.
```

Saving a File

To save a file, type

```
C-x C-s <filename>
```

Where C-x means Control-X and C-s means Control-s. You may be prompted to enter a file name if this is a new file, otherwise Emacs will automatically supply it.

Quitting Emacs

To quit Emacs, type the following and you will be asked if you wish to save your file (if it hasn't already been saved):

```
C-x C-c
```

To merely suspend Emacs, so that you can return to it later without having to restart the entire program, type:

`C-z`

Invoking Emacs and Editing an Existing File

To invoke Emacs to edit an existing file just type:

`emacs filename`

For instance, the following command will load in the message of the day file:

`emacs /etc/motd`

Loading an Existing File From Emacs

To load a file into an Emacs buffer, type:

`C-x C-f filename`

You can load in the message of the day file by typing:

`C-x C-f /etc/motd`

Moving the Cursor

The following keys are the fundamental cursor movement keys:

`C-f`	Move Forward one character.
`C-b`	Move Backward one character.
`C-p`	Move up one line to the Previous line.
`C-n`	Move down one line to the Next line.
`C-v`	Move forward by one page.
`M-v`	Move back by one page.

Editing Text

After placing the cursor where you wish to insert text, all you have to do is type. The characters you type will be inserted at the cursor. You can delete text by using the DEL key to delete the character before the cursor.

Additional Emacs Tricks

Since a large portion of the power of Emacs is involved with creating and changing buffers and windows, this section would not be complete without a brief description of some of the commands that can be used to accomplish this.

Since each time you load a file, you are creating a new buffer, it would be nice to find a way to manage these buffers. You can list all current buffers by typing:

`C-x C-b`

You can switch the current window to another buffer by typing:

```
C-x b <buffername>
```

Hint: You will be prompted to enter the name of the buffer you wish to switch to.

You can remove a buffer by typing:

```
C-x k <buffername>
```

Hint: You will be prompted to enter the name of the buffer you wish to switch to to delete. This will not affect an actual file.

To split your current window in two vertically, type:

```
C-x 2
```

To split your current window in two horizontally, type:

```
C-x 5
```

To move to another window, type:

```
C-x o
```

Hint: This is a small oh.

To delete the current window, type:

```
C-x 0
```

Hint: This is a zero.

Common Desktop Environment (CDE)—Text Editor

The Common Desktop Environment (CDE) is the result of combined efforts of IBM, HP, SUN, and Novell to create a common user interface that would have the same look and feel on any UNIX system.

Since CDE provides all of the necessary tools to do a wide range of work, it is only natural that one of these tools should include a text editor. The CDE text editor is a fairly easy to use, fairly powerful text editor, that is available on platforms that support CDE. The Common Desktop Environment (CDE) comes standard with all AIX 4.1 or later systems in fileset X11.Dt.rte, so there is no need to install anything special in order to use the CDE text editor.

Using the CDE Text Editor

The CDE text editor is a Graphical User Interface (GUI) based application that can use either the mouse or the keyboard in an intuitive fashion. There are no particular modes to worry about; all operations are menu driven. Although all commands can be typed with a keyboard, the mouse can be used as well.

Invoking the CDE Text Editor

There are several methods to invoke the CDE text editor. Perhaps the easiest is to press the Note Pad icon on the lower left of the CDE Front Panel. It is also possible to run the CDE text editor under any X-Windows or CDE session by typing /usr/dt/bin/dtpad.

Adding Lines

As with Emacs, adding text is a matter of simply typing. After invoking the text editor, you can start typing text right away. Using the return key between lines, try typing the following:

```
The quick brown fox
jumps over the
lazy dog.
```

Saving a File

You can either use the keyboard or the mouse to save a file:

Mouse:	Keyboard:
Click <File>	ALT-F
Click <Save as...>	A
type the filename	type the filename
Click <OK>	press <return>

Hint: When the "Save As" screen shows up, you may wish to change the path or folder name.

Hint: If you save an existing document, you don't have to use Save As, you can use Save, which will not prompt you for file names or paths or anything. It will just save the file.

Quitting the CDE Text Editor

Note the two methods of quitting the CDE text editor:

Mouse:	Keyboard:
Click <File>	ALT-F4
Click <Close>	

Invoking the CDE Text Editor and Editing an Old File

To start editing a file in an existing CDE text editor session, do the following:

Mouse:	**Keyboard:**
Click <File>	ALT-F
Click <Open...>	O
Type path and filename in the appropriate spots	Type path and filename in the appropriate spots
Click <OK>	Press <return>

You can also specify the filename as an argument when starting the CDE text editor from the command line, for example:

```
/usr/dt/bin/dtpad /etc/motd
```

Moving the Cursor

Cursor movement is a snap with the CDE text editor. If you like keyboards, you can use the arrow keys, along with the page up and page down keys to move the cursor.

If you like the mouse, you can use the scroll bar to move through the document. You can also point the mouse where you want the cursor to be and then press the mouse button.

Editing Text

Editing text with CDE text editor is a breeze. To add text, just point the mouse, click where you want to add text, and start typing. If you want to delete, you can either point and click and start pressing the backspace key a number of times, or you can highlight the text you want to delete (click and drag) and just press the backspace key once. In other words, this is the sort of intuitive, easy-to-use functionality we have come to expect from PC-based word processors. In fact, as you explore and experiment with this editor, you will find many of the features one has come to expect from word processors, including mouse-based cut and paste, spell checker, on-line help, formatting, and so on.

INed

Similar to the other editors in this chapter, INed is a screen-based text processing system. INed has a lot of on-line help and documentation available. INed is installed on AIX 4.3 by installing the bos.ined fileset. See Chapter 5, Installing AIX, for more information.

Using INed

Since the many key strokes used to control INed change drastically depending on your terminal type, I would recommend using another text editor such as the CDE text editor. If you get an error message, press CANCEL to continue. CANCEL is Scroll Lock on aixterm, and F4 on dtterm.

Invoking INed

INed can be invoked by typing in the name e, optionally followed by a file name to edit, or a directory:

```
e
```

or

```
e filename
```

When you do not specify a file name, INed will start the file manager. You can use the file manager to select a file to edit. Place the cursor on the file (using the arrow keys) and press ZOOM-IN (or F-11).

To create a new text file, type:

```
e filename
```

Then, select "Create a text file (without history)", with the up/down arrow keys. Then press EXECUTE (CTRL/ACT on aixterm, and Control-a enter on dtterm).

To edit an existing file use the same syntax as for creating a file.

```
e filename
```

Adding Lines

Adding lines to a file can be done by simply typing text. For example, you can type the following, pressing the return key between lines:

```
The quick brown fox
jumps over the
lazy dog.
```

Saving a File and Quitting INed

Saving a file is accomplished by typing ALT-s on an aixterm, or Control-a s on a dtterm.

You can quit INed by typing Control-\ on either terminal.

Moving the Cursor and Editing Text

Cursor movement is done with the arrow keys. You move to the next page by using page up and page down on aixterm, and Control-a plus either page up or page down on dtterm.

The default mode is insert, so adding text can be accomplished by placing the cursor at the desired position, and simply typing. Pressing the insert key on either terminal will toggle the mode between insert and overwrite, so you can change a word by switching into overwrite mode and typing over it.

INed documentation makes continual references to nonexistant keys or "editor functions" that often have very little to do with your actual keyboard. The following Tables 4–1 and 4–2 map INed virtual keys (editor functions) to actual key sequences used for aixterm, dtterm, and the LFT. For example, the documentation may talk about ZOOM-IN, but if you look at these tables, you will see they actually mean F11.

Editor FAQs

Subtitled: Give Me a Couple Wizardries to Impress My Friends!

This section answers commonly asked questions, and includes tidbits that will help you use these editors productively in short time.

I lost power before I got a chance to save a fifty page report I just typed in. What can I do?

vi

> `vi -r` should list files. Then use `vi -r filename` to reload the backup version of your document.

Emacs

> Since Emacs makes a point of saving backups fairly often, you can just edit the last backup. Backups have a tilde (~) appended to the filename.

CDE

> The CDE text editor creates a recovery file if it can that has a pound sign added before and after your file name. For example, if your filename is `foo`, then the recovery file will be called `#foo#`. To use the recovery file, simply load it in as you would a normal file.

INed

> INed creates *.bak files as backups. So, if your file was `foo`, then try reading `foo.bak`. In addition, after abnormal program termination, INed will attempt to recover lost data if invoked without any arguments, i.e., just type `e`.

How do I spell check my document?

vi

> I simply use the spell command to test spelling of documents created with `vi`. Then I go back into vi to fix up the spelling.

Table 4–1 INed Functions and Key Sequences for aixterm and LFT

Editor Function	Key Sequence	Editor Function	Key Sequence
BACKSPACE	Backspace	PAGE UP	Alt-Page Up
BACKTAB	Shift Tab	PICK COPY	F9
BEGIN LINE	Alt-Left arrow	PICK UP	F7
BOX MARK	Alt-b	PREVIOUS	Alt-F11
BREAK	Ctrl-c	PRINT	Alt-Print Screen
CANCEL	Scroll Lock	PUT COPY	F10
CENTER	Alt-c	PUT DOWN	F8
CURSOR RIGHT	Right arrow	QUIT	Ctrl-\
CURSOR UP	Up arrow	QUOTE	Alt-q
DELETE CHAR	Delete	REFRESH	Alt-z
DELETE LINE	Alt-Delete	REPLACE	Alt-End
DO	Alt-x	RESTORE	Alt-Insert
END LINE	Alt-Right arrow	RETURN	Enter
ENTER	Ctrl/Act	RIGHT	Alt-r
EXECUTE	Ctrl/Act	SAVE	Alt-s
EXIT	Alt-d	SEARCH DOWN	Alt-Down arrow
FONT	Alt-f	SEARCH UP	Alt-Up arrow
FORMAT	F5	SET TAB	Alt-v
GO TO	End	TAB	Tab
HELP	F1	TEXT MARK	Alt-t
HOME	Home	(1)	Alt-F1
INSERT LINE	F6	(2)	Alt-F2
INSERT MODE	Insert	(3)	Alt-F3
LAST ARG	Alt-a	(4)	Alt-F4
LEFT	Alt-l	(5)	Alt-F5
LINE DOWN	Page Down	(6)	Alt-F6
LINE UP	Page Up	(7)	Alt-F7
MARGIN	Alt-m	(8)	Alt-F8
MENU	F3	USE	Alt-u
NEXT	Alt-F12	WINDOW	Alt-w
NEXT WINDOW	Alt-n	ZOOM IN	F11
PAGE DOWN	Alt Page Down	ZOOM OUT	F12

Table 4–2   INed Editor Functions and Key Sequences for dtterm

Editor Function	Key Sequence	Editor Function	Key Sequence
(1)	CTRL-a F1	LOCAL-MENU	F3
(2)	CTRL-a F2	MARGIN	CTRL-a m
(3)	CTRL-a F3	MENU	F2
(4)	CTRL-a F4	NEXT	F12
(5)	CTRL-a F5	NEXT-WINDOW	CTRL-a n
(6)	CTRL-a F6	PAGE DOWN	CTRL-a Page Down
(7)	CTRL-a F7	PAGE UP	CTRL-a Page Up
(8)	CTRL-a F8	PICK-COPY	F9
BACKSPACE	BACKSPACE	PICK-UP	F7
BEGIN-LINE	CTRL-a Left arrow	PREVIOUS	CTRL-a F11
BOX-MARK	CTRL-a b	PRINT	CTRL-a p
BREAK	CTRL-c	PUT-COPY	F10
CANCEL	F4	PUT-DOWN	F8
CENTER	CTRL-a c	QUIT	CTRL-\
DELETE-CHARACTER	Delete	QUOTE	CTRL-a q
DELETE-LINE	CTRL-a Delete	REFRESH	CTRL-a z
DO	CTRL-a x	REPLACE	CTRL-a =
DOWN-ARROW	Down arrow	RESTORE	CTRL-a i
END-LINE	CTRL-a Right arrow	RETURN	Enter
ENTER	CTRL-a Enter	RIGHT	CTRL-a r
EXECUTE	CTRL-a Enter	RIGHT-ARROW	Right arrow
EXIT	CTRL-a d	SAVE	CTRL-a s
FONT	CTRL-a f	SEARCH DOWN	CTRL-a Down arrow
FORMAT	F5	SEARCH UP	CTRL-a Up arrow
GO-TO	CTRL-a g	SET-TAB	CTRL-a v
HELP	F1	TAB	Tab
HOME	CTRL-a h	-TAB	CTRL-t
INSERT-LINE	F6	TEXT-MARK	CTRL-a t
INSERT-MODE	Insert	UP-ARROW	Up arrow
LAST-ARG	CTRL-a a	USE	CTRL-a u
LEFT	CTRL-a l	WINDOW	CTRL-a w
LEFT-ARROW	Left arrow	ZOOM-IN	F11
LINEFEED	LINEFEED	ZOOM-OUT	F12
LINES DOWN	Page Down		
LINES UP	Page Up		

Emacs

Type M-x spell-buffer.

CDE

With the mouse click <Edit>, then click <Check Spelling...>. Or with a keyboard type ALT-E, then press k.

INed

Like vi, INed does not have a built-in spell checker.

You said there are public domain versions of vi. How can I get a copy for my DOS machine? Can I get Emacs for DOS?

vi

Try using anonymous ftp to get the contents of /usenet/comp.sources.unix/volume15/stevie on ftp.wustl.edu. (See the chapter on Internet for more information on anonymous ftp. You may also want to use archie to look for other or newer sites.)

Emacs

See the section on installing Emacs.

How do I search for text?

vi

From the command mode type /string<return> to search for a string "string".

Emacs

Type C-s <ESC> string <RET>.

CDE

With the mouse click <Edit>, then click <Find/Change...>, then you can type the text to search for, and click <Find>. Or with a keyboard, you can just type Control-F, and then type the text to look for and press <return>.

INed

Press ENTER string +SEARCH, or on aixterm, type Ctrl/act string Alt-Down arrow, and on dtterm type Control-a Enter string Control-a Down arrow.

I made a mistake, how do I undo my last entry?

vi

Type u from the command mode. vi can only remember one change, so the second time you press u in a row, the undo is undone.

Emacs

Type C-x u. The nice thing about undo in Emacs is that you can continue to type C-x u and it will continue to undo your changes (unlike vi which will only undo a single change).

CDE

With the mouse, click <Edit>, then click <Undo>. Or with a keyboard, just type Control-Z.

INed

Well, you could go back to a prior saved version of your document...

How do I replace every occurrence of "evrone" with "everyone"?

vi

Type 1,$s/evrone/everyone/g.

Emacs

Type M-x replace-string <RET> evrone <RET> everyone <RET>.

CDE

With the mouse, click <Edit>, then click <Find/Change...>, then specify the text to search for ("evrone") and the text to replace it with ("everyone"), and then click <Change all>. With a keyboard type Control-F, then type in the text to search for, press tab, then type in the text to replace it with ("everyone"), and press <return>.

INed

First, go to the beginning of the document, then type

ENTER 99991 "evrone" "everyone" DO

On aixterm

Ctrl/Act 99991 "evrone" "everyone" Alt-x

On dtterm

Control-a Enter 99991 "evrone" "everyone" Control-a x

What kind of on-line help or tutorials are available?

vi

Well, you can use InfoExplorer to look up the man pages for vi.

Emacs

Try C-h t to invoke the Emacs tutorial, or just typing C-h will give you some on-line help.

CDE

With the mouse, click the Help button in the upper right hand corner of the screen. With a keyboard, type ALT-H.

INed

Press F1 on either terminal, then using arrow keys select an entry, press ENTER (aixterm: Ctrl/Act, dtterm: Control-a Enter), and follow the on screen directions.

The following reference charts (Tables 4–3 to 4–13) give you a quick way to lookup how to perform common operating with each of the editors discussed in this chapter.

Reference Charts

Invoking

Table 4–3   Invoking Editors with Optional File Name

vi	Emacs	CDE	INed
vi [file]	emacs [file]	dtpad [file]	e [file]

Exiting

Table 4–4   Exiting an Editor

Description	vi	Emacs	CDE	INed
quit and save	<ESC>ZZ	C-x C-c	ALT-F4	EXIT
quit no save	<ESC>:q!<RET>	C-x C-c	ALT-F4	ENTER q EXIT

Cursor Movement

Table 4–5 Moving the Cursor

Description	vi	Emacs	CDE	INed
Previous char	h	C-b	left arrow	LEFT-ARROW
Next Char	l	C-f	right arrow	RIGHT-ARROW
Previous Line	k	C-p	up arrow	UP-ARROW
Next Line	j	C-n	down arrow	DOWN-ARROW
Previous Screen	C-b	M-v	page up	PAGE UP
Next screen	C-f	C-v	page down	PAGE DOWN
Beginning of Line	0	C-a	home	BEGIN-LINE
End of Line	$	C-e	end	END-LINE
Beginning of File	:0<RET>	M-<	Control-Home	GOTO
End of File	:$<RET>	M->	Control-End	ENTER GOTO
goto line x	:x<RET>	C-x goto-line <RET>x<RET>	Control-G, new # <ret> (if needed, ALT-o s shows status)	ENTER x GOTO

Searching

Table 4–6 Searching for Text

Description	vi	Emacs	CDE	INed
Forward search	/text<RET>	C-s text	Control-F text <RET>	ENTER text SEARCH DOWN
Backward search	?text<RET>	C-r text	—	ENTER text SEARCH UP

File Manipulation

Table 4–7 File Manipulation Commands

Description	vi	Emacs	CDE	INed
Save current file	<ESC>:w!<RET>	C-x C-s	ALT-F s	SAVE
Save As	<ESC>:w! file <RET>	C-x C-w file	ALT-F A file <RET>	ENTER file SAVE
Load File	<ESC>:e file <RET>	C-x C-f file	ALT-F O file <RET>	ENTER file USE

Insertion (*vi* Only)

Table 4–8   Inserting Text with vi

Description	vi	All Other Editors
Insert at cursor	i	Just position cursor and type!
Insert at end of line	A	Just position cursor and type!
Start new line below cursor	o	Just position cursor and type!

Deletion

Table 4–9   Deleting Text

Description	vi	Emacs	CDE	INed
Delete character	x	C-d	backspace and delete	DELETE-CHARACTER
Delete entire line	dd	C-a C-k	home control-delete	DELETE-LINE

Miscellaneous

Table 4–10   Miscellaneous Editor Commands and Information

Description	vi	Emacs	CDE	INed
Meta-	—	<ESC>	—	—
Cancel Command	<ESC>	C-g	<ESC>	CANCEL
Undo	u	C-x u	Control-z	—
Refresh Screen	<ESC> C-l	C-l	automatic	REFRESH
Spell Check	—	M-x spell-buffer<RET>	ALT-e k	—
Shell Command	:! <cmd> <RET>	M-! <cmd> <RET>	—	ENTER <cmd> MENU

Help

Table 4–11 On-line Help

Description	vi	Emacs	CDE	INed
Help	—	C-h	Control-Z	HELP
Tutorial	—	C-H t	—	—
Documentation	InfoExplorer	C-h i	—	Infoexplorer

Buffer (Emacs Only)

Table 4–12 Buffer Management Commands (Emacs only)

Description	Emacs
List Buffers	C-x C-v
Switch to buffer	C-x b buffername <RET>
Kill buffer	C-x k buffername <RET>

Windows (Emacs Only)

Table 4–13 Windows Management Commands (Emacs only)

Description	Emacs
Split horizontal	C-x 2
Split vertical	C-x 5
Return to one window	C-x 1
Move to other window	C-x o (letter oh)
Close current window	C-x 0 (zero)

Table 4–1   INed Functions and Key Sequences for aixterm and LFT

Editor Function	Key Sequence	Editor Function	Key Sequence
BACKSPACE	Backspace	PAGE UP	Alt-Page Up
BACKTAB	Shift Tab	PICK COPY	F9
BEGIN LINE	Alt-Left arrow	PICK UP	F7
BOX MARK	Alt-b	PREVIOUS	Alt-F11
BREAK	Ctrl-c	PRINT	Alt-Print Screen
CANCEL	Scroll Lock	PUT COPY	F10
CENTER	Alt-c	PUT DOWN	F8
CURSOR RIGHT	Right arrow	QUIT	Ctrl-\
CURSOR UP	Up arrow	QUOTE	Alt-q
DELETE CHAR	Delete	REFRESH	Alt-z
DELETE LINE	Alt-Delete	REPLACE	Alt-End
DO	Alt-x	RESTORE	Alt-Insert
END LINE	Alt-Right arrow	RETURN	Enter
ENTER	Ctrl/Act	RIGHT	Alt-r
EXECUTE	Ctrl/Act	SAVE	Alt-s
EXIT	Alt-d	SEARCH DOWN	Alt-Down arrow
FONT	Alt-f	SEARCH UP	Alt-Up arrow
FORMAT	F5	SET TAB	Alt-v
GO TO	End	TAB	Tab
HELP	F1	TEXT MARK	Alt-t
HOME	Home	(1)	Alt-F1
INSERT LINE	F6	(2)	Alt-F2
INSERT MODE	Insert	(3)	Alt-F3
LAST ARG	Alt-a	(4)	Alt-F4
LEFT	Alt-l	(5)	Alt-F5
LINE DOWN	Page Down	(6)	Alt-F6
LINE UP	Page Up	(7)	Alt-F7
MARGIN	Alt-m	(8)	Alt-F8
MENU	F3	USE	Alt-u
NEXT	Alt-F12	WINDOW	Alt-w
NEXT WINDOW	Alt-n	ZOOM IN	F11
PAGE DOWN	Alt Page Down	ZOOM OUT	F12

Table 4–2   INed Editor Functions and Key Sequences for dtterm

Editor Function	Key Sequence	Editor Function	Key Sequence
(1)	CTRL-a F1	LOCAL-MENU	F3
(2)	CTRL-a F2	MARGIN	CTRL-a m
(3)	CTRL-a F3	MENU	F2
(4)	CTRL-a F4	NEXT	F12
(5)	CTRL-a F5	NEXT-WINDOW	CTRL-a n
(6)	CTRL-a F6	PAGE DOWN	CTRL-a Page Down
(7)	CTRL-a F7	PAGE UP	CTRL-a Page Up
(8)	CTRL-a F8	PICK-COPY	F9
BACKSPACE	BACKSPACE	PICK-UP	F7
BEGIN-LINE	CTRL-a Left arrow	PREVIOUS	CTRL-a F11
BOX-MARK	CTRL-a b	PRINT	CTRL-a p
BREAK	CTRL-c	PUT-COPY	F10
CANCEL	F4	PUT-DOWN	F8
CENTER	CTRL-a c	QUIT	CTRL-\
DELETE-CHARACTER	Delete	QUOTE	CTRL-a q
DELETE-LINE	CTRL-a Delete	REFRESH	CTRL-a z
DO	CTRL-a x	REPLACE	CTRL-a =
DOWN-ARROW	Down arrow	RESTORE	CTRL-a i
END-LINE	CTRL-a Right arrow	RETURN	Enter
ENTER	CTRL-a Enter	RIGHT	CTRL-a r
EXECUTE	CTRL-a Enter	RIGHT-ARROW	Right arrow
EXIT	CTRL-a d	SAVE	CTRL-a s
FONT	CTRL-a f	SEARCH DOWN	CTRL-a Down arrow
FORMAT	F5		
GO-TO	CTRL-a g	SEARCH UP	CTRL-a Up arrow
HELP	F1	SET-TAB	CTRL-a v
HOME	CTRL-a h	TAB	Tab
INSERT-LINE	F6	-TAB	CTRL-t
INSERT-MODE	Insert	TEXT-MARK	CTRL-a t
LAST-ARG	CTRL-a a	UP-ARROW	Up arrow
LEFT	CTRL-a l	USE	CTRL-a u
LEFT-ARROW	Left arrow	WINDOW	CTRL-a w
LINEFEED	LINEFEED	ZOOM-IN	F11
LINES DOWN	Page Down	ZOOM-OUT	F12
LINES UP	Page Up		

Table 4–3 Invoking Editors with Optional File Name

vi	Emacs	CDE	INed
vi [file]	emacs [file]	dtpad [file]	e [file]

Table 4–4 Exiting an Editor

Description	vi	Emacs	CDE	INed
quit and save	<ESC>ZZ	C-x C-c	ALT-F4	EXIT
quit no save	<ESC>:q!<RET>	C-x C-c	ALT-F4	ENTER q EXIT

Table 4–5 Moving the Cursor

Description	vi	Emacs	CDE	INed
Previous char	h	C-b	left arrow	LEFT-ARROW
Next Char	l	C-f	right arrow	RIGHT-ARROW
Previous Line	k	C-p	up arrow	UP-ARROW
Next Line	j	C-n	down arrow	DOWN-ARROW
Previous Screen	C-b	M-v	page up	PAGE UP
Next screen	C-f	C-v	page down	PAGE DOWN
Beginning of Line	0	C-a	home	BEGIN-LINE
End of Line	$	C-e	end	END-LINE
Beginning of File	:0<RET>	M-<	Control-Home	GOTO
End of File	:$<RET>	M->	Control-End	ENTER GOTO
goto line x	:x<RET>	C-x goto-line <RET>x<RET>	Control-G, new # <ret> (if needed, ALT-o s shows status)	ENTER x GOTO

Table 4–6   Searching for Text

Description	vi	Emacs	CDE	INed
Forward search	/text<RET>	C-s text	Control-F text <RET>	ENTER text SEARCH DOWN
Backward search	?text<RET>	C-r text	—	ENTER text SEARCH UP

Table 4–7   File Manipulation Commands

Description	vi	Emacs	CDE	INed
Save current file	<ESC>:w!<RET>	C-x C-s	ALT-F s	SAVE
Save As	<ESC>:w! file <RET>	C-x C-w file	ALT-F A file <RET>	ENTER file SAVE
Load File	<ESC>:e file <RET>	C-x C-f file	ALT-F O file <RET>	ENTER file USE

Table 4–8   Inserting Text with vi

Description	vi	All Other Editors
Insert at cursor	i	Just position cursor and type!
Insert at end of line	A	Just position cursor and type!
Start new line below cursor	o	Just position cursor and type!

Table 4–9　Deleting Text

Description	vi	Emacs	CDE	INed
Delete character	x	C-d	backspace and delete	DELETE-CHARACTER
Delete entire line	dd	C-a C-k	home control-delete	DELETE-LINE

Table 4–10　Miscellaneous Editor Commands and Information

Description	vi	Emacs	CDE	INed
Meta-	—	<ESC>	—	—
Cancel Command	<ESC>	C-g	<ESC>	CANCEL
Undo	u	C-x u	Control-z	—
Refresh Screen	<ESC> C-l	C-l	automatic	REFRESH
Spell Check	—	M-x spell-buffer<RET>	ALT-e k	—
Shell Command	:! <cmd> <RET>	M-! <cmd> <RET>	—	ENTER <cmd> MENU

Table 4–11　On-line Help

Description	vi	Emacs	CDE	INed
Help	—	C-h	Control-Z	HELP
Tutorial	—	C-H t	—	—
Documentation	InfoExplorer	C-h i	—	Infoexplorer

Table 4–12 Buffer Management Commands (Emacs only)

Description	Emacs
List Buffers	C-x C-v
Switch to buffer	C-x b buffername <RET>
Kill buffer	C-x k buffername <RET>

Table 4–13 Windows Management Commands (Emacs only)

Description	Emacs
Split horizontal	C-x 2
Split vertical	C-x 5
Return to one window	C-x 1
Move to other window	C-x o (letter oh)
Close current window	C-x 0 (zero)

References

1. Cameron, Debra and Roseblatt, Bill, *Learning GNU Emacs*, Sebastopul, CA: O'Reilly & Associates, 1991.

2. Lamb, Linda, *Learning the vi Editor,* Sebastopul, CA: O'Reilly & Associates, 1986.

3. Stallman, Richard, *GNU Emacs Manual*, Cambridge, MA: Free Software Foundation, 1987.

4. IBM, *AIX V4.1: The INed User's Guide,* Form number SC23-2524-00.

5. CDE Documentation Group, *Common Desktop Environment 1.0 User's Guide,* Reading, MA: Addison-Wesley, 1995 (see chapter 10).

CHAPTER
5

- How to Get AIX Up and Running

- How Is AIX Packaged?

- All Right! Installation Assistance!

- Network Installation Manager

Installing AIX

T he nitty-gritty of AIX installation is thoroughly covered in the *AIX Installation Guide* (SC23-2550). In this chapter, we're going to tell you how AIX installation just got easier and how network installation is now a possibility. We'll touch on the AIX installation highlights, and then we're going to dig into the GUI tools that make installation entertaining—the Install Assistant, the Install and Update Software Manager, and the Maintain Installed Software Manager. We'll show you how to do a network install—undertaking a network install is extremely useful when you're ready to knock 'em dead. So, sit back, tighten your AIX headgear, and get ready to take off!

How to Get AIX Up and Running

Unlike those wimpy shrink-wrapped operating systems you can just buy off the shelf, AIX offers you significant installation functionality (Figure 5–1). You can install AIX on stand-alone systems (a system that starts up by itself); you can manage the installation and configuration of diskless, dataless, or stand-alone systems from a network installation server; or you can get AIX preinstalled at the factory. Refer to the *AIX Installation Guide* if you're installing a stand-alone machine; see the *AIX Network Installation Management Guide and Reference* if you're tackling a network install; and refer to your *Start-up Instructions for Preinstalled Systems* if you took the easy way out and had your system preinstalled.

If you're installing AIX from a CD-ROM or tape, load the tape or CD into the appropriate drive and get going—you can accept default settings and begin installation immediately. Or, you can verify or change system settings before beginning the installation. You also have the option of customizing the BOS Install

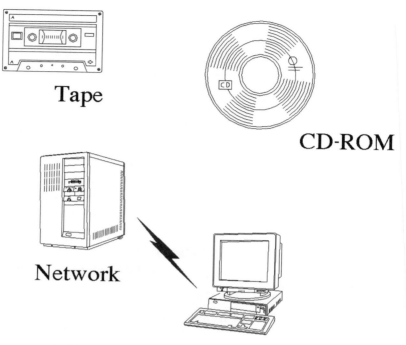

Figure 5–1 AIX Installation Options

program. (BOS is an acronym for *base operating system* and is used interchangeably with AIX by seasoned AIX system administrators.) AIX system administrators can modify the `bosinst.data` file, enabling installation without the set of menus usually displayed—this might speed up installation, but be careful that you don't get misdirected in the process.

You can also install optional software and service updates. The latter are "fixes" that the AIX development team makes available for bugs discovered between major releases. AIX installation also includes a migration path that allows you to move from AIX Version 3.2.x to the most recent version, while keeping customized configuration information and installed optional software. Any configuration files that cannot be migrated will be saved in a specific directory.

The AIX Version 4.3 software license management system allows an application to operate in compliance with the terms and conditions of its license agreement. For example, when you load your AIX CSet++ compiler, you will be asked for your license or "key" to the code. You obtain this code through your point of sale.

How Is AIX Packaged?

Software products include those shipped with AIX and those purchased separately. For example, the AIX client package includes Motif and AIXwindows; however, if you wanted the AIX multimedia product, Ultimedia, you would purchase that software package separately from the AIX base operating system.

AIX is organized into small, installable filesets. You can install only what you need! AIX 4 has approximately 2,200 filesets. Each fileset can be serviced separately—fixes are delivered in fileset packages and are cumulative.

A function previously installed automatically with **bos.obj** (hardware diagnostics, extended RAS) for example, is packaged separately and installed only if you select it. To simplify installation (by helping you determine which filesets to install), filesets are now grouped into bundles; sets of filesets (of a certain type) that are apt to be installed by most users.

Packaging Definitions

The following terms are packaging definitions:

- **Fileset**   Filesets provide a specific function. For example, **bos.net.tcp.nfs** is a fileset in the **bos.net** package. A fileset is the smallest individually installable unit.

- **Package**   A group of filesets with common function.

- **Bundle**   A collection of filesets and fileset updates that provide specific functions. Predefined bundles contain a specific set of filesets. Now this is a cool idea—you can create your own bundle by using the SMIT Custom Install path or the Install and Update Software Manager graphical application. Bundle definitions are stored in the **/usr/sys/Inst.dat/sys_bundles** directory.

- **Product Offering**   Selected sets of packages are grouped together to meet the needs of specific customers. Product offerings contain all of the filesets that go on the media, while a bundle defines some subset of these filesets to actually install on a system. For example, AIX 4.3 for Clients is a product offering.

- **Licensed Program Products (LPPs)**   Complete software product including all packages and filesets associated with the LPP. For example, the Base Operating System (BOS) is an LPP.

  Example of Packaging Term Usage

  Licensed Program Product
  bos

Package
```
bos.diag
```

Fileset
```
bos.diag.rte
```

Product Offerings

Filesets are grouped together into different sets to meet the needs of different customers. AIX product offerings include the following:

- AIX for Advanced Servers
- AIX for Workgroup Groups
- AIX for Clients
- AIX for Entry Clients
- AIX for Clients
- AIX for Servers
- Licensed Program Products
- DES (Data Encryption Standard)
- InfoExplorer Hypertext
- Diagnostics
- OpenGL and GL32
- PEX and graPHIGS

AIX bundles include these offerings:

- Client Bundle
- Personal Productivity Bundle
- Server Bundle
- Hardware Diagnostics Bundle
- Application Development Bundle

Understanding AIX Version Control

AIX release numbering indicates the Version Release Modification Fix level (VRMF); for example, the AIX 4.1.1 bos.rte.up fileset had a VRMF of 4.1.1.0, indicating Version 4, Release 1, Modification Level 1, Fix Level 0.

Version numbers are incremented to indicate a new product. Major functional enhancements occur every one to two years. Release numbers are incremented to show a product enhancement and generally fall one year apart.

The modification level is incremented for two reasons: accumulation of maintenance and support of new processors or devices that DO NOT change the behavior of the product on existing systems. This occurs generally three to six months
apart.

The fix level field is incremented when a fix is added to a fileset. Fixes for AIX 4
are produced on customer demand. Note that maintenance and fix levels for AIX
4 do not change application interfaces; applications that are written to documented interfaces should function identically on different maintenance and fix
levels.

After installing the AIX base operating system, AIX will run with default settings: one user (root); the date and time set for where the system was manu-
factured; and other general settings. To change some or all of these settings and
to provide system and network information for communication with other systems, use the Installation Assistant.

All Right! Installation Assistance!

Installation Assistant supports software installation and the initial configuration
of RS/6000s. The task of supporting installations is divided into three applications: Installation Assistant, Install and Update Software Manager, and Maintain
Installed Software Manager.

Installation Assistant

Installation Assistant is displayed when you first start-up your system; Installation Assistant walks you through the tasks needed to install options (the software you want to install) and configure the system for use. You can also bring up
the Installation Assistant by entering install_assist on the command line.

Use the Installation Assistant for the following purposes:

- Set date and time
- Set root password
- Set installation device
- Configure network communications
- Manage system storage and paging space
- Manage language environment
- Create users
- Define printers
- Import existing volume groups

- Install license passwords and software applications
- Backup the system

The Installation Assistant start-up screen is shown in Figure 5–2. The Installation Assistant task list provides the following for each task:

- Task title
- Numbered steps on how to perform each task
- Suggested reading
- Hypertext link to proceed to the next task
- Hypertext link to return to the initial menu

How Do I Get Started?   To make changes to the system configuration during installation, you can choose one of two paths. Clicking on the *i* icon (shown in Figure 5–3) before each task walks you through the information path, explains why each task should be executed, and then provides step-by-step instructions. For example, if you click on the iconified *i* next to the **Set Date and Time** task, you would see the informational screen shown in Figure 5–4.

Clicking on the airplane (shown in Figure 5–5) leads you directly to the action listed on the screen. Using this path, the application related to the selected topic can be started and displayed beside the Installation Assistant. Completing tasks by clicking on the airplane enables you to simultaneously read and execute instructions step-by-step.

If you'd like more information on how the Installation Assistant works before beginning your system configuration, click on Using Installation Assistant (it's underlined indicating that it's a hypertext link). Selecting Using Installation Assistant invokes the screen shown in Figure 5–6.

Easy Install and Install and Update Software Manager

Easy Install enables you to install a software bundle already created to meet specific needs—installing through Easy Install requires minimal decision making. First, you select how the software bundle is to be installed (either from tape, directory, or CD). Then select which software bundle is to be installed (for example, the client or server bundle). If all the functionality you want from AIX is in a particular bundle, use this application. This application only installs the software for which you have a license or that does not require a license. The software is committed at the same time it is installed without saving the previous version of the software. (Note that once you have *committed* software, there is no turning back to the previous level.) Bring up Easy Install by entering

```
xinstallm -ez
```

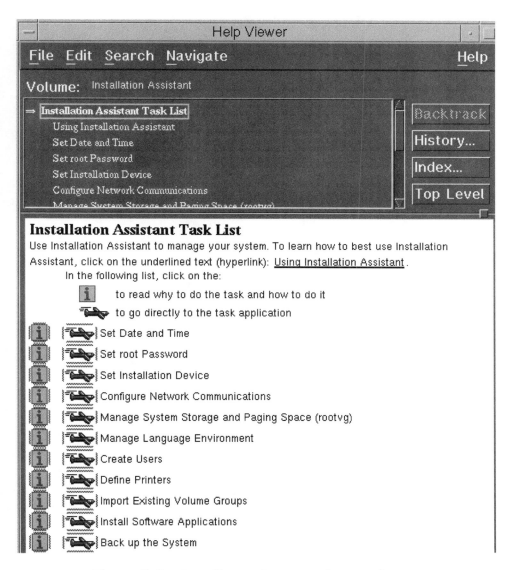

Figure 5–2   Installation Assistant Startup Screen

Figure 5–3   Information Path Icon

Set Date and Time

💡 Why Do This Task

Before you begin, determine the geographic time zone and if Daylight Savings Time is in effect.

⚠️ *Caution:* Complete all the steps before selecting OK. Selecting OK closes the Set Date and Time application. The system time is set to what is displayed in the time fields. Since the time fields are static, reset the time just before selecting OK.

Instructions

1.

   Click the picture and wait for the Set Date and Time graphical dialog to open.

2. At the top of the window, locate the Current System Time field. If the date is not correct, locate the Date area and set the correct date using the Year, Month, and Day fields provided.

3. Add new step.

4. At the right of the Selected Time field, locate the Time Notation option menu. Make sure the displayed notation is correct.

   For example, if it is set to 24–hour and your network uses the 12–hour clock, specify AM or PM depending on your current 12–hour clock.

5. In the lower right side of the window, locate the Time Zone field. Make sure the displayed geographical time zone and standard time indicator are correct. (If daylight savings time is in effect, the DST indicator should be displayed.)

   To change the standard time indicator or the time zone, click List.

   a. To change the daylight savings time indicator, click the Daylight Savings Time check box.

Figure 5–4   Set Date and Time Information Screen

You can also bring up Easy Install by clicking on the Easy Install icon in the Application Manager System_Admin directory. The Easy Install interface is shown in Figure 5–7.

The Install and Update Software Manager enables users to understand the relationships between licensed products, installable filesets, maintenance levels, enhancements, and fixes.

Figure 5–5   Task Execution Icon

Using Installation Assistant

Installation Assistant simplifies customizing your system by guiding you through post-installation tasks and, in some cases, automatically installing software packages for you. In addition, the Installation Assistant introduces you to various interfaces, providing only the help you need, when you need it. If you are unfamiliar with using a mouse or with terms like "click" and "drag and drop," select the following hyperlink: Using a Mouse.

How to Use the Installation Assistant Task List
You can follow the learning path or the fast path.

i   Learning Path – Click the "i" for information on why you would want to do a task, what the prerequisites are, and how to complete a task. Click the "i" for the first task "Set Date and Time," then select the" To Continue" button at the end of each task to step through the tasks in the suggested order.

    Fast Path – If you are familiar with the tasks and know how to use SMIT and graphical interfaces, then click the airplane to skip the instructions and go directly to the task application.

How to Use the Task Instructions
Each task contains the following sections:

Title	Identifies the task. Some tasks lead into subtasks.
? Why Do This Task	The reasons for performing the task, and its advantages. Click the ?.
Prerequisites	Prerequisites or suggestions to consider.
Instructions	A picture (graphic hyperlink) to start the task application and instructions to complete the task. Read through the instructions once, click the picture, adjust the windows so you can read the instructions as you complete the task. To learn how to manage your windows, select the following hyperlink: Moving and Resizing Windows
To Continue:	The suggested order for completing the tasks. For instance, you should make all the changes to the system before you make a backup copy of it. If you choose not to follow the suggested order, select tasks from the Installation Assistant Task List or the topic tree in the upper pane of this window.

Figure 5–6   Using Installation Assistant Startup Screen

You can use the Install Update Software Manager for the following tasks:

- Install or update software packages
- Set default install settings
- Preview size/options required for install packages (prerequisites)
- Copy install images for use in future installs
- Create new install bundles

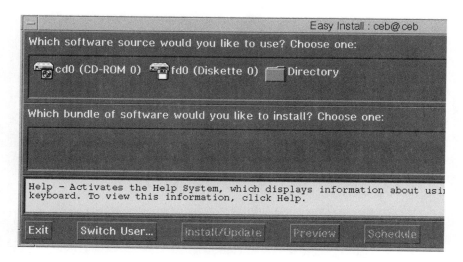

Figure 5–7   Easy Install Startup Screen

The Install and Update Software Manager provides users with a Visual System Manager application to execute the `installp` command. Bring up the Install and Update Software Manager by clicking on the **Install Software Applications** task on the Installation Assistant start-up screen. Clicking on the **Install Software Applications** task brings up the Software Installation & Maintenance SMIT screen. You can also bring up the Install and Update Software Manager by entering

`xinstallm`

From the Installation & Maintenance SMIT screen, select **Install Selectable Software (Custom Install)** to bring up the Install and Update Software Manger. You can also bring up the Install and Update Software Manager by clicking on the Install Manager icon in the Application Manager System_Admin directory. The Install and Update Software Manager startup screen is shown in Figure 5–8.

The Install and Update Software Manager helps users select the correct install device (for example, tape, CD-ROM, or diskette) and bundle (for example, client, server, or personal productivity) for installation. See the information on AIX packaging for more information on AIX software bundles.

After you select the installation device you want to use, the installation device is read and the list of software available on the media is displayed in the work area.

When a user selects a bundle, the Install and Update Software Manager selects all of the software titles in the bundle that are also on the install media enabling you to quickly select the software you want to install.

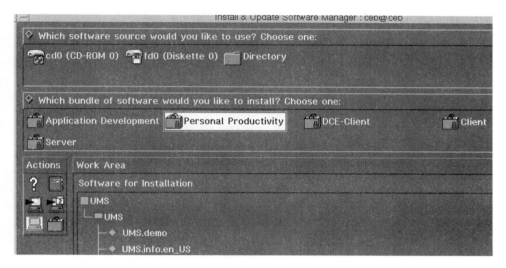

Figure 5–8 Install and Update Software Manager
Startup Screen

Using the Install and Update Manager, you can select or deselect additional software titles, or specify any of the following actions for the selected titles:

- Install the selected software
- Schedule the installation to occur later
- Preview the selected software for size
- Save the selected objects as a new bundle (create your own bundle)

The relationship between the filesets, files, and fixes is presented in a tree view. You can also specify any of the following actions for the installation task:

- Show the following install settings

  Apply and commit

  Install requisite software

  Extend the filesystem if needed

  Include language packages
- Show or change the scheduled activities
- Delete the bundle or object

Maintain Installed Software Manager

The Maintain Installed Software Manager manages software that has already been installed. Users can select objects from the product list and specify any of the following actions:

- Commit the selected software
- Reject the selected software
- Cleanup installed software
- Verify that the selected software is complete

You can also find specific objects by name and delete software (de-install). Bring up the Maintain Installed Software Manager by clicking on the Application Manager located on the CDE Front Panel. Double-click on the System_Admin icon, then the Maintain Software icon. Or, you can enter

```
xmaintm
```

Clicking on the Maintain Software icon brings up the Maintain Installed Software Manager start-up screen as shown in Figure 5–9.

Network Installation Manager

You can install AIX using tape or CD-ROM or by using the Network Installation Manager (NIM). NIM is not only an excellent tool for installing multiple ma-

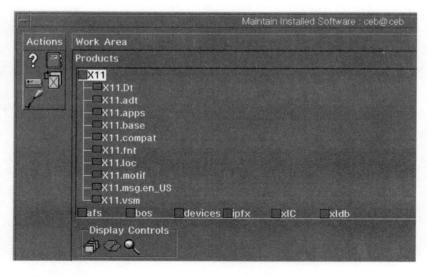

Figure 5–9   Maintain Software Manager Start-up Screen

chines over a network, it can also be used for software maintenance and machine customizations. Using NIM, you can set up an installation once for machines with identical requirements or customize the specific needs of given machines. The number of machines you install simultaneously depends on the throughput of your network, the disk access throughput of the installation servers, and the platform type of your servers. System administrators can perform tasks for multiple machines from NIM including running diagnostics and installing fixes. Note that the Network Installation Manager utility is thoroughly discussed in the *AIX Network Installation Management Guide and Reference.*

Advantages of network installation include the ability to share installation images. Since the installation images are on the network, it is easier to share them between machines. Installation can be initiated by either the NIM master or a NIM client. If the master initiates it, it is called a push install. If the client initiates it, it is called a pull install.

With push capability, an administrator can update machines for people. If some new software comes in, the administrator can push the files onto his client machines. The machine users do not have to get involved. With pull capability, the clients can customize their own machines. A NIM resource server can be used as a software library. Since it is on the network, the installer does not have to hunt down the media.

What do you gain by using NIM? If your organization has strong central network administration, NIM is extremely useful for updating machines. NIM is also great for environments where many machines are installed/updated simultaneously because machines can share the installation media on the network. Using NIM also reduces installation time—network communication is faster than tape and CD-ROM input/output. How big can your NIM environment be? You can define the size; the NIM environment is easily expandable from your development lab to your multiple corporate sites to your international offices (Figure 5–10).

NIM Environment

The NIM environment is composed of two basic machine roles: *master* and *client*. The NIM master manages the installation of the rest of the machines in the NIM environment. The master is the only machine that can remotely execute NIM commands on the clients. All the other machines participating in the NIM environment are clients to the master, including machines that may also serve resources. A smallscale NIM environment is shown in Figure 5–11.

The types of machines you can install are *stand-alone*, *diskless*, and *dataless*. A stand-alone machine is one that can boot (start up) by itself. Diskless and dataless systems cannot boot by themselves. They must use remote resources to boot.

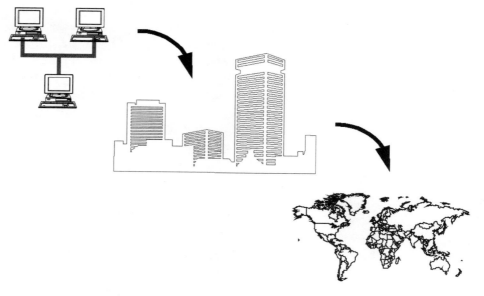

Figure 5–10   Expandable NIM Environment

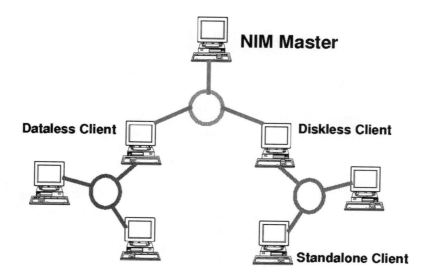

Figure 5–11   Small-scale NIM Environment

Diskless systems have no disk drive. Dataless systems have a local disk drive but they cannot boot from it. This book provides concepts and procedures for setting up the NIM environment and initiating the installation of stand-alone machines and the initialization of resources for diskless and dataless machines.

Most installation tasks in the NIM environment are performed from one server, called the *master*. A set of installation tasks can also be performed from NIM clients. Once the administrator completes the network installation setup, users of stand-alone clients can, from the client, install software that is available on NIM servers.

The machines you want to manage in the NIM environment, their resources, and the networks through which the machines communicate are all represented as *objects* within a central database that resides on the master. Each of these objects has *attributes* that give it a unique identity, such as the network address of a machine or the location of a file or directory. With this information, you can install the base operating system and optional software on multiple machines, managed from a central location.

NIM Master.   There is only one NIM master per NIM environment. The master is fundamental for all operations in the NIM environment. This machine must be set up and functional before you can perform any NIM operations. The master must be a stand-alone machine, running AIX Version 4.3, with the NIM master fileset installed. The master manages the NIM configuration database and provides the central point of administration for the NIM environment.

The rsh command is used to remotely execute commands on clients. To use the rsh command, the .rhosts file on the client is configured automatically by NIM so that the master has the permissions required to execute commands on the client. Once a NIM client is running, a user with root authority on a client can disable the master's permissions to push commands onto the client. A user with root authority on a client can also enable the master's push permissions for the client.

NIM Clients.   NIM clients can have the following configurations:

*   Stand-alone
*   Diskless
*   Dataless

Stand-alone clients have all the required file systems on a local disk after installation. Diskless clients access all their resources from servers in the network. Dataless clients have a combination of local and remote resources.

The installation processing that occurs on diskless and dataless clients involves populating the root directory for the client with files from a resource known as a Shared Product Object Tree (SPOT) that is located on a NIM server. A SPOT is a /usr file system or an equivalent file system that is exported by servers in the NIM environment for remote client use.

While the master can push installation resources onto NIM clients, a running stand-alone NIM client can also initiate the installation by *pulling* resources from another NIM machine.

Diskless and dataless clients cannot initiate installations because these resources are not stored on the client.

NIM Objects

NIM stores information about the physical environment as objects in the NIM database. There are three *classes* of objects:

- Networks
- Machines
- Resources, which are files and directories required to perform NIM operations

Network Objects

Network objects represent information about each local area network (LAN) that is part of the NIM environment. These objects and their attributes reflect the physical characteristics of the network environment. This information does not affect the running of a physical network but is used internally by NIM for configuration information.

There are three types of network objects. These objects represent the following types of networks that are supported in the NIM environment:

- Token-Ring
- Ethernet
- Fiber Distributed Data Interface (FDDI)

Each network object contains the following information:

- The network interface type: Token-Ring, Ethernet, or FDDI
- The Internet Protocol (IP) address of the network
- The subnet mask of the network
- The NIM routing information for the network, if required.

Clients use resources that are usually provided by other machines in the NIM environment. The NIM routing information is required to define which gateways should be used when establishing communication with clients on different networks.

On Network objects you can perform the following management operations:

1. **Define:** Creates a new object.

2. **Change:** Adds new attributes or changes the existing attributes of the object.

3. **Remove:** Removes the network object from the database.

Machine Objects

There are three types of machine objects. These objects represent the following machine configurations that are supported in the NIM environment:

- Stand-alone
- Diskless
- Dataless

Each machine object in the NIM database has associated attributes representing information about each client that participates in the NIM environment. This information includes the following:

- The type of machine: diskless, dataless, or stand-alone
- The hardware address of the client's network interface
- The TCP/IP host name for the client
- The name of the network object that represents the network to which the client is connected
- The ring speed of the Token-Ring network or the cable type for the Ethernet network connection.

A client can have multiple network interfaces. The first interface that is defined is called the *primary interface*. This attribute of the machine object specifies the interface that a client must use to access NIM resources.

There are two types of operations that can be performed on machine objects: *management* and *control* operations. The management operations manipulate the object instances in the NIM database. The control operations initiate an action to be performed on the client.

Resource Objects

Resource objects represent the available resources in the NIM environment. All operations on clients in the NIM environment require one or more resources. NIM resource objects represent files and directories that are used to support some type of NIM operation. Because NIM resources are ordinary file system objects in the AIX operating system, most of them are provided to clients with standard Network File System (NFS) software. This means that many resources must reside locally on the servers providing these resources, because NFS can only export file system objects that are stored on local media in the machines from which they are exported.

Shared Product Object Tree

The Shared Product Object Tree (SPOT) is a fundamental resource in the NIM environment. It is required to install or initialize all machine configuration types. A SPOT provides a /usr file system for diskless and dataless clients, as well as the network boot support for all clients.

Everything that a machine requires in a /usr file system, such as the AIX kernel, executable commands, libraries, and applications, is included in the SPOT. Machine-unique information or user data is usually stored in the other file systems. A SPOT can be located on any stand-alone machine within the NIM environment, including the master. The SPOT is created, controlled, and maintained from the master, even though the SPOT can be located on another system.

There are two ways to create a SPOT. You can convert the /usr file system (/usr SPOT) or you can locate the SPOT elsewhere within the file system (non-/usr SPOT) on the server.

A SPOT is also used to create and maintain the network boot images and the support for network boot processing. The network boot images are created using the files that reside in the SPOT and reside in the /tftpboot directory on the SPOT server. Network boot images are limited in size and cannot include all the code necessary to boot a system. A SPOT provides these files for the client boot process by exporting the resources with NFS.

The Network Boot Process

The AIX boot process brings a machine to a specific execution state. Every machine requires a *boot image* that can be loaded after the machine is turned on or reset. A boot image contains the AIX kernel and a RAM file system containing libraries and programs necessary to reach a specific state. Stand-alone machines use a boot image stored on the local disk. Network-dependent systems, such as diskless or dataless systems, retrieve a boot image from a server on the network every time the system is turned on. The boot image is called a *network boot image*.

To obtain a network boot image, NIM clients use the BOOTP and TFTP protocol. The BOOTP protocol consists of a client sending a request to a server for a boot image, which enables the client to achieve a specific state.

In the NIM environment, a network boot image is also required to install stand-alone machines over the network. After installation, the stand-alone machines boot using the boot image that resides on the local disk.

Initial Program Load (IPL) Read Only Memory (ROM) Emulation

The Initial Program Load (IPL) Read Only Memory (ROM) is a piece of firmware in each machine that is responsible for locating and loading an AIX boot image. After the boot image is located and loaded, the IPL ROM's role is complete. It is the loaded boot image that brings the machine to a specific state.

All versions of IPL ROM can search local devices for an AIX boot image. However, only some versions, known as BOOTP-enabled IPL ROM, can use a network communications adapter to search for a remote boot image. The BOOTP-enabled versions use the boot protocol (BOOTP) to find a network boot image and retrieve it using Trivial File Transfer Protocol (TFTP).

Some machines do not have a BOOTP-enabled IPL ROM. These machines must use the IPL ROM emulation program, which enables the machine to search for a remote boot image. The IPL ROM emulation program can be stored on a diskette (or a tape). The program is created on the NIM master.

The client machine will boot from the media to provide the same function as the BOOTP-enabled IPL ROM. The IPL ROM emulation media should be left in the drive of the target machine so the machine can be rebooted remotely from the master.

CHAPTER
6

- Using SMIT to Install Devices
- Printers

Setting up
Peripherals

I n this chapter we will explain how to use SMIT to set up devices such as CD-ROMs, generic devices, and most importantly, printers. Since printers are so crucial to everyday work, we will go into detail on how to set up, administer, use, and troubleshoot your printer under AIX.

Using SMIT to Install Devices

The Software Management Interface Tool (SMIT) is a useful graphical interface for nearly all system management tasks. After you have physically plugged in any new devices (be sure the power is off first!), log into your computer as root and run SMIT with the command `smit devices` (you can also select "devices" from the main SMIT menu). If you run SMIT from a graphical environment such as the CDE desktop, or from an X-Windows session, you will see the screen in Figure 6–1, otherwise you will see a text-based version with the same prompts and labels.

Adding, removing, and configuring peripherals is easily done by selecting the type of device you wish to work with from the menu above. Although each device has its own unique installation quirks, there are several concepts that apply to all devices that you should be familiar with. Devices can be defined, supported, and available. Nearly all device menus have options to display supported and defined devices. A supported device is one that AIX knows how to use. An unsupported device can also be used on AIX if additional software or configuration data is loaded. A defined device is one that has actually been configured to work on your system; your system knows about that particular device. To "define" a device on your system you must select one of the "add xyz device"

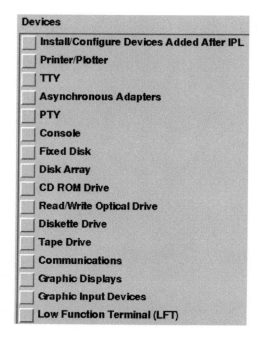

Figure 6–1   SMIT Devices Screen

options. An available device is one that is supported, defined, and on-line. It is available for immediate use.

Let's take a look at some examples. You can see all supported devices (all devices that your system is preprogrammed to deal with), by selecting "List Devices" from the "Devices" menu in SMIT (Figure 6–2). Now select "List All Supported Devices" (Figure 6–3).

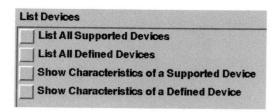

Figure 6–2   List Devices SMIT Screen

```
Output:

adapter    colorgda    mca        Color Graphics Display Adapter
adapter    fda         sio        Standard I/O Diskette Adapter
adapter    fda_2       sio        Standard I/O Diskette Adapter
adapter    fda_iod     sio        Standard I/O Diskette Adapter
adapter    hscsi       mca        SCSI I/O Controller
adapter    hscsi       sio        Standard SCSI I/O Controller
adapter    keyboard    sio        Keyboard/Tablet Adapter
adapter    keyboard_2  sio        Keyboard Adapter
adapter    mouse       sio        Mouse Adapter
```

Figure 6–3   All Supported Devices SMIT Screen

You can also take a look at all defined devices (the ones that your system is explicitly aware of) by selecting "List Devices" from the "Devices" menu, and then selecting "List all Defined Devices" (Figure 6–4).

You will notice that with this list, some devices have the status "available" where as others simply have the status "defined." This is because available devices are also by definition "defined." This list can be used to answer such questions as, "exactly how much disk space or memory is installed on my system?"

Using SMIT to Install a CD-ROM

Since the concepts behind installing a CD-ROM are applicable to almost all other devices, we will use this as a detailed example. After physically plugging in the CD-ROM, and typing in `smit devices` as the root user, you should select "CD-ROM Drive" (Figure 6–5).

The first step is to add the CD-ROM, so that it will be "defined," then you can configure the CD-ROM, and it will become "available." As illustrated by Figures

```
Output:

lvdd     Available           LVM Device Driver
mem0     Available 00-0A     16 MB Memory Card
mem1     Available 00-0B     8 MB Memory Card
mem2     Available 00-0C     16 MB Memory Card
mem3     Available 00-0E     16 MB Memory Card
mem4     Available 00-0F     8 MB Memory Card
mem5     Available 00-0G     16 MB Memory Card
mouse0   Available 00-00-0M-00  3 button mouse
```

Figure 6–4   All Defined Devices SMIT Screen

CD ROM Drive

	List All Defined CD ROM Drives
	List All Supported CD ROM Drives
	Add a CD ROM Drive
	Change / Show Characteristics of CD ROM Drive
	Remove a CD ROM Drive
	Configure a Defined CD ROM Drive
	Generate an Error Report
	Trace a CD ROM Drive

Figure 6–5   CD-ROM Drive SMIT Screen

6–6 through 6–10, installing a CD-ROM is a simple matter of clicking on buttons and answering appropriate questions. This example is for a SCSI device. (Hint: you may need to look at the setting of switches on the back of any SCSI device for the SCSI address. The manual that comes with your device will have useful information. Read it!)

First click on "Add a CD-ROM Drive" (Figure 6–6) then select the type of CD-ROM devices you wish to add.

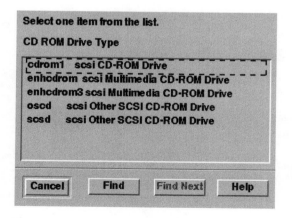

Figure 6–6   Select CD-ROM Drive Type SMIT Screen

Select one item from the list.

Parent Adapter

scsi0 Available 00-08 SCSI I/O Controller

| Cancel | Find | Find Next | Help |

Figure 6–7   Select Parent Adapter SMIT Screen

Selecting the Parent Adapter on the next screen is a no-brainer (Figure 6–7). After answering the following questions on the screen shown in Figure 6–8 click "OK". Press "List" or "Help" if you are not sure of something.

Now that you have added, and thus "defined" your CD-ROM drive, you will need to configure it, in order to make it "available." From the "smit cdrom" menu select "Configure a Defined CD-ROM," and select the device you have just defined (Figure 6–9).

After you have defined a device, you can change its characteristics by selecting "Change/Show Characteristics of CD-ROM Drive." First you will need to select

CD ROM Drive type	cdrom1	
CD ROM Drive interface	scsi	
Description	CD-ROM Drive	
Parent adapter	scsi0	
* CONNECTION address		List
RESERVE device on open	no	List ▲ ▼
PREVENT ejection of media when open	no	List ▲ ▼

| OK | Command | Reset | Cancel | ? | Help |

Figure 6–8   Describe CD-ROM SMIT Screen

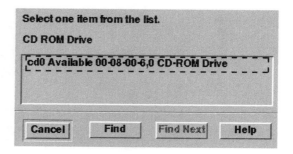

Figure 6–9   Select CD-ROM Drive Screen

the CD-ROM drive you wish to change or show. You can then view and modify the attributes shown in Figure 6–10.

Printers

Installing and Configuring a Local Printer

Although there are a variety of techniques that could be used, we will introduce the most straightforward method which will allow you to define the printer and create new queues in the same step. The technique we describe here is new in AIX Version 4. In AIX 3.2 it was necessary to define and configure the printer, then create and start a queue. This required a number of seemingly unrelated

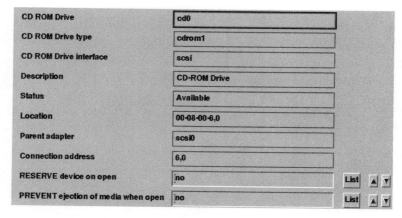

Figure 6–10   View/Modify CD-ROM Attributes SMIT Screen

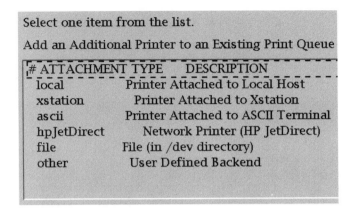

Figure 6-11   Select Attachment Type SMIT Screen

steps to be executed in precision by the user. I think you will agree that the new path is a snap to use!

From the command line type `smit mkpq`, and you will see the screen shown in Figure 6–11.

Although it is possible to add a variety of different printer types, for this example, we will add a local printer. After clicking "local" you will see a menu of selections that looks something like those in Figure 6–12 (the exact printer names may be different on your system).

In our example, we selected "IBM". The next screen is a long list of possible printer types. In this example, we will truncate the list to the last five items, and select the generic printer at the end (Figure 6–13).

The following screen attempts to identify the exact printer being installed. In this case, the answer is simple since there is only a single option (Figure 6–14).

After selecting "Generic Printer", we are given a selection that may look like that shown in Figure 6–15. This screen will show all currently defined queues. If you wish to add the printer to an existing queue, for instance "lp0", then click that queue name. Otherwise if you wish to add a new queue then select, "+ Add NEW Printer." For this example we will add a new printer.

Next, select the interface to use. In this example, we will use a parallel interface (Figure 6–16). Then select the adapter type (Figure 6–17).

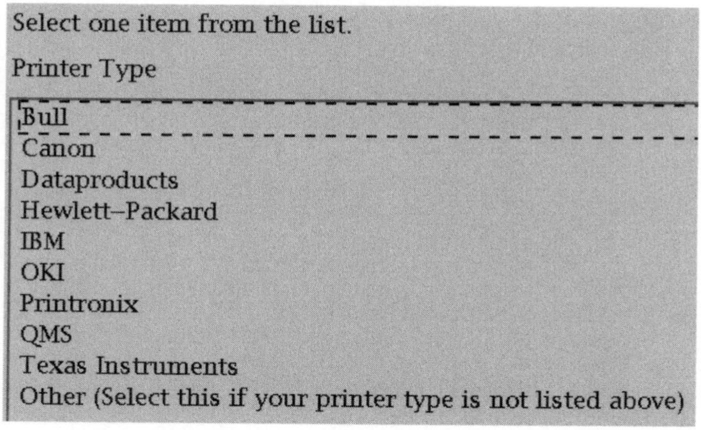

Select one item from the list.

Printer Type

Bull
Canon
Dataproducts
Hewlett–Packard
IBM
OKI
Printronix
QMS
Texas Instruments
Other (Select this if your printer type is not listed above)

Figure 6–12   Select Printer Type SMIT Screen

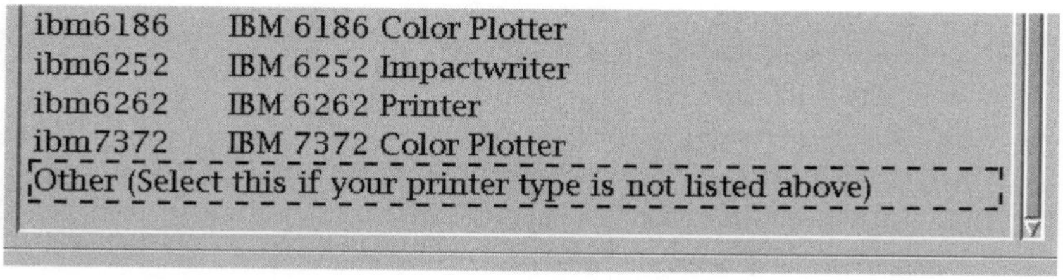

ibm6186   IBM 6186 Color Plotter
ibm6252   IBM 6252 Impactwriter
ibm6262   IBM 6262 Printer
ibm7372   IBM 7372 Color Plotter
Other (Select this if your printer type is not listed above)

Figure 6–13   Select Printer Model SMIT Screen

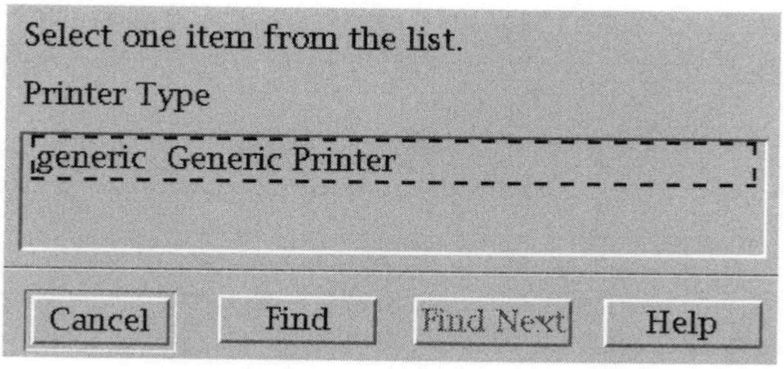

Select one item from the list.

Printer Type

generic Generic Printer

| Cancel | Find | Find Next | Help |

Figure 6–14   Select Printer SMIT Screen

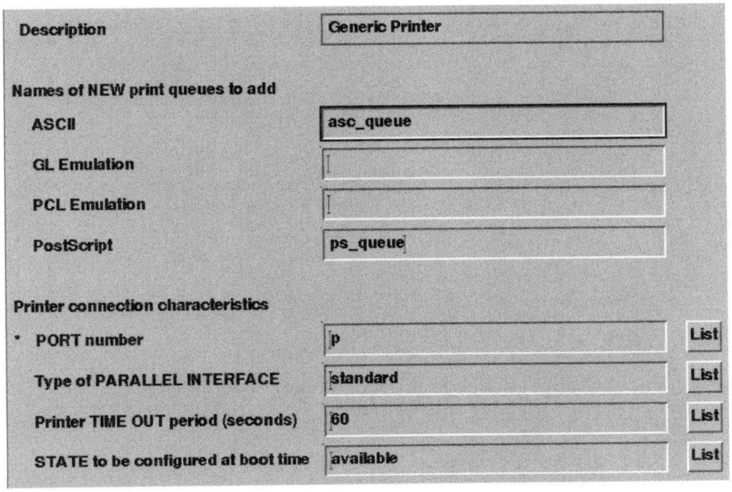

Figure 6–15 Select Printer Queue SMIT Screen

You will now see the screen shown in Figure 6–18. In general the default values are usually OK to use. The "List" option is very useful when selecting other values. In this case we added two queues for this printer; an ASCII queue called "asc_queue" and a postscript queue called "ps_queue". (Generally queue names are much shorter, for instance "lp1" or "ps1" and so on.) After you are satisfied, select the OK button, and printer configuration and its queues will be added (Figure 6–18).

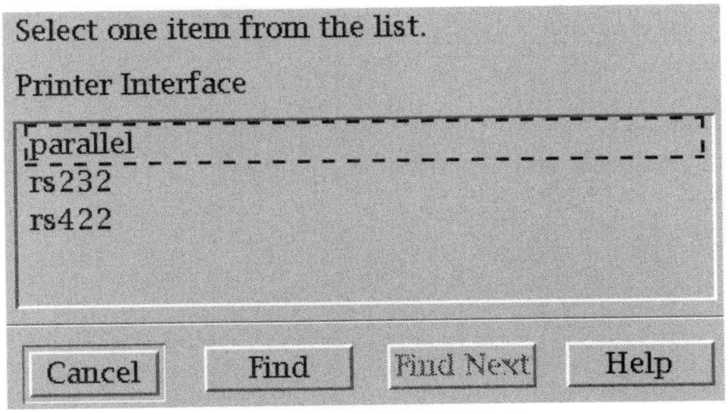

Figure 6–16 Select Printer Interface SMIT Screen

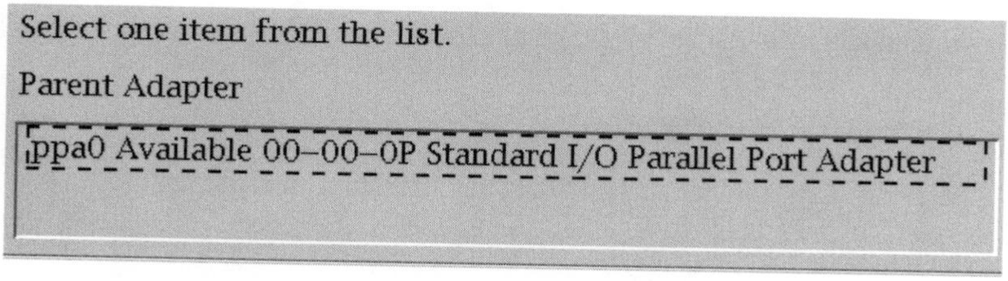

Select one item from the list.

Parent Adapter

ppa0 Available 00–00–0P Standard I/O Parallel Port Adapter

Figure 6–17   Select Printer Parent Adapter SMIT Screen

We have now added a printer and its queues. Before you use it, you may wish to try the `smit chpq` command, and see if there are any details that you wish to configure. You may now use your printer with any of the printer commands supplied with AIX.

Creating a Remote Printer Queue

If your computer is connected to a local area network, then you may have access to printers connected to other computers on your network. For example, many

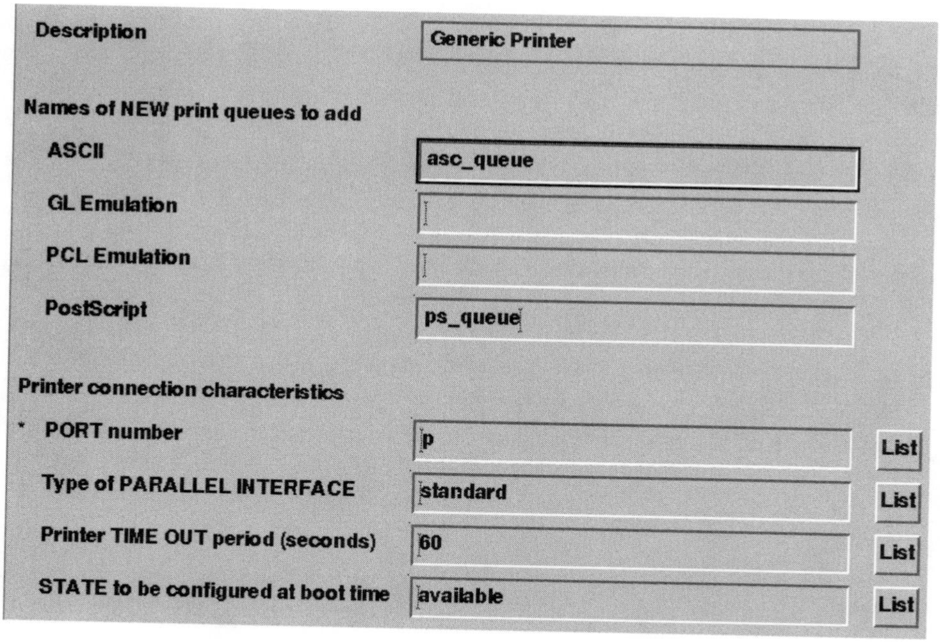

Description	Generic Printer
Names of NEW print queues to add	
ASCII	asc_queue
GL Emulation	
PCL Emulation	
PostScript	ps_queue
Printer connection characteristics	
* PORT number	p
Type of PARALLEL INTERFACE	standard
Printer TIME OUT period (seconds)	60
STATE to be configured at boot time	available

Figure 6–18   Printer Configuration SMIT Screen

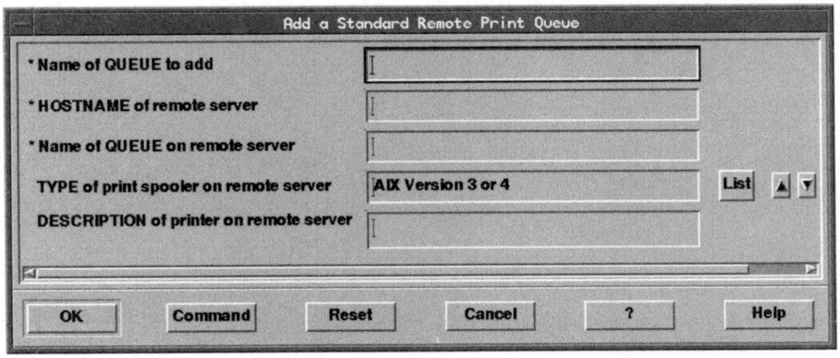

Figure 6–19   Add Remote Printer Queue SMIT Screen

companies and schools have a central printer server with a number of printers connected to it that all users in an organization can share. In order to use a remote printer you must ask the administrator of the printer server to give you access to the printer queue. The administrator should tell you the host name of the printer server as well as the name of the printer queue on that machine. Once you have done this, you should run SMIT as before (type in `smit mkpq` from the command line). First select "remote," next select "Standard Processing." You will see the screen in Figure 6–19.

At this point you should type in the name you wish to use for your local queue (Name of QUEUE to add), the name of the machine that is acting as the printer server (HOSTNAME of remote server), and the name of QUEUE on remote server. You may optionally specify a one-line description of this queue; for example, "Jim's color postscript holograph generator".

Common Questions about Common Printer Commands

How do I see the print jobs on the queue?

Use either the `qchk` or the `lpq` command:

```
$ lpq
Queue Dev   Status Job Files     User      PP % Blks    Cp Rnk
---- ---   ----- -- ------- ---- ---- - ----- --- ---
pr    @prin READY
pr    b906p READY
```

How do I remove a print job from the queue?

Use either the qcan or lprm commands:

```
$ lprm 1
Message from qdaemon:
Job number 1 has been deleted from the queue.<EOT>
```

What commands can I use to print with?

Use either the qprt, enscript, lp, or lpr commands. Commands lp and lpr are fairly simple commands that are good for printing text files without adornment. These commands are also the commands to use when printing postscript files. Commands qprt and enscript are slightly more powerful commands for printing. I like to use the enscript -Gr2f Courier6 command to print program listings since it prints sideways in two columns with a small font. You can also use the enscript command to generate postscript files by specifying the -p ps.file option.

How can I print graphics files?

I recommend using a utility such as xv (available via anonymous ftp from ftp.cis.upenn.edu in directory /pub/xv) to save the file as a postscript file. You can then print the postscript file with lpr.

Troubleshooting

First, make sure that the printer itself is OK. Double check that it is properly connected to your computer, plugged in to the power outlet, and turned on. Next, be sure that the printer has enough paper, is not jammed, or is not low on toner (or needs a new ribbon). The manual that comes with your printer should offer other suggestions. You may wish to run any self-tests that come with the printer to be sure that it is working properly.

In some cases, the printer will notify the spooling system when certain errors occur (such as running out of paper or jamming). When this happens, a diagnostic error message is usually displayed on the console, and the print queue "goes down." You can bring the queue back up by typing the following command as root (be sure to substitute <queuename> with the name of the queue you are using!):

```
qadm -U <queuename>
```

You can generally send files directly to your printer by copying text straight to the printer file. Default printer files are /dev/lp, /dev/lp0, /dev/lp1, and so on. For example, this command would print the message of the day file directly:

```
cat /etc/motd >> /dev/lp0
```

If this does not work then there is something wrong with the printer itself, the physical connection to the printer, or the printer is not configured. If this does work, but normal print spool commands do not work, then the problem is in the spooler configuration.

In some cases, you may get the error, "cannot awaken qdaemon." If you notice that the qdaemon process is not running when you do a `ps -ef | grep qdaemon` command, then you may wish to try running `startsrc -s qdaemon`.

I recommend reading the book, *AIX Guide to Printers and Printing,* available from IBM (order number SC23-2783) to guide you in troubleshooting.

CHAPTER 7

- AIX Web Browsers & Servers: AIX WebExplorer, Netscape, Mosaic

- AIX Welcome Center

- AIX 4.3 Bonus Pack: Java, Adobe Acrobat, Ultimedia, etc.

- AIX Connections Bring Them All Together

- File Transfer, Remote Login

- E-Mail

- Distributed File Systems

Communicating
with the World

In the global environment we now live in, it's more and more important to be able to connect to other systems. AIX provides many methods to connect to all kinds of computer systems, whether they are IBM systems or not. AIX 4.2 includes a great deal of Internet software not available in prior releases. There is so much new code that AIX 4.2 is shipped on multiple CD's instead of just one!

AIX Web Browsers & Servers: AIX WebExplorer, Netscape, Mosaic

Of the currently available Web browsers, we will briefly describe how to obtain and use the three main ones for AIX. These are the AIX WebExplorer, Netscape, and Mosaic. Browsers give you an easy way to access information that is on the Internet. Menus, help text, and lots of colorful pictures are all accessible at the click of a mouse!

Selecting the right browser and client/server setup is very important. Sometimes you might want to connect to a Website that is literally on the other side of the world. This means that it could take a very long time to get the connections through and get large files (graphic images) sent over just to view the home page. If your system is a client, then the files are sent to your server first to be stored and then displayed on your client.

AIX WebExplorer

The AIX WebExplorer is shipped with the standard install media for AIX Version 4.1.4 and 4.1.5. To use it, you need to ensure that the X11.internet fileset is installed. You can check this by typing in lslpp -L all | grep internet on the command line. If it is not installed, then follow these directions:

- Insert your install media (CD-ROM, tape, or so on) in the appropriate device.

- As the root user, type `smit install_latest`, and select the input device/directory (Hint: use the LIST button).

- On the next screen specify "X11.internet" as the package to install. You can use the LIST button here to keep things easy.

After installing the software, take a look at any readme files in `/usr/lpp/explorer` regarding configuration or other important issues. When you are ready to try out WebExplorer, just type `explorer` at the command line. One of the nice things about the AIX WebExplorer is that it displays pictures and text as they are being loaded. It also contains a clickable map of where you have been (see Figure 7–1).

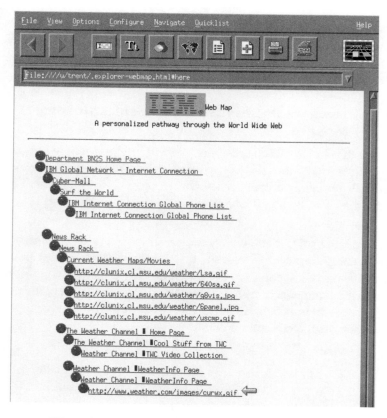

Figure 7–1   AIX WebExplorer Map Screen

AIX 4.2 includes a Web Server as well as the browser. The server code allows your system to act as an Internet server that can be shared by many users and other systems.

Netscape

The Netscape browser and server applications are part of the AIX 4.2 and later packages. Just use the CD with Netscape on it and install it normally (see the install chapter) with SMIT.

Prior to AIX Version 4.2, obtain the Netscape Web browser for AIX by calling 1-415-528-2555 (USA) between 7:00 A.M. and 5:00 P.M. PST to order an official package. If you already have a Web browser running, you can take a look at http://www.netscape.com/. Alternatively, you can download a copy via `ftp`. To use `ftp`, first read about how to use it later on in this chapter, then, using your new-found knowledge, do an anonymous `ftp` to `ftp10.netscape.com`. First get any `README` files for late breaking information. After typing `bin` in `ftp` to ensure that the binary download works, download the AIX version of Netscape. At the time of writing, the latest full version was `/pub/communicator/4.06/shipping/english/unix/aix4/base-install/communicator-V406-export.pc_rs6000-ibm-aix4.tar.gZ`. After downloading this file, type `gZip-C_d <filename> |tar-xvf-| tar -vxf -` to uncompress and untar the files. After reading the `README` file, you can try Netscape by simply typing `netscape` at the command line.

When you get Netscape up and running, you can expect to see a Netscape Home Page (see Figure 7–2).

Mosaic

To obtain the Mosaic Web browser for AIX, first read about how to use `ftp` later on in this chapter, then using your newfound knowledge, do an anonymous `ftp` to `ftp.ncsa.uiuc.edu`, and take a look at directory /Mosaic/Unix/binaries. Currently the available versions are 2.6 and 2.7b. Next, I would recommend obtaining the `README` file in the directory you are interested in. If you wanted to get Version 2.6, then you can get file `/Mosaic/Unix/binaries/2.6/Mosaic-ibm-2.6.Z`. Be sure to type `bin` in `ftp` to make sure that the binary file is unaltered on download. After downloading the file to your system, uncompress the file by typing `uncompress Mosaic-ibm-2.6`, and then make the file executable by typing `chmod a+x Mosaic-ibm-2.6`. You can run the program by typing `Mosaic-ibm-2.6`. You can obtain documentation and further information in one of two ways. If you have a Web browser of some kind working, you can connect to the NCSA Mosaic Home Page (http://www.ncsa.uiuc.edu/SDG/Software/ Mosaic/MCSAMosaicHome.html), as shown in Figure 7–3, or you can `ftp` documentation from directory /Web/Mosaic/Unix/Documents on `ftp.ncsa.uiuc.edu`.

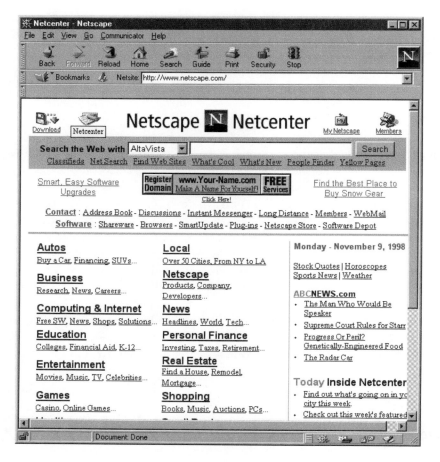

Figure 7–2   Netscape Home Page

AIX Welcome Center

The AIX Welcome Center has a fun and interesting way of taking you around the system with graphics artwork and images, with audio clips that will surprise you, with service information, pointers to Internet sites dedicated to AIX, and everything else you wanted to know about IBM and AIX but were afraid to ask . . .

You need to order the Welcome Center when you order AIX and ask for feature code 0598. You can also see it by pointing your Web browser at
http://www.rs6000.ibm.com/support/welcome

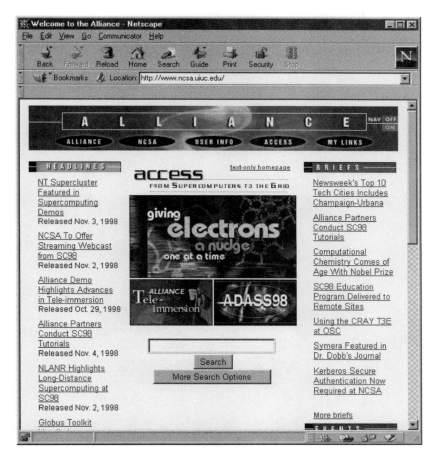

Figure 7–3   Mosaic Home Page

AIX 4.3 Bonus Pack: Java, Adobe Acrobat, Ultimedia, etc.

AIX 4.3 includes additional applications on several different CD "Bonus Packs".

The Bonus Pack CD's fall into two main categories, just as the AIX operating system does. Those categories are Client and Server. Some of the neat stuff found on the client CD includes:

• The Adobe Acrobat reader.

• The Java development kit, runtime environment, and samples.

• The AIX Ultimedia services package.

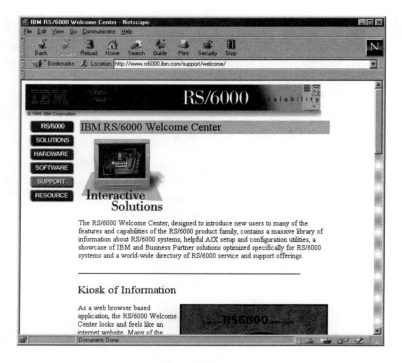

Figure 7–4　The IBM RS/6000 Welcome Center

Some of the neat stuff found on the server CD includes:

- The Adobe Acrobat reader.
- The Java development kit, runtime environment, and samples.
- The AIX Ultimedia services package.
- The IBM internet Connection Server.

Yes, you can use the server Bonus Pack CD to set up your very own web server!

Bonus Pack Software Installation

Installing any of these packages is fairly straightforward and simple. However, you may wish to review the chapter on installation if this sounds confusing.

1. Insert the CD-ROM into your CD-ROM drive, and start SMIT as root.
2. Select "Software Installation and Maintenance".
3. Select "Install and Update Software".
4. Select "Install and Update Software from all Available Software".

5. Select the input media. (Hint: use the "List" button.)

6. Press the "List" button and select which packages you want to install.

7. Click "OK" when you are ready.

What's on the CD?

Let's briefly describe a couple of the packages included.

JAVA

In a nutshell, the developers of Java describe it as a "simple, object-oriented, distributed, interpreted, robust, secure, architecture neutral, portable, high-performance, multithreaded, and dynamic language". (I've seen some claims that it is also buzz-word compliant.) What does this mean? It's a neat new programming language whose objects will run on all major platforms, and it is ideal for development of applets which can be loaded and run in a Java compliant browser such as the latest version of Netscape. You can find more information by checking out http://java.sun.com/.

After you have installed the Java distribution package, take a look at the `readme` file in /usr/lpp/Java/README, and then try running the demo applets. First you need to add /usr/lpp/Java/bin to your path. You can either do this in your `.profile` file, or type (in `ksh`):

```
export PATH=$PATH:/usr/lpp/Java/bin
```

Then change to the `/usr/lpp/Java/demo` directory and take a look at the files. You will see a number of subdirectories, including: `BouncingHeads` and `Tic-TacToe`. To run my favorite, the bouncing heads demo do this: (Remember to set your path to include /usr/lpp/Java/bin!)

```
cd /usr/lpp/Java/Demo/BouncingHeads
appletviewer example1.html
```

Since the source code to each of these demos (`*.java` files) is included along with a Java interpreter, you can try your hand at creating your own Java applets!

Adobe Acrobat Reader

Another neat application is Adobe's Acrobat Reader. It is a program that displays audio, video, and multimedia images from scripted file type. The power of Adobe Acrobat is that any Adobe Portable Document Format (`*.pdf`) file can be viewed on any major platform, including Macintosh, Windows, DOS, and UNIX. For more information about Adobe Acrobat, you may want to take a look at their homepage on the Internet: http://www.adobe.com/

To use Acrobat, after installing it from the bonus pack CD, type the following:

1.   cd /usr/Adobe/acrobat.

2.   Read any readme or information files such as `AIX.CDE.README` and `INSTGUID.TXT`

3.   type `INSTALL` and follow the directions.

Run the program by typing: `/usr/lpp/AcroRead/bin/acroread`.

AIX Ultimedia Services (UMS)

The AIX Ultimedia services include software and demonstrations that show off speech recognition, text to speech generation, and, of course, the usual multimedia presentation that we have all gotten used to.

After installing UMS, you can play with the different multimedia samples included. You can either use the CDE file manager to go into /usr/lpp/UMS/samples and start clicking on interesting files, or you can use the command line and type the following:

```
cd /usr/lpp/UMS/samples
/usr/lpp/UMS/bin/run_ums dtmedia_player
```

Now use the GUI interface to select and display interesting-looking files.

If you have a sound card, you can also play with the text to speech program. For example:

```
echo "Shall we play a game?" | /usr/lpp/UMS/Demos/tts/bin
```

AIX Connections Bring Them All Together

The AIX Desktop Connectivity Server (ADCS for short) gives you the ability to get more from your PC's by hooking them up to an AIX system. ADCS will let you connect to many different kinds of PC operating systems and network software, such as the following:

- DOS
- OS/2
- NT
- Windows
- Macintosh AppleShare
- Novell NetWare
- SPX Clients
- SMB Compatible Servers

ADCS allows these remote systems to store their files on the AIX system server. Both systems may access the files with their own operating system commands. ADCS also allows multiple different systems to share printers and terminals.

You can customize the AIX Desktop Connectivity Server with the SMIT application so that makes it easy to set up. There's plenty of help from the InfoExplorer on-line publications system, and PostScript files. It comes with AIX 4.1.4 and later only if you select it with your order.

LSserver

The LSserver allows an AIX computer to provide file, print, terminal emulation, and other network services to client PCs running DOS, OS/2, NT, or Windows. It uses the ServerMessage Block (SMB) protocol and is compatible with IBM's LAN Server and Microsoft LAN Manager specifications for LAN servers. Other servers may participate on the same network using SMB-compatible software; for example, an IBM LAN Server.

MACserver

MACserver runs on AIX allowing it to act as a Macintosh AppleShare server host, providing file and print services to Macintosh client computers on an Ethernet network. It also manages network connections and user accounts.

NWserver

NWserver running on AIX allows it to provide file, print, and terminal emulation services to NetWare-compatible PCs. It also includes an SPX protocol stack to support SPX clients.

TNclient

TNclient provides access from AIX to NetWare-compatible and SMB-compatible servers for file and print services. TNclient allows AIX workstations to participate in LANs as well as behave as clients. PC file attributes are preserved when accessed by AIX users. TNclient also provides the capability to mount Netware volumes, LAN Manager shared resources, and LAN Server shared resources.

Additional References

AIX Desktop Connectivity Server LSserver User's Guide, SC23-1759

AIX Desktop Connectivity Server MACserver User's Guide, SC23-1760

AIX Desktop Connectivity Server NWserver User's Guide, SC23-1761

AIX Desktop Connectivity Server TNclient User's Guide, SC23-1762

NetBIOS for AIX: Administration Guide, SC23-2685

NetBIOS API Reference, SC23-2758

File Transfer, Remote Login

FTP and `telnet` are popular commands that are a part of TCP/IP. These are very commonly used on the Internet, so it's a good idea to learn them. This section is marked with a hot pepper because you'll be hot stuff when you've mastered it, but it's almost a basic on the Internet.

FTP

The `ftp` and `tftp` commands (file transfer protocol) allow you to get and put files from your system to and from another system across the wire. This isn't like e-mail that adds a header for the To, From, Subject, and so on. This is like a file copy. With FTP you won't have to use "Sneaker-Net"! That's when you copy a file to a diskette, run it over to someone else's computer, and copy it in.

When you use the `ftp` command on a machine that you don't have a login or password to, often times it is set up for "anonymous `ftp`". You login with the name "anonymous" and use your full electronic mail address as the password.

Anonyomous `ftp` is used commonly on the Internet to allow users to grab public files.

The `ftp` command puts you into a mode where you have limited commands into the remote file system. The following passage is an example of logging in, asking for help, getting the directory name, listing the files, and getting a file.*

First, start the file transfer program with `remotehost`:

```
$ ftp remotehost
Connected to remotehost.
220 remotehost FTP server (Version 4.1 Thu Jun 15 12:28:17 CDT
1995) read
Name (remotehost:carolynj):
```

If this is your login name, press enter; otherwise, type in your login ID.

```
331 Password required for carolynj.
Password:
```

The password is invisible.

```
230 User carolynj logged in.
```

Now, get some help on available commands.

```
ftp> ?
```

---

*   The **bold** statements are book commentary and the other statements are from `ftp`.

Commands may be abbreviated. Commands are:

!	help	recv
$	image	reinitialize
account	lcd	remotehelp
append	local	rename
ascii	ls	reset
bell	macdef	restart
binary	mdelete	rhelp
block	mdir	rmdir
bye	mget	rstatus
carriage-control	mkdir	runique
case	mls	send
cd	mode	sendport
cdup	modtime	site
close	mount	size
copylocal	mput	status
cr	nmap	stream
delete	nlist	struct
debug	non-print	sunique
dir	ntrans	system
disconnect	open	telnet
ebcdic	prompt	tenex
exp_cmd	proxy	trace
file	put	type
form	pwd	user
get	quit	verbose
glob	quote	
hash	record	

Print working directory:

```
ftp> pwd
257 "/home/carolynj" is current directory.
```

List the files:

```
ftp> ls
200 PORT command successful.
150 Opening data connection for ..
```

```
.profile
.sh_history
fminit
.dt
.dtprofile
book
.Xauthority
226 Transfer complete.
```

Change the working directory to "book":

```
ftp> cd book
250 CWD command successful.
```

Now the important part, get the file `chapt5` from remotehost and it will be copied onto the working directory of localhost:

```
ftp> get chapt5
200 PORT command successful.
150 Opening data connection for chapt5 (7330 bytes).
226 Transfer complete.

ftp> quit
221 Goodbye.
$
```

In the session shown, we logged into the system called "remotehost". Then we asked for help by typing "?" at the `ftp` command line, and it listed all the commands available in the FTP mode. We printed the working directory (`pwd`), listed the files there (`ls`), changed directories to the `book` directory, and then finally got the filenamed `chapt5`. The file was sent across the wire to the local system and copied into the current directory. Then we quit the `ftp` session, which logged us out.

That wasn't hard! The difficulty for some people is keeping a clear head about the local and remote hosts. The key is remembering the host you start from. We did a `get` from the remote host during the `ftp` session because we wanted to get it and copy it to the local host.

TFTP

The `tftp` command is more like other commands with parameters expected versus the `ftp` command which puts you into a logged-in mode in the remote system. The default for the system is for the `tftp` command to be disabled for security reasons. To turn it back on, you or the system administrator should edit the `/etc/inetd.conf` file and take the comment (#) off the line that starts the `tftp` program as the root user. Then refresh the program with the command

```
refresh -s inetd
```

If we do the same function we just finished with `ftp`, but use `tftp` instead, it would look like the following to get help and then get the file:

```
        tftp -?
        usage: tftp {-r|-g|-o|-w|-p} <local file> <host> <for-
eign file> [netascii|image]
            tftp -g chapt5 remotehost /home/book/chapt5
```

Ping

The `ping` command refers to the sound a sonar makes. AIX will send a *ping* over to another system across the wires and wait for a response. That's how you can find out if the other system is up. Let's see if the system `austin.ibm.com` is up and running with `tcp`:

```
ping austin.ibm.com

PING austin.ibm.com: (129.35.208.96): 56 data bytes

64 bytes from 129.35.208.96: icmp_seq=0 ttl=255 time=0 ms

64 bytes from 129.35.208.96: icmp_seq=1 ttl=255 time=0 ms
```

(Enter `Ctrl c` to stop the pinging, or it will continue forever!)

```
- - - - austin.ibm.com PING Statistics - - - -

2 packets transmitted, 2 packets received, 0% packet loss
```

This shows that two "pings" were sent and two "responses" were sent back. The system is up and running.

Remote Login and Execution

There are three similiar commands to login to someone else's system:

- `tn`
- `telnet`
- `rlogin`

These commands are easy to use. Just type the command and the system name and you will be prompted for your user login name and password. Then you are on the remote system and can do most of the normal stuff. You will be using the environment set up on the remote system and it could be different than the one you are used to; you may also have limited directory access.

What if Casey has a really clever program set up on her system that you'd like to try out? You could install it on your system, but why not just use hers (if it's OK with her)? You will need a login and password on her machine and the exact name of her system.

Here comes a tricky part. If the program uses graphics or other fancy output, you'll need to set a couple things up. Let's use the remote host name "casey" in our example, and the local hostname of "me":

```
xhost +casey
tn casey
(login and password)
export DISPLAY=me:0.0
```

(Now invoke that clever program!)

The `xhost` command gives permission to allow casey to put stuff on this display (after all, we don't just allow anyone displaying who-knows-what on our display). Then we telnet'd into the casey remote system (and entered the remote login and password). The export `DISPLAY` command tells the remote system to display all output on the "me" system instead of on the "casey" system.

The application will execute on the "casey" system using Casey's files and memory. Your system will show the application on your display using some of your memory and resources.

You can execute totally on the remote system by telnetting in without the export DISPLAY command, but you will be limited to commands and applications that are not graphical in nature.

Other TCP/IP Commands

There are many useful TCP/IP commands. Read the appendix if you want more details on the following commands:

- `rexec`—remote execution of commands
    You can enter the command on your local system and have it totally run on the remote system, including the output.

- `rsh`—remote execution shell
    Similar to the `rexec` command but you get more of the shell with it.

- `rcp`—remote copy
    You can copy files to someone else's file system from your system.

- `on`—unauthenticated remote execution
    Uses NFS (network file system) to run commands on a remote system with the current environment passed on over.

- `finger, f, rusers`—query remote users
    This command displays information about people logged into remote systems.

- `talk`—carry on a conversation from the keyboard and screen
  - Two people invoke this command and can have a computerized conversation back and forth.

- `rwall`—remote broadcast message
  - Sends messages to all users on the remote system (remote worn all).

E-Mail

I Can Send Mail My Way !

The AIX system offers several electronic mail (e-mail) programs that users may choose from. Like editors, mail programs are a personal choice. Different strokes for different folks! The e-mail choices include the following:

MH (Mail Handler)

Berkeley Mail

Desktop Mail

There are additional mailer programs that are available in the public domain (not shipped in AIX), such as `elm`, `pine`, `mutt`, and `emacs`, etc.

Some mailer programs have different (incompatible) mail storage systems. If you choose one, you can't always switch between one and the other and expect your mail to be converted.

There is a program that runs in the background, invisible to you, that waits for mail to come in. It's called "sendmail". When a mail message is received, send-mail appends the message to a long file, called the spool, in the directory `/usr/spool/mail`. There is one spool file for each user. When you invoke the mailer of your choice, it breaks up that long spool file into messages and allows you to act on each message separately.

Each mailer gives at least the basic operations on mail:

- Create a new message and send it
- View a message
- Remove a message
- Reply to the sender of a message
- Forward a message to another user
- List your messages

New users will probably like the desktop mail program the best. It's easy to learn and shows you all the prompts from menus. It has help screens and shows you the list of mail (your inbox) on the screen at all times. To invoke the desktop mailer, select the mail icon at the bottom of the desktop. (See the section on the Common Desktop Environment for more information.)

The MH mail handler concepts are used in the desktop mail program but it's a set of commands rather than menu screens. The common desktop mail application cannot be used interchangeably with MH shell commands. Advanced users like MH because it is so flexible and can be used with shell functions. Each action in MH is a shell command.

The Berkeley mail system is also pretty easy to use. There is one main command and several subcommands with help.

E-Mail Etiquette

Some general tips about e-mail will keep you from being unpopular. When you get a message and you're one of a long list on the "To" or "Cc" list, don't reply to the whole group unless you're sure that they all want to hear it, just reply to the sender. Pay attention to the folks on the mailing list.

If you are sending a message to a very long list of e-mail addresses, send to them as a "blind copy" or "Bcc:". It's not that you don't want them to know who's getting the message; the issue here is that the people receiving the message will tire of reading through all the e-mail names and addresses before getting to the meat of the message. It's a waste of time. You can let folks know who you're sending the message to by using "X-to:<comment>" such as

```
X-to: Screen-Team
```

Don't get into mail wars! That's when you pop off some terse snippy reply without cooling off first and then they reply back, and on and on. It's better to cool off, keep it professional, and just pick up the phone or drop by to talk about the problem. This is also known as a "flame".

Here's another tip. DON'T SHOUT. If you use all uppercase characters, it reads as if you are shouting!

What's the Address?

When you send electronic mail, you need to pay attention to the address. The Internet follows a convention for addresses across the world. Reading left to right, the address starts specific and becomes more general, kind of like name, street, town, state. Typically used addresses have "com" for commercial companies, "gov" for government, "edu" for educational institutes, and so on.

The address of bozo@austin.ibm.com goes to a commercial company "com", IBM, in Austin, to the user, "bozo". Mail will be delivered to "bozo" "at" Austin IBM.

There are other address forms that aren't as common that use a different format. The safest way to get mail there is to get the exact address you are sending to or to reply to a message from them!

Another address type, a Universal Resource Locator (URL), is used for an Internet browser to bring up World Wide Web home pages. These addresses use the location part of the e-mail address with the directory name and a protocol type attached; for example:

```
http://www.ibm.net/inter.html
```

The http stands for hypertext transfer protocol. "www.ibm.net" is the address of a computer, and then a sometimes optional directory name and/or filename follows. In this case, `inter.html` is the filename.

Berkeley Mail

Bring up the Berkeley mail program with the command `mail`. You'll then be inside the mail program and have its sub-commands to use until you "quit" and go back to the AIX command line. The mail prompt is a question mark (?). The AIX commands may be used while you're inside the mail program if you precede the AIX command with an exclamation point (!).

The mail is received into a mail spool file, one for each user in `/usr/spool/mail/<user>`. The Berkeley mail program leaves the mail in the spool and acts on it there.

This is what the Berkeley mail program looks like with two messages queued:

```
> mail
Mail [5.2 UCB] [AIX 4.1] Type ? for help.
"/var/spool/mail/carolynj": 2 message
> 1 carolynj Sat Sep 16 16:11 32/806 "hello, it's me"
> 2 carolynj Sat Sep 16 16:11 34/808 "2nd message"
```

Ask for a list of the mail commands by entering a "?" or "help" and you'll get the following displayed:

- Control Commands:

q	Quit—apply mailbox commands entered this session
x	Quit—restore mailbox to original state
! <cmd>	Start a shell, run <cmd>, and return to mailbox
cd [<dir>]	Change directory to <dir> or $HOME

- Display Commands:

t [<msg_list>]	Display messages in <msg_list> or current message
n	Display next message
f [<msg_list>]	Display headings of messages
h [<num>]	Display headings of group containing message <num>

- Message Handling:

e [<num>]	Edit message <num> (default editor is ex)
d [<msg_list>]	Delete messages in <msg_list> or current message
u [<msg_list>]	Recall deleted messages
s [<msg_list>] <file>	Append messages (with headings) to <file>
w [<msg_list>] <file>	Append messages (text only) to <file>
pre [<msg_list>]	Keep messages in system mailbox

- Creating New Mail:

m <addrlist>	Create/send new message to addresses in <addrlist>
r [<msg_list>]	Send reply to senders and recipients of messages
R [<msg_list>]	Send reply only to senders of messages
a	Display list of aliases and their addresses

MH (Mail Handler)

The Mail Handler (MH) is a set of commands you use from the command line. For experienced command line users, the MH commands can be very powerful when combined with other AIX commands.

MH Startup. The first thing to do is an "inc" to incorporate the mail messages from the spool in /usr/spool/mail/<user> (where <user> is your login name) to your local mail directories. The directory "Mail" in your home directory will contain an "inbox" directory where each new mail message will be kept as a separate file.

You may "refile" messages into as many different folders (directories) as you want. If this is the first time, it will ask you whether you want to set MH up now;

answer "yes". It will copy a hidden profile (.mh_profile) and create the directories needed into your home directory. It will show you a list of mail message headers: the message number, the date, sender, and subject:

```
inc
Create folder "/home/carolynj/Mail/inbox" <yes/no>? y
Incorporating new mail into inbox...
   1+ 09/16 carolynj@austin 1st message << Hello, It's me !
   2+ 09/23 carolynj@austin Meeting Notice <<Project Status
```

Message Identifiers.   The message identification number is used extensively with the MH commands. One of the messages is kept as the "current" one which is the default. The message number is used as the filename when the messages are stored. Message number ranges may be used to perform one action on multiple messages. That's handy for junk mail! For example, you can refile messages in the range 3 to 11 in the mail folder named `followup`. You can also remove messages 45 through 53 with one command.

```
refile 3-11 +followup
rmm 45-53
```

Folders.   You can set up folders for each topic you get mail on and want to keep for your records. Then you can scan a specific folder and get a list of messages in that folder, refile into it, forward from it, remove mail or any of the regular actions. You designate the folder name with a plus "+":

```
scan +action
30 09/29 ceb@AUSVM6.AUSTIN ART files needed <<FROM THE DE
31 09/28 trent@austin.ibm.co Re: prototype ready (forw)


refile 31 +followup
folder +fyi
fyi+ has 201 messages (4269-5496); cur=5316; (others).
```

This scans the folder named `action` and displays a list of stored messages, then files message number 31 from the `action` folder to the `followup` folder. Then we changed folders to the `fyi` folder. The `fyi` folder has 201 messages waiting, from message number 4269 to number 5496 with the current message being number 5316. Looks like there's a lot of mail stacking up!

MH Commands.   These MH commands are the most frequently used:

inc	Incorporate from the spool into the local mail
scan	Scan the mail messages and show a list of them
show	Show a message contents
forw	Forward a message on to another
rmm	Remove mail message
next	Show the next message
prev	Show the previous message
refile	Refile message from the inbox into a different folder
comp	Compose a new message to send
folder	Show a summary status of the current folder; can also change folders with this command
folders	Show a list of mail folders

You can use these commands on the inbox, or on one of the mail folders. This lets you get a list of new or old messages and show, forward, or remove, the messages there.

The comp command allows you to compose a new message. It prompts for the mailing address with "To:", carbon copy (no real carbons with electronic mail these days !) with "Cc:", file copy with "Fcc:", the message subject with "Subject:", and then you can type in your message body. Whether all these prompts are displayed is determined by each user's customization. When you are finished, type <Ctrl> <d> (hold down the <Ctrl> key and then press the "&" key). It will ask, "What now? If you need help, type '?' " and you'll get the following:

```
What now? ?
Options are:
display [<switches>]
edit [<editor> <switches>]
list [<switches>]
push [<switches>]
quit [-delete]
refile [<switches>] +folder
send [<switches>]
whom [<switches>]
```

You can get help with each of the commands by adding -help to the command. It will show you the options available for that command.

Advanced MH Commands. There are over thirty more commands for the advanced user. You can pack the messages into a single file. You can set up digests and bulletin boards. You can also write shell scripts and use AIX commands on these mail messages with MH commands. This is due to the MH design where messages are stored as separate files and each of the MH actions is separate commands. This is especially useful for people who get huge amounts of mail.

Here are some ideas for MH users with gobs of mail:

```
scan | fgrep -i meeting      Look for all meetings
scan | sort +2               Sort messages by sender
```

Removed messages aren't really erased; they are renamed to the same filename but preceded with a comma ",". New messages you send are kept in a filenamed `draft` or in a folder (if you create it) named "drafts".

XMH. XMH is a sample program that is an X-Windows user interface to the MH mail system (see Figure 7–5). It has the same terminology and functionality, but instead of AIX commands, it uses menus with point and click. It looks a lot like the Common Desktop Mail application. Menu selections are shown as buttons at the top of the screen. The body of the window shows the folders as buttons and then the list of mail messages.

Common Desktop Mail

The Common Desktop Mail Manager uses the same terminology as MH and is integrated into the Common Desktop Environment (see Figure 7–6). Invoke it by selecting the Mail icon from the control panel. Some of the underlying directory structure is different. It uses the "mbox" directory and a different profile file. The menu selections are available as buttons. The body of the window contains a list of mail messages and then the contents of the current message. See the CDE. chapter for more information.

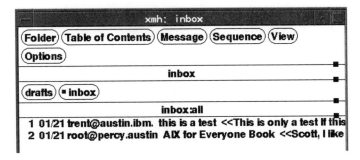

Figure 7–5   Sample XMH Screen

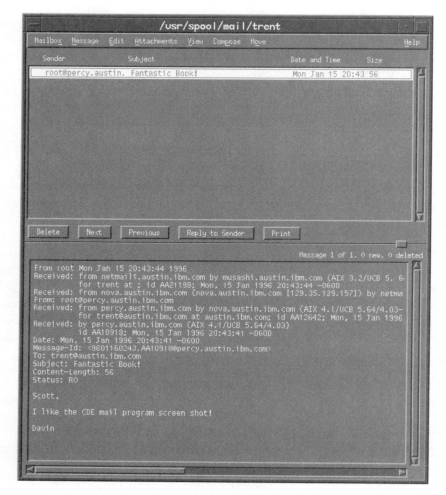

Figure 7–6   CDE Mail Manager Sample Screen

Distributed File Systems

Copying files using `ftp` and `tftp` is really nice, but it surely would be nice if the operating system would take care of that for you! That's what distributed file systems do. You tell the operating system that the files are really across the network, but they look like they are on the computer in your office! Not just you, but all your co-workers can share files this way.

So if you get organized, you can set up one computer system with a lot of hard file storage; that's your "server," sometimes also called a "host." Everyone in the office can use the files on the servers from their local systems, the "clients" (sometimes also called a "slave"). There are a couple different types of distributed file systems available in the industry and on AIX. RS/6000 systems with AIX make great servers and clients!

Network File System (NFS)

Originally developed by Sun Microsystems, NFS has become a defacto networking standard. NFS is independent of hardware, operating systems, and network architectures. So you can share files with coworkers that have computers from many different companies using various network wiring. This independence was achieved through the use of two sets of protocols:

- Remote procedure call (RPC) protocols
- Data standardizing External Data Representation (XDR) protocols

In addition to the RPC and XDR, NFS uses the TCP/IP protocol to implement data transmission. NFS requires TCP/IP to be installed, configured, and operational. The NFS facility can be started upon request or simply configured to start up when the operating system is booted.

NFS Has Daemons! NFS functions are controlled by a set of daemons. The master daemon associated with NFS is called inetd. inetd is not just for NFS but is also the master for other daemons on the system. It essentially triggers the startup of the following daemons when/if needed:

- portmapd
- mountd
- nfsd
- pcnfsd
- biod

The biod daemon is required to run on all of the machines that are serving as NFS clients. The pcnfsd daemon is needed on the server machine only if a PC's files are mounted. The rest of the daemons run on the server machine.

File Permissions. NFS also supports access control lists (ACL). ACLs are used with the read/write/execute permission structures that are part of the UNIX operating systems. That's because there are so many systems, there could be users named "carolyn" on more than one. I don't want her looking at my files just because we share the same name!

Mapped Files. Mapped files are also supported under NFS running AIX. This feature allows programs on clients to be accessed as if they were in real memory instead of on disk storage. That makes them much faster to access! You have to write a program to use the shmat system call, and that maps areas of a file into memory address space.

Secure NFS. Secure NFS is also implemented under AIX in addition to the standard UNIX authentication. NFS uses the Data Encryption Standard (DES) and public key cryptography to authenticate users and machines in networks. A DES key is generated from two components: a public key published for general availability and a private key used to encrypt and decrypt data.

Locking Keeps Things Straight. The NFS-compatible Network Lock Manager supports file and record locking over the network (records are rows of the file). The network lock manager contains both the client and server functions. The status monitor performs *health-check* duties and keeps a record of relevant failures at the client and the server end. This is a list of frequently used NFS commands:

Command	Description
exportfs	Exports and unexports directories to NFS clients
mount	Makes a file system available for use
nfsstat	Displays statistics pertaining to the ability of client/ server to receive calls
on	Executes commands on remote systems
rusers	Displays a list of users currently logged in on remote machines
rup	Displays status of a remote host
rpcinfo	Reports the status of RPC servers
rpcgen	Generates C code to implement an RPC protocol
rwall	Sends message to all users on the network
showmount	Displays a list of all clients that have remotely mounted a file system spray; sends a specific number of packets to a host to report performance statistics.

High Availability for Network File System (HANFS)—It's Done with Mirrors

Let's face it, hardware wears out sometimes and systems have occasional problems. HANFS makes sure that your data will be safe in spite of Murphy's Law.

HANFS is an extension to NFS that supports higher availability of data than that provided by a standard NFS configuration. The main feature of HANFS is improved availability of servers through disk impersonation. Data availability is optimized through an option to mirror disks. It can survive planned outages and failures of the operating system, system planar, adapters, and internal and external disks.

In addition to the NFS daemons, HANFS requires three additional daemons to facilitate configuration and reconfiguration of the system and of Object Data Manager (ODM) databases. The additional daemons are hanfsd, hacfgd, and hapngd.

It takes some extra hardware to use mirrors! Hardware required by HANFS includes a backup server with multiple shared volume groups with external disks that are individually connected to a disk adapter of the server on one end and to the backup machine on the other. HANFS requires that both the server and its backup must be POWERstation or POWERserver computers. There is a redundant set of network adapters, also. The server and backup use four network adapters: one each for normal operations, the third to impersonate the server by the backup in case of server failure, and the fourth to impersonate the backup by the server in case of backup failure. Whew! That should cover a really unlucky day!

Network Information Service (NIS)—The Old Yellow Pages

NIS is a centralized database service that offers centralized control of networked machines. NIS was formerly known as "Yellow Pages" (YP). Rather than having to manage each host's files (for example /etc/hosts, /etc/passwd, and /etc/group), system administrators maintain one database for each file on one central server. Machines that are using NIS retrieve information as needed from these databases.

NIS consists of clients and servers, logically grouped together in domains using maps (databases) that provide information such as host names or passwords. An NIS slave is a client that uses the maps to share information.

NIS reduces the effort of maintaining repetitive databases of information. It also helps users by making their password, directories, and files available on other systems. Network administration becomes easier and less time consuming.

Typical information stored in an NIS database includes password files and host files whose contents are essentially the same for different nodes on a single network.

The following is a list of frequently used NIS commands:

Commands	Description
domainname	Lists the name of the current NIS domain system for a NIS host
makedbm	Creates the NIS database maps
ypbind	Enables a client process to connect to a server
ypcat	Lists the contents of NIS maps
ypinit	Builds and installs NIS maps on an NIS server
ypmatch	Displays the values of one or more keys within an NIS map
yppasswd	Allows users to change NIS passwords from any NIS host
yppoll	Identifies the version of a NIS map on the NIS server
yppush	Forces propagation of updated NIS maps from the master server to slave servers
ypserv	Looks up information in the local NIS databases
ypset	Points the ypbind process to a specific server
ypwhich	Identifies which machine is the NIS server of an NIS client
ypxfr	Transfers an NIS map from an NIS server to a local host

Andrew File System

The distributed Andrew file system (AFS) machines allows users to access information stored anywhere on a network. The AFS file system uses a client/server model—file server machines store data and transfer it to client machines.

AFS uses a hierarchical file structure—a tree with /afs as the root. The next level of directories consist of *cells*. Cells are subtrees of the AFS file space and consist of related directories and files. The cell controlling a specific user workstation is termed a local cell; other cells in the AFS file space are termed foreign cells. The directories and files under /afs make up the AFS *file space*.

AFS client machines use a Cache Manager to access information stored in the AFS file space. When a user accesses a file, the Cache Manager stores the file as a copy on the client workstation's local disk. This enables the client to use the local copy of the cached file rather than continuously sending network requests to the file server machines for data. When the file closes, the Cache Manager sends the changed file back to the appropriate file server, and the changed version replaces the file stored on the server.

Because AFS is a distributed file system, several security techniques are used to protect the many users: passwords, mutual authentication, and access control lists (ACLs). ACLs allow individual users to restrict access to their own directories. Each ACL entry has two parts: a user or group name and the access control rights. Access control rights include:

r   read

l   lookup

i   insert

d   delete

w   write

k   lock

a   administer

For example,

```
fs setacl . jenny rl
```

would give Jenny read and lookup permission only on the current directory.

Frequently used AFS commands follow:

Command	Description
`fs listacl`	Lists a directory's ACL
`fs setacl`	Sets one directory's ACL
`fs setacl -dir`	Sets multiple directories' ACLs
`fs copyacl`	Copies a directory's ACL to one or more other directories
`kpasswd`	Changes AFS password
`fs whereis`	Lists the file server housing a file or directory
`fs checkservers`	Checks the status of file servers
`klog`	Authenticates with Server to obtain tokens
`tokens`	Displays all tokens
`pts`	Sets up and lists group membership

You can get help for each of the commands by typing the command and then help. This will give you a list of all the parameters for that command with a description. You can get help on the syntax for the command and parameter by entering the command, the parameter, and then –help; for example,

```
$ fs sa -help

Usage: fs sa -dir <directory>+ -acl <access list entries>+
[-clear ] [-negative ] [-id ] [-if ] [-help ]
```

CHAPTER
8

- System Management Interface Tool (SMIT)

- Distributed System Management (or Why Just Worry About One Machine When You Can Multitask?!)

- Web-based System Manager

- Backup—and Make Restore an Option!

SMIT Happens! Administering AIX

No, it's not a misspelling! AIX Version 4.3 system administration has a suite of system management tools, including the System Management Interface Tool (SMIT), a menu-driven system management tool. DSMIT, Distributed SMIT, is available for distributed environments. AIX also includes Web-based System Manager, an object-oriented, drag-and-drop graphical interface for managing devices, printers, storage, users, and lots of other system management tasks. We'll review some system backup and restore commands you can use at the command line to impress your friends and boss—we don't want this to look too easy!

Read through this chapter to find out about these topics:

- System Management Interface Tool (SMIT)
- Distributed System Management Interface Tool (DSMIT)
- Web-based System Manager
- Backup and restore

To get started, boot the operating system. (*Boot*?! Computer terminology for *turn the system on*.) During the boot process, the system tests the hardware, loads and executes the operating system, and configures devices. The system finds all information necessary to the boot process on its disk drive.

When the system is first installed, the `bosboot` command creates a boot image from a RAM (random access memory) disk file system image and the operating system kernel. The boot image is transferred to a particular media such as the hard disk. When the machine is rebooted, the boot image is loaded from the media into memory.

To shut down your system, type `shutdown` and press the Enter key. The system shuts down; the system waits one minute before stopping the user processes and the init process. There are several reasons for shutting down the system:

- After installing new software or changing the configuration for existing software

- When a hardware problem exists

- When the system is hung

- When system performance is degraded (slow)

- When the file system is possibly corrupt

System Management Interface Tool (SMIT)

SMIT is a tool for managing the system that presents a natural-language, task-oriented interface, enabling you to quickly perform tasks that might otherwise require MANY typed commands.

SMIT steps you through adding a user or mounting a file system (only two of many tasks) with the use of menus, selectors, and dialogs. What does this mean to you? You don't have to remember the details of complex command syntax, valid parameter values, and system command spelling. Because you might need help remembering how you added a user yesterday, SMIT creates log files that you can use to duplicate work you did yesterday or to learn how to use specific commands. SMIT help is available on each menu and field label. "Using SMIT" on the main menu discusses how to use the interface and some of the features.

Note that for most system management SMIT tasks, you must have root authority. Use SMIT for the following reasons:

- Reduce need for memorization and need for documentation

- Make system administration easy to learn

- Structure your decision-making process

- Shorten training for novice system administrators:

  Use the F6 function key and command output window to see the commands you built while completing a SMIT task

  Use the F8 function key to capture SMIT screens in your `smit.log`

- Reduce keystrokes (and typing errors!)

- Review the `smit.log` file in your home directory and identify:

  Menu paths taken to complete SMIT tasks

  Fast paths

  Command output needed to complete a SMIT task from the command line

- Access Help!

But Why Should I Care About SMIT?

You should care about SMIT, because SMIT enables you to configure and administer AIX like a pro. Consider the following options:

- Software Installation & Maintenance

  Use this option to install products fixes, list installed software, and verify your software installation.

- Devices

  Use this option to add, move, change, remove, configure, and trace devices (for example, printers, CD-ROM drives, and tape drives).

- Physical & Logical Storage

  Use this option to mount and unmount file systems as well as to backup and restore file systems; add and/or activate paging space; and manage your physical and logical volumes.

- Security & Users

  Use this option to add, remove, list, and change users and groups and to assign passwords to users.

- Communications Applications and Services

  Use this option to configure TCP/IP and NFS.

- Spooler (Print Jobs)

  Use this option to start, cancel, and prioritize print jobs; to manage print queues; and to manage local and remote printer subsystems.

- Problem Determination

  Use this option to generate error reports, manage dump devices, run hardware diagnostics, and validate software.

- Performance & Resource Scheduling

  Use this option to set system run level, report system activity, and to list and schedule jobs.

- System Environments

  Use this option to stop the system, set the date and time, broadcast messages, and to change the language environment.

- Processes & Subsystems

  Use this option to show or remove processes and to query, start, stop, and trace subsystems and subservers.

- Using SMIT (Information Only)

  Use this option for help on the SMIT windows and features.

How to Get SMIT Up and Running

To start up GUI SMIT, enter `smit` on the command line. Your output will look like the screen shown in Figure 8–1.

To start up ASCII SMIT, enter `smitty` or `smit -C` on the command line. Your output will look like the screen shown in Figure 8–2.

When you are using the ASCII version of SMIT, the valid functions are displayed at the bottom of the screen. Only those functions that are valid for the specific menu, selector, or dialog are displayed. Table 8–1 describes all functions in SMIT. If you use a key sequence (Esc+*Number*), press and release the Esc key, then immediately press the number key.

Use SMIT to Add a Tape Drive

You can use SMIT to add a tape drive. We're going to add the tape drive using ASCII SMIT. Begin by logging in as root, enter `smitty`, then click on Devices. Your output will look like the screen in Figure 8–3.

Scroll down to Tape Drive on the Devices menu. Select Tape Drive. The Tape Drive menu pops up (Figure 8–4).

We want to add a tape drive, so scroll down to Add a Tape Drive and select the highlighted function. When you select Add a Tape Drive, you'll see the menu shown in Figure 8–5.

This menu shows the tape drive configured with your system. Which of these tape drives do you have attached to your system? I have physically attached (and powered on) a 5GB tape drive, so I'll select that option. Once I've selected that option, SMIT asks me to give it some more information (indicated by the + to the right of some of the fields). Once you've done this, hit Enter.

```
 ┌──────────────────────────────────────────────────────┐
 │═══            System Management Interface Tool         │
 ├──────────────────────────────────────────────────────┤
 │ Exit  Edit  Show                                       │
 ├──────────────────────────────────────────────────────┤
 │ Return To:                                             │
 │                                                        │
 │                                                        │
 │                                                        │
 │                                                        │
 │                                                        │
 │                                                        │
 │                                                        │
 │                                                        │
 │                                                        │
 │ System Management                                      │
 │  ┌─┐                                                   │
 │  │ │ Software Installation & Maintenance               │
 │  └─┘                                                   │
 │  ┌─┐                                                   │
 │  │ │ Devices                                           │
 │  └─┘                                                   │
 │  ┌─┐                                                   │
 │  │ │ Physical & Logical Storage                        │
 │  └─┘                                                   │
 │  ┌─┐                                                   │
 │  │ │ Security & Users                                  │
 │  └─┘                                                   │
 │  ┌─┐                                                   │
 │  │ │ Diskless Workstation Management & Installation    │
 │  └─┘                                                   │
 │  ┌─┐                                                   │
 │  │ │ Communications Applications and Services          │
 │  └─┘                                                   │
 │  ┌─┐                                                   │
 │  │ │ Spooler (Print Jobs)                              │
 │  └─┘                                                   │
 │  ┌─┐                                                   │
 │  │ │ Problem Determination                             │
 │  └─┘                                                   │
 │  ┌─┐                                                   │
 │  │ │ Performance & Resource Scheduling                 │
 │  └─┘                                                   │
 │  ┌─┐                                                   │
 │  │ │ System Environments                               │
 │  └─┘                                                   │
 │  ┌─┐                                                   │
 │  │ │ Processes & Subsystems                            │
 │  └─┘                                                   │
 │  ┌─┐                                                   │
 │  │ │ Applications                                      │
 │  └─┘                                                   │
 │  ┌─┐                                                   │
 │  │ │ Using SMIT (information only)                     │
 │  └─┘                                                   │
 └──────────────────────────────────────────────────────┘
```

Figure 8–1   GUI SMIT Startup Screen

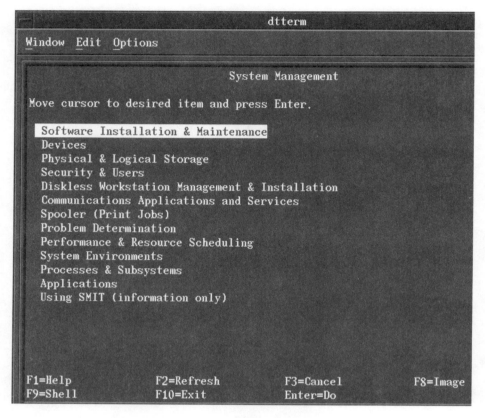

Figure 8–2   ASCII SMIT Start-up Screen

The OK following "Command" indicates that you have successfully added the tape drive. Congratulations! You have completed your first of many SMIT tasks.

What Are All of Those Weird Symbols on the Screen?

Oh right, I forgot to tell you about those. Table 8–2 will help you figure them out.

What Do I Do If I Need More SMIT Help?

For a general overview of how to use SMIT, select the Using SMIT option (in either ASCII or GUI) to access the following information:

- Overview
- Understanding the Menu Window
- Understanding the Dialog Window
- Understanding the Path Window
- Understanding the Command Output Panel

Table 8–1   Functions in SMIT

Function Key	Command	Description
F1 or Esc+1	`Help`	Gives more information on the topic to which the cursor points.
F2 or Esc+2	`Refresh`	Redraws the screen. Use if console messages overwrite the screen.
F3 or Esc+3	`Cancel`	Returns to the previous screen. F3 in the main menu exits SMIT.
F4 or Esc+4	`List`	Presents a list of choices for the highlighted entry field. A pop-up selector screen displays a scrollable list of choices.
F5 or Esc+5	`Reset`	Resets the entry field to the original setting.
F6 or Esc+6	`Command`	Displays the command that SMIT is building.
F7 or Esc+7	`Edit`	Presents the highlighted text-entry field in a wide, pop-up selector screen for editing.
	`Also: Select`	Makes individual selections on multiselect lists.
F8 or Esc+8	`Image`	Displays the *FastPath* parameter for the current menu or dialog screen. Also saves a screen image in the smit.log file so that you can print it later.
F9 or Esc+9	`Shell`	Escapes to a shell. A confirmation pop-up menu or message is displayed.
F10 or Esc+0	`Exit`	Exits SMIT.
Enter	`Do`	Executes the command built by SMIT or commits list entries to a dialog.

- Making Selections from a List of Choices
- Using SMIT Functions
- Using SMIT Fastpath
- Related Information in InfoExplorer

Distributed System Management (or Why Just Worry About One Machine When You Can Multitask?!)

The Distributed System Management Interface Tool (DSMIT) adds functionality to SMIT by enabling the SMIT interface to build commands for system management and distribute them to other clients on a network. DSMIT has most of the functionality of the SMIT program, such as fast paths, log files, and flags.

DSMIT works in a Client/Server model. One RS/6000 running AIX 4.1 must be defined as a DSMIT Server machine. This machine will be the single point to per-

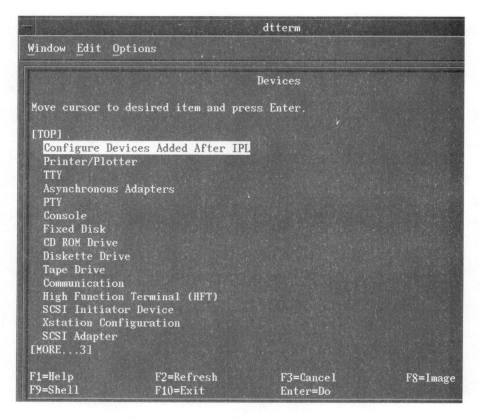

Figure 8-3   Select Devices Screen

form all the systems management tasks, sending commands over the network to DSMIT Client machines. These client machines could be RS/6000, Sun, or Hewlett-Packard workstations. A heterogeneous DSMIT environment would look like that shown in Figure 8–6.

DSMIT runs in both concurrent and sequential modes. Concurrent mode means that the DSMIT server builds a command and routes it to the clients simultaneously. Sequential mode means that the DSMIT server builds a command and routes it to the clients one machine at a time. After you build a command on the server and press the Enter key, a menu appears asking in which mode you wish to run DSMIT.

Start DSMIT by entering the `dsmit` command for the ASCII interface or `mdsmit` for the GUI interface at the command line. When you start the DSMIT program, you must define the working collective of clients. DSMIT provides a simple

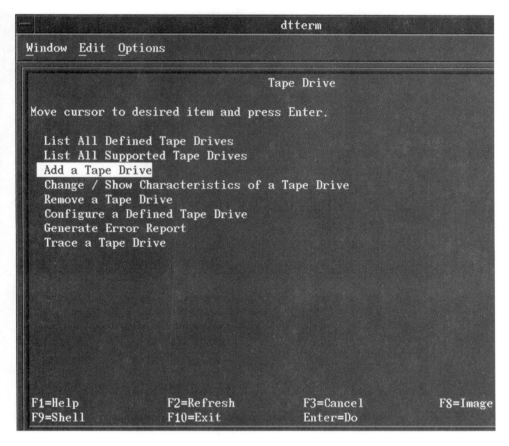

Figure 8–4 SMIT Tape Drive Menu

mechanism for exiting. The function keys enable you to exit a particular screen or to stop DSMIT when you complete a task.

DSMIT allows you to change a domain. You can add a new client to the domain, delete a client from the domain, or redefine the domain's member list entirely. Use the `chdsmitd` command or the interface to change a domain. When you use the interface, you can view the domain and any changes you are making to them. The Manage Domains of Machines menu provides options to assist in altering domains.

Defining clients for the Distributed System Management Interface Tool (DSMIT) program enables clients to run commands built by the DSMIT server. To define a

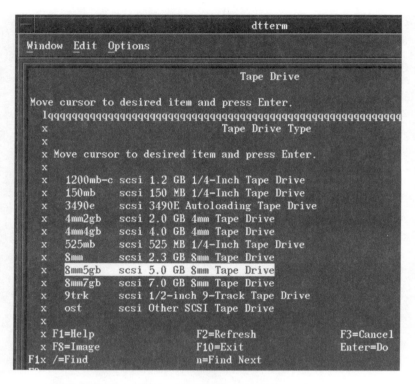

Figure 8–5   SMIT Tape Drive Information Menu

client, you must add it to the `/usr/share/DSMIT/hosts` file by editing the file directly or with the DSMIT interface.

The working collective specifies the current list of clients that receive commands built by the Distributed System Management Interface Tool (DSMIT) program. The working collective is a temporary list of clients and must be respecified with each new DSMIT session. By default, the server is the only machine in the working collective when you start DSMIT. For more information on DSMIT, see *Distributed SMIT 2.2 for AIX: Guide and Reference*, SC23-2667.

Web-based System Manager

With Web-based System Manager, you can manage AIX systems from anywhere in the Internet/intranet. Web-based System Manager is a comprehensive system management environment that takes advantage of Web technology. Web-based

Table 8–2 Symbols

Symbol	Symbol Name	Meaning
*	Asterisk	An entry is required. Appears to the left of the field name or prompt.
#	Number sign	Enter a number.
X	The letter X	Enter a hexadecimal number.
/	Slash	Enter a file name.
+	List of options or Option ring	Displays a list of current, available choices generated by the system. To view list, press the List key (F4 or Esc+4). An option ring offers a fixed set of options, such as Yes or No. Press the Tab key to display ring options individually in the entry field.
[ ]	Brackets	Beginning and end of an editable field.
<	Less than sign	More text to the left of the visible field.
>	Greater than sign	More text to the right of the visible field.

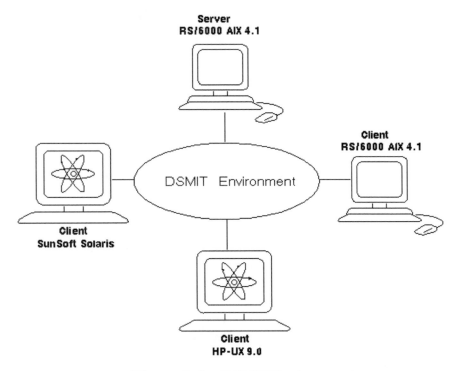

Figure 8–6   DSMIT Environment

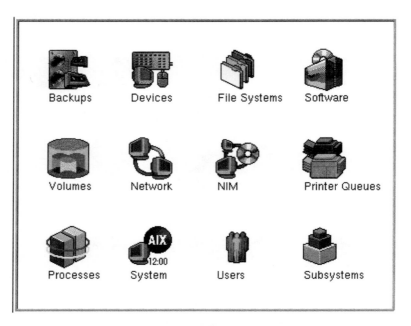

Figure 8–7   Web-based System Manager Icons

System Manager provides the following features to help you easily manage your system:

- **Ease of Use.**   Quite simply, systems should be easier to administer. Ease of use can reduce training costs and those caused by human error. It also enhances productivity and work satisfaction.

- **Comprehensiveness.**   With this extensive and consistent administrative environment, you can manage your system without having to manually edit configuration files or use UNIX commands.

- **Familiarity.**   A first-time user of Web-based System Manager, accustomed to the graphical user interface style, needs little or no training to learn how to interact with it. Using a style consistent with both Windows and the Common Desktop Environment (CDE) gives Web-based System Manager a look and feel consistent with the platform you are using.

- **Client Independence.**   Web-based System Manager offers you the choice of client operating systems and platforms. You should be able to use your available client platforms to manage AIX systems.

- **Location Independence.** Using Web-based System Manager, you can manage an RS/6000 using a locally attached graphical terminal or a remote client with equal ease. The same familiar graphical user interface is available whether the client is a personal computer or RS/6000 workstation.

With Web-based System Manager, any operating system and platform for which a Java 1.1 enabled browser is available can be used to manage an RS/6000 system. However, Web-based System Manager has been tested only on AIX Version 4.3, Windows 95, and Windows NT clients.

The graphical, object-oriented user interface of Web-based System Manager promotes ease of use. Graphical interfaces provide the visual keys for performing administrative tasks on AIX. Web-based System Manager features graphical user interfaces based on Java technology for most system management tasks.

TaskGuides simplify complex or unfamiliar tasks by stepping you through your task in a friendly interface, reducing the need for expert knowledge.

You can run Web-based System Manager in local, remote, or applet mode using any AIX Version 4.3 system. No Internet/intranet connection is needed to run Web-based System Manager from the command line or CDE desktop.

The Web-based System Manager can also be remotely run on any AIX host known to the system. In remote mode, the user interface is managed locally, but the operations are performed on the remote host.

Finally, Web-based System Manager can be run on a remote AIX host through any Java 1.1, Alternative Window Toolkit (AWT) 1.1-enabled Web browser. This mode gives you the ability to administer an RS/6000 running AIX 4.3 with a variety of client platforms.

What Tasks Can I Do with Web-based System Manager?

Applications provide the Web-based System Manager with the power to manage the AIX system. Web-based System Manager provides the user with 12 applications that can be run in local, remote, or applet (browser-based) mode. The applications are:

- Backups
- Devices
- File Systems
- Network
- NIM (if NIM product is installed)
- Printer Queues

- Processes
- Software
- Subsystems
- System
- Users
- Volumes

File Systems.   Creates and manages the hierarchical structure of files and directories. The file system organizes data and programs into groups, allowing the management of several directories and files at the same time. This application supports several file system types, including: journaled file systems, network file systems, and CD-ROM file systems. Figure 8–8 is an example of what the Web-based System Manager File Systems container might look like on your system.

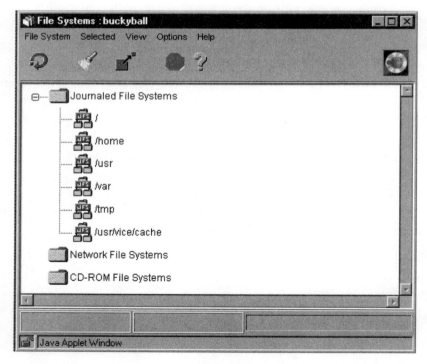

Figure 8–8   Web-based System Manager File Systems Container

NIM. If the Network Installation Manager product is installed on your system, you can use the application to manage software across the network. It also provides the support for managing diskless or dataless machines. Figure 8–9 is an example of what the Web-based System Manager NIM container might look like on your system.

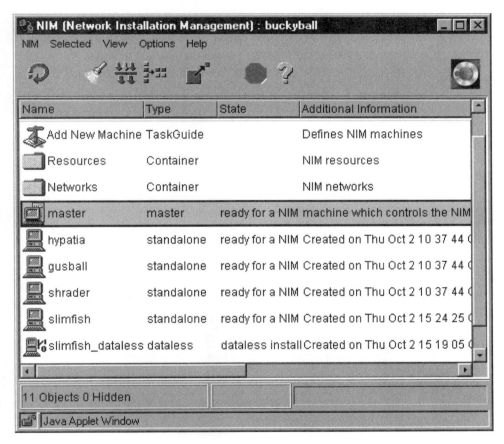

Figure 8–9 Web-based System Manager NIM Container

Printer Queues.   Provides you with managers for printers, print queues, and print jobs in the queues. Support for both local and remote queues is provided. Figure 8–10 is an example of what the Web-based System Manager Printer Queues container might look like on your system.

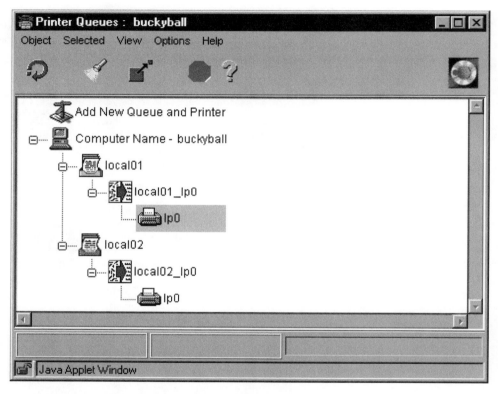

Figure 8–10   Web-based System Manager Printer Queues Container

Users. Manages users or groups of users in the AIX environment. You can show or change user properties such as passwords, group membership, and disk quotas. Figure 8–11 is an example of what the Web-based System Manager Users container might look like on your system.

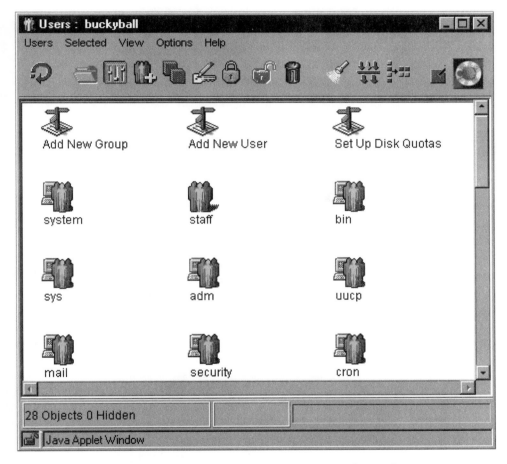

Figure 8–11   Web-based System Manager Users Container

Subsystems. Manages the program or process or set of programs or processes that operate independently or with a controlling system. Subsystems are often called "daemons". This application can refresh, start, stop, start a trace, and stop a trace. Figure 8–12 is an example of what the Web-based System Manager Subsystems container might look like on your system.

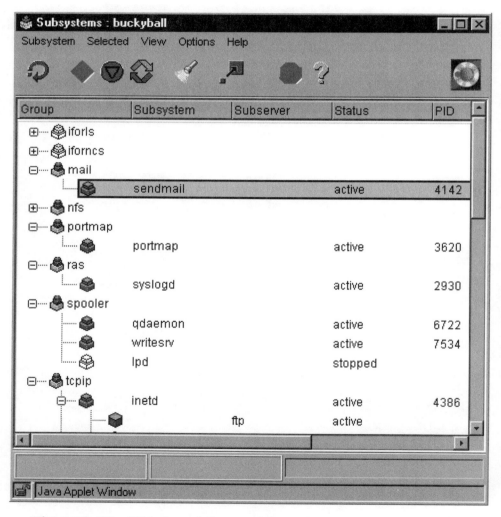

Figure 8–12   Web-based System Manager Subsystems Container

Processes.   Manages the single programs running in their own address space
(processes). This application also assesses the processes use of system resources.
Processes are distinct from a job or command which can be composed of many
processes working together to perform a specific task. Figure 8–13 is an example
of what the Web-based System Manager Processes container might look like on
your system.

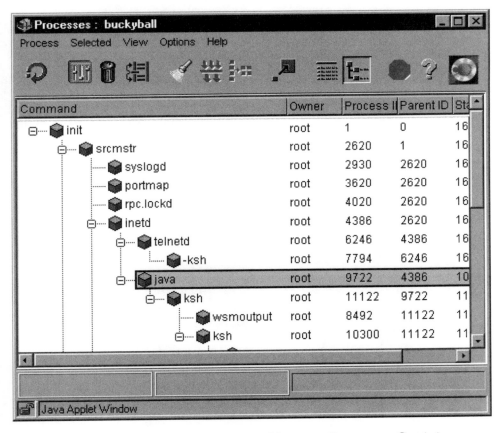

Figure 8–13   Web-based System Manager Processes Container

Volumes.   Defines and manages the logical volumes, including volume groups, physical volumes, and paging space. Figure 8–14 is an example of what the Web-based System Manager Volumes container might look like on your system.

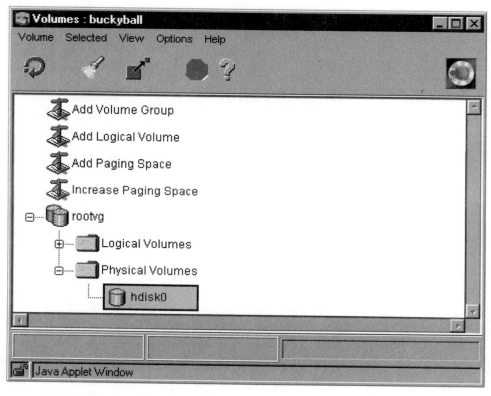

Figure 8–14   Web-based System Manager Volumes Container

Backup—and Make Restore an Option!

Congratulations! You are up and running—but just in case you delete a file (or files) or work with any unhappy employees possibly interested in destroying your data, keep a spare copy of your data on hand (well, on a tape, CD-ROM, or another hard disk). This spare copy of your information is called a *backup*. Tape drives are commonly used for backup due to their speed and large data capacity. You can also use a CD-ROM attached to your system to download system files.

AIX Version 4 provides multiple ways of backing up your systems. You can use SMIT or the command line. Backup commands available include `cpio`, `tar`, `pax`, `dd`, `backup`, `restore`, and `mksysb`. SMIT also provides a menu-driven method of backing up and restoring AIX files or the entire rootvg volume group. After restoring your files using SMIT, you can use the `fsck` command to check the integrity of the file system.

backup *Command*

The `backup` command creates copies of your files on a backup medium, such as a magnetic tape or diskette, in one of two backup formats:

1.   Specific files backed up by name using the -i flag. The `backup` command reads standard input for the names of the files to be backed up. You can generate filenames with the `find` command, then pipe the list into the `backup` command.

2.   You can also backup your entire file system by i-node using the *Level* and *FileSystem* parameters.

Before a file system is backed up, you should unmount the file system. This will ensure that files being backed up are not in the process of being changed. The default backup device is `/dev/rfd0` (or, your diskette drive). If flags are specified that are not appropriate for the specified backup device, the `backup` command displays an error message and continues with the backup. Note that a single backup can span multiple volumes.

The following command options will be extremely useful:

•   -#: Level of backup (0=entire system)

•   -f: Device to backup to

•   -u: Update /etc/dumpdates

•   -i: Backup by name

File types can be special files, regular files, or directories. When the file type is a directory, only the directory is backed up. The files under the directory are not backed up, unless they are explicitly specified:

1. To backup all the files and subdirectories in the /home directory using full path names, enter

```
find /home -print | backup -i -f /dev/rmt0
```

The -i flag specifies that files will be read from standard input and archived by filename. The find command generates a list of all the files in the / home directory. The files in this list are full path names. The | (pipe symbol) causes this list to be read from standard input by the backup command. The -f flag directs the backup command to write the files to the / dev/rmt0 tape device. Because the files are archived using full path names, they will be written to the same paths when restored.

2. To backup all the files and subdirectories in the /home/mike directory using relative path names, enter

```
cd /home/mike
find . -print | backup -i -v -q
```

Each filename in the list generated by the find command is preceded by ./ (dot, slash). Because the files are backed up using relative path names, they will be written to the current directory when restored. The -v flag causes the backup command to display additional information about the backup. The files are written to the default backup device /dev/rfd0.

3. To backup the / (root) file system, enter

```
backup -0 -u -f /dev/rmt0 /
```

The 0 level specifies that all the files in the / (root) file system be backed up. The -u flag causes the backup command to update the /etc/dumpdates file for this backup.

restore **Command**

The restore command reads backup files created by the backup command and extracts the files stored on them. These backed up files can be in either filename or file-system format. Backups can be stored on disk, diskette, or tape. Files must be restored using the same method by which they were backed up (so knowing whether relative path names or complete path names were used when backing up your files is important). The backed up format can be determined by examining the backed up volume header information that is displayed when using the -T flag. When using the -x, -r, -T, or -t flags, the restore command automatically determines the archive format.

The Command options include the following:

- -f: Device to restore from
- -T: Table of contents
- -r: Restores an entire file system
- -v: Verbose
- -x: Restores files specified, or all files if none specified

Individual files can be restored from either filename or filesystem archives by using the -x flag and specifying the filename. The filename must be specified as it exists on the archive. Files can be restored interactively from filesystem archives using the -i flag. The names of the files on an archive can be written to standard output using the -T flag.

The diskette device, /dev/rfd0, is the default media for the restore command. To restore from standard input, specify a - (dash) with the f flag. You can also specify a range of devices, such as /dev/rmt0-2.

If you are restoring from a multiple-volume archive, the restore command reads the volume mounted, prompts you for the next volume, and waits for your response. After inserting the next volume, press the Enter key to continue restoring files.

If an archive, created using the backup command, is made to a tape device with the device block size set to 0, it may be necessary for you to have explicit knowledge of the block size that was used when the tape was created in order to restore from the tape.

Multiple archives can exist on a single tape. When restoring multiple archives from tape, the restore command expects the input device to be a no-retension-on-open, no-rewind-on-close tape device. Do not use a no-rewind tape device for restoring unless either the -B, -s, or -X flag is specified. For more information on using tape devices, see the rmt special file.

Note the following operations:

1. To list the names of files in either a filename or file-system archive on the diskette device /dev/rfd0, enter

   ```
   restore -Tq
   ```

   The archive is read from the /dev/rfd0 default restore device. The names of all the files and directories contained in the archive are displayed. For file-system archives, the filename is preceded by the i-node number of the file as it exists on the archive. The -q flag tells the restore command that the first volume is available and is ready to be read. As a result, you are not prompted to mount the first volume.

2.   To restore a specific file, enter:

```
restore -xvqf myhome.bkup system.data
```

This command extracts the file system.data into the current directory from the archive myhome.bkup. The archive in this example is in the current directory. File and directory names must be specified as they are displayed when using the -T flag. The -v flag displays additional information during the extraction. This example applies to both filename and file-system archives.

3.   To restore a specific directory and the contents of that directory from a filename archive, enter

```
restore -xdvqf /dev/rmt0 /home/mike/tools
```

The -x flag tells restore to extract files by their filename. The -d tells restore to extract all the files and subdirectories in the /home/mike/ tools directory. File and directory names must be specified as they are displayed when using the -T flag. If the directories do not exist, they are created.

How to backup and restore through SMIT

SMIT provides you with a menu-driven method of backup and restoring AIX files or the entire rootvg volume group. Unmount a file system prior to backup to ensure data integrity. After you have unmounted the file system, enter smitty on the command line. Select:

- Physical and Logical Storage
- File Systems
- Backup Files in a File System (smit backup)
- Backup the System (smit mksysb)

The Backup the System option will prompt you for the pathname of the directory you want to back up as well as the backup device.

To restore files, mount the file system you want to restore data to and enter:

- Physical and Logical Storage
- File Systems
- Restore Files in a File System

After the files have been restored, use SMIT and select the Verify a File System option. This option uses the `fsck` command to check the integrity of the file systems after you have restored them.

mksysb Command

The `mksysb` command creates a backup of the operating system (that is, the root volume group). This backup can be used to reinstall a system to its original state after it has been corrupted. If the backup is created on tape, the tape is bootable and includes the installation programs needed to install from the backup.

The file-system image is in backup-file format. The tape format includes a boot image, a bosinstall image, and an empty table of contents followed by the system backup (root volume group) image. The root volume group image is in backup-file format, starting with the data files and then any optional map files.

The `mksysb` command also creates the /bosinst.data file from the system default file if the `/bosinst.data` file does not exist. To generate a system backup to a tape device named /dev/rmt1, enter

```
mksysb /dev/rmt1
```

CHAPTER 9

AIX Speaks Your Language: Internationalization

Just the way you expect to be able to look up a person's name and number in a phone book, you expect the computer to do things in a way that makes sense. You expect the computer to be able to display and process the letters in your alphabet; you expect it to give understandable messages. Although an error message of "Invalid offset" may not help much, you certainly would not expect the computer to come back with the following:

無効なオフセットです。

You expect your computer to be a useful and usable tool. Since AIX users throughout the world feel the same way, AIX has been designed to be easily configured to "do the right thing" for over forty different "locales."

In AIX, a "locale" is an environment that you specify that tells AIX which language and cultural conventions you want to use. AIX Version 4 supports over forty of these. Some of them are defined in Table 9–1.

If you want AIX to display messages in Japanese, it will! If you want to see date and time displayed in the German format, you can! If you want to enter and print Chinese characters, you can! If you want to use French accent characters in your files, no problem!

Figure 9–1 is a brief example of how the operation of AIX changes depending on the "locale."

To be a little bit more technical, AIX internationalization is based on the industry standard X/Open Portability Guide Version 4 (known as XPG4) model which was created by industry standard gurus at X/Open with help from other industry standard gurus from throughout the world. For what it's worth, this is the

Table 9–1 Did Somebody Say Locale?

Locale	Description
C	This is for UNIX programmers anywhere!
POSIX	Same as C
ar_AA	Arabic
bg_BG	Bulgarian in Bulgaria
ca_ES	Catalan in Spain
cs_CZ	Czech in Czechoslovakia
da_DK	Danish in Denmark
de_CH	German in Switzerland
de_DE	German in Germany
el_GR	Greek in Greece
en_GB	English in Great Britain
en_US	English in the United States
es_ES	Spanish in Spain
fi_FI	Finnish in Finland
fr_BE	French in Belgium
fr_CA	French in Canada
fr_CH	French in Switzerland
fr_FR	French in France
hr_HR	Croatian in Croatia
hu_HU	Hungarian in Hungary
is_IS	Icelandic in Iceland
it_IT	Italian in Italy
iw_IL	Hebrew in Israel
ja_JP	Japanese in Japan
ko_KR	Korean in Korea
mk_MK	Macedonian in Macedonia
nl_BE	Dutch in Belgium
nl_NL	Dutch in the Netherlands
no_NO	Norwegian in Norway
pl_PL	Polish in Poland
pt_BR	Portuguese in Brazil
pt_PT	Portuguese in Portugal
ro_RO	Romanian in Romania

Table 9–1 *(Continued)*

Locale	Description
ru_RU	Russian in the Soviet Union
sh_SP	Serbian Latin in Serbia
sk_SK	Slovak in Slovakia
al_SI	Slovene in Slovenia
ar_SP	Serbian Cyrillic in Serbia
sv_SE	Swedish in Sweden
tr_TR	Turkish in Turkey
zh_CH	Simplified Chinese in China
zh_TW	Traditional Chinese in Taiwan

```
[trent@musashi] /u/trent > export LANG=En_US
[trent@musashi] /u/trent > date
Mon Jan  1 12:30:42 CST 1996
[trent@musashi] /u/trent > cat foo
cat: 0652-050 Cannot open foo.

[trent@musashi] /u/trent > export LANG=Ja_JP
[trent@musashi] /u/trent > cat foo
cat: 0652-050 fooがオープンできません。

[trent@musashi] /u/trent > export LANG=es_ES
[trent@musashi] /u/trent > date
Lu  1 Ene 12:31:30 1996
[trent@musashi] /u/trent > cat foo
cat: 0652-050 No se puede abrir foo.
```

Figure 9–1   AIX Locale Example

same model used in industry standard POSIX P1003.2 from the IEEE Computer Society. This model contains six categories of information that tend to vary from country to country and from language to language. The purpose of defining these categories is to provide a foundation for a database of cultural conventions that users can easily pick and choose from. Oh, by the way, people who do internationalization for a living find that the word, "internationalization", is too long to type, too cumbersome to read, and certainly too much of a tongue twister to say. Thus they tend to type "i18n", and say I-eighteen-N, since there are 18 characters between the I and the N.

The first category is known as "LC_CTYPE". X/Open describes this as, "Character classification and case conversion." This category specifies what characters you can use, which are uppercase, which are lowercase, which are alphabetic, which are numeric, which are control, and . . . well, I think you get the picture. This category also specifies how case conversion is done; that is to say, there is a list of all lowercase characters, and which uppercase characters they can be mapped to, and vice versa.

The second category is known as "LC_COLLATE". X/Open describes this as "Collation order." Information in this category specifies exactly how words should be sorted. This is much more complicated and interesting than one might suppose. Many languages have their own special rules regarding sorting that are just as important as placing Apple before Zebra in an English sort. For instance, Spanish has "multicharacter collating symbols" such as "ch", "cz", and "ll". "ch" must collate between "c" and "d", unless it is in the middle of a word, in which case it collates after "cz" and before "d". Got that? We may have a pop quiz on this . . . Just kidding. Seriously, computers are supposed to keep track of details like this so that YOU don't have to.

The third category is known as "LC_TIME." X/Open describes this as, "Date and time formats." Each country and language tends to have its own words for days of the week and names of months. Often there are special formatting requirements for different countries on how dates and times should be displayed. These kind of things are specified in this category. (Time zones are handled with the TZ environment variable and can be specified in SMIT rather than in this category.)

The fourth category is known as "LC_NUMERIC." X/Open describes this as, "Numeric, non-monetary formatting." This category contains just a couple of pieces of information: which character to use as the decimal point, which character to use to group, and how to group digits. That is, do you want to see 1,500.1 or 1500.1 or 1.500,1 or 1500,1?

The fifth category is known as "LC_MONETARY." X/Open describes this as, "Monetary formatting." This category contains information similar to

LC_NUMERIC. Since this is for formatting currency figures, it also includes which symbol to use (i.e., $ in the U.S., the yen symbol in Japan, and so on). It also specifies exactly how to format the number. That is, where exactly should the minus sign be placed? The plus sign? The currency symbol?

The sixth category is known as "LC_MESSAGES." X/Open describes this as, "Formats of informative and diagnostic messages and interactive responses." This category tells AIX two things: which language you want messages displayed in, and what it should consider a "yes" or a "no" response to a yes/no question.

I know all these different categories seem complicated, but trust me, generally you don't need to worry about it. Usually it is sufficient to simply specify a single locale that you wish to use, and AIX understands that you want the overall behavior specified by all of these different categories. The advantage of all these different locale categories is that by setting only LC_COLLATE to German, you can do things like sort a list of data in German, but if you don't actually speak German, you can have program prompts and messages displayed in English. Nifty, isn't it?

Why Should I Care About Speaking Your Language?

If you speak only one language, and your customers speak only your language, and if you think this will never change, then you probably don't need to care, and you can skip to the next chapter.

If you would like to have AIX operate in a language other than English, or if you have customers who would like to have information processed in some way other than the "United States" way, then you should care deeply.

For what it's worth, large computer software and hardware companies make more than 50% of their profits from customers outside of the United States. Savvy programmers and hardware manufacturers design their products so that they work well in as many countries as possible. In fact, it is not enough to have a separate version localized for each country. For both scales of economy and ultimately customer satisfaction, it is best to ship a single product world-wide that can be easily configured by the user to adapt to any locale. This is the goal of both the XPG locale model, and its AIX implementation.

I'm Convinced! How Do I Get AIX to Speak My Language?

The first step is to ensure that the right pieces of AIX were installed on your system. Since this was all covered in the chapter on installing your system, this should not be a problem.

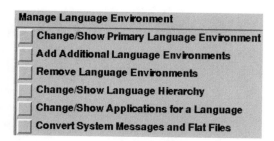

Figure 9–2   Manage Language Environment SMIT Screen

Before we begin, we need to define a few terms you will see as we use SMIT to configure your system. A *codeset* is simply the name for the set of characters that a language uses. IBM-850 was the default English codeset in AIX 3.2. ISO8859-1 is the default English codeset in AIX Version 4. Both are based on ASCII. Other codesets are used as defaults for other languages. The term *cultural convention* refers to how you want your computer to behave when it sorts, displays dates, and so on. In fact, the term, "cultural convention" includes all of the categories discussed above except for the message translation used. *Language translation* specifies which language you want AIX to display messages in. Since AIX supports a variety of keyboards for each country, there is also an option to specify what kind of *keyboard* you are using.

All right, let's use SMIT to configure system language defaults. Once this is complete, you can configure user defaults, or even change things on the fly! First, start SMIT as root and select "System Environments." Next, select "Manage Language Environment" (Figure 9–2). This is where all the action takes place for configuring your system to speak different languages.

Now select "Change/Show Primary Language Environment" (Figure 9–3). Next select "Change/Show Cultural Convention, Language, or Keyboard" (Figure 9–4).

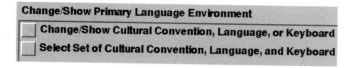

Figure 9–3   Change/Show Primary Language Environment SMIT Screen

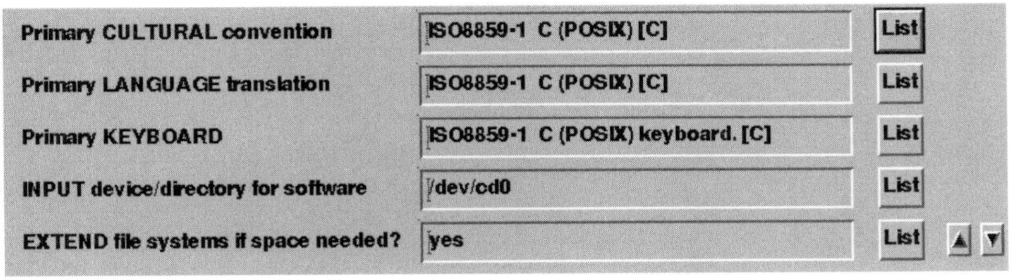

Primary CULTURAL convention	ISO8859-1 C (POSIX) [C]	List
Primary LANGUAGE translation	ISO8859-1 C (POSIX) [C]	List
Primary KEYBOARD	ISO8859-1 C (POSIX) keyboard. [C]	List
INPUT device/directory for software	/dev/cd0	List
EXTEND file systems if space needed?	yes	List ▲ ▼

Figure 9–4 Change/Show Cultural Convention, Language, or Keyboard SMIT Screen

To keep things simple, press the LIST button to the right of "Primary CULTURAL convention" and select either the country you are in or the conventions you wish to use. This will specify all of the locale category behavior information we just discussed. Figure 9–5 is a partial list of cultural conventions.

Now select the LIST button to the right of "Primary LANGUAGE translation", and select the language you wish to see messages in. Then select the LIST button to the right of "primary KEYBOARD" and select the value that corresponds to the keyboard you have on your system. Next, select the "INPUT device". This should be the device that has your AIX install media, probably /dev/rmt0 if you used a tape or /dev/cd0 if you used a CD-ROM to install. I recommend selecting "yes" for the question, "EXTEND file systems if space needed?" Now SMIT will install and configure your request. After this is done, shutdown your computer. When you reboot, your computer will be speaking your language!

For the curious among us, Figure 9–6 shows what the Manage Language Environment SMIT menu looks like in Japanese. Figure 9–7 shows what the same menu looks like in German.

The screens in Figures 9–6 and 9–7 were created simply by typing, LANG=ja_JP smit lang and, LANG=de_DE smit lang from the desktop on a system that had Japanese and German message translations installed. It's that easy!!

This Is Interesting! Tell Me More!

Here are some nifty tidbits. If you forget what language you are using, you can use the locale command to see what it is:

Figure 9–5   Partial List of Cultural Conventions

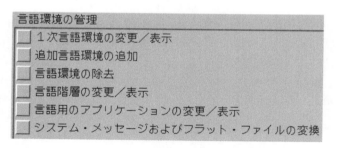

Figure 9–6   Japanese Manage Language Environment
SMIT Screen

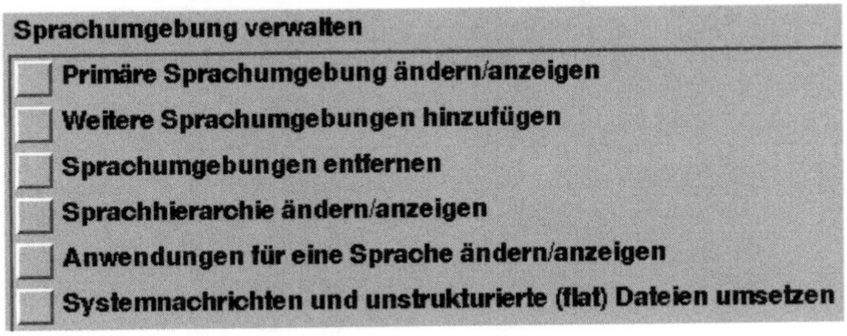

Sprachumgebung verwalten

☐ **Primäre Sprachumgebung ändern/anzeigen**

☐ **Weitere Sprachumgebungen hinzufügen**

☐ **Sprachumgebungen entfernen**

☐ **Sprachhierarchie ändern/anzeigen**

☐ **Anwendungen für eine Sprache ändern/anzeigen**

☐ **Systemnachrichten und unstrukturierte (flat) Dateien umsetzen**

Figure 9–7 German Manage Language Environment SMIT Screen

```
[trent@musashi] /u/trent > locale
LANG=Ja_JP
LC_COLLATE="Ja_JP"
LC_CTYPE="Ja_JP"
LC_MONETARY="Ja_JP"
LC_NUMERIC="Ja_JP"
LC_TIME="Ja_JP"
LC_MESSAGES="Ja_JP"
LC_ALL=
```

This example shows that we are using the Japanese locale. OK, suppose you want to know what other locales can you use? Try typing `locale -a`. This will list all of the locales installed on your system. You might see something like this:

```
        [trent@musashi] /u/trent > locale -a
C
POSIX
Sv_SE
Da_DK.IBM-850
De_CH.IBM-850
De_DE.IBM-850
En_GB.IBM-850
En_US.IBM-850
Es_ES.IBM-850
Fi_FI.IBM-850
Fr_BE.IBM-850
Fr_CA.IBM-850
Fr_CH.IBM-850
Fr_FR.IBM-850
Is_IS.IBM-850
It_IT.IBM-850
```

```
Pt_PT
Nl_BE.IBM-850
Nl_NL.IBM-850
No_NO.IBM-850
Pt_PT.IBM-850
Sv_SE.IBM-850
No_NO
Nl_NL
Nl_BE
It_IT
Is_IS
Fr_FR
Fr_CH
Fr_CA
Fr_BE
Fi_FI
Es_ES
En_US
En_GB
De_DE
De_CH
Da_DK
Ja_JP
Ja_JP.IBM-932
zh_TW
ar_AA.ISO8859-6
bg_BG.ISO8859-5
cs_CZ.ISO8859-2
da_DK.ISO8859-1
de_CH.ISO8859-1
de_DE.ISO8859-1
el_GR.ISO8859-7
en_GB.ISO8859-1
en_US.ISO8859-1
es_ES.ISO8859-1
fi_FI.ISO8859-1
fr_BE.ISO8859-1
fr_CA.ISO8859-1
fr_CH.ISO8859-1
fr_FR.ISO8859-1
hr_HR.ISO8859-2
hu_HU.ISO8859-2
is_IS.ISO8859-1
it_IT.ISO8859-1
iw_IL.ISO8859-8
ja_JP.IBM-eucJP
ko_KR.IBM-eucKR
mk_MK.ISO8859-5
```

```
nl_BE.ISO8859-1
nl_NL.ISO8859-1
no_NO.ISO8859-1
pl_PL.ISO8859-2
pt_PT.ISO8859-1
ro_RO.ISO8859-2
ru_RU.ISO8859-5
sl_SI.ISO8859-2
sk_SK.ISO8859-2
sh_SP.ISO8859-2
sr_SP.ISO8859-5
sv_SE.ISO8859-1
tr_TR
tr_TR.ISO8859-9
zh_TW.IBM-eucTW
pt_BR.ISO8859-1
sv_SE
sr_SP
sl_SI
sk_SK
sh_SP
ru_RU
ro_RO
pt_PT
pt_BR
pl_PL
no_NO
nl_NL
nl_BE
mk_MK
ko_KR
ja_JP
iw_IL
it_IT
is_IS
hu_HU
hr_HR
fr_FR
fr_CH
fr_CA
fr_BE
fi_FI
es_ES
en_US
en_GB
el_GR
de_DE
de_CH
```

```
da_DK
cs_CZ
bg_BG
ar_AA
Iw_IL
Ar_AA.IBM-1046
Iw_IL.IBM-856
Ar_AA
```

You notice how some of these have a dot and some text added? This tells you exactly what codeset this locale uses. Notice that we have four Japanese locales. Ja_JP and Ja_JP.IBM-932 are really the same, they both use IBM-932 as the codeset. (This is also known as Shift-JIS.) ja_JP and ja_JP.IBM-eucJP are also the same. They use IBM-eucJP (also known as Japanese EUC) as the codeset. You can temporarily change your language on the fly by changing the LANG environment variable to one of those values.

To set your language to English (with ksh or bsh) type

```
export LANG=en_US
```

If you use csh type

```
setenv LANG=en_US
```

To set your language to German (with bsh or ksh) type

```
export LANG=de_DE
```

or for csh:

```
setenv LANG=de_DE
```

If you wish to change your language permanently, the `chlang` command is a good way to do this. For example this would change your default language to German, effective next time you login:

```
chlang de_DE
```

OK, now for something really out of the ordinary. Suppose you want to see what kind of information is actually IN the locale. This can be done with the locale command. Try this:

```
[trent@musashi] /u/trent > locale -ck LC_TIME

LC_TIME

abday="Sun";"Mon";"Tue";"Wed";"Thu";"Fri";"Sat"

day="Sunday";"Monday";"Tuesday";"Wednesday";"Thursday";
"Friday";"Saturday"

abmon="Jan";"Feb";"Mar";"Apr";"May";"Jun";"Jul";"Aug";"Sep";
"Oct";"Nov";"Dec"
```

```
    mon="January";"February";"March";"April";"May";"June";
"July";"August";"September";"October";"November";"December"

    d_t_fmt="%a %b %e %H:%M:%S %Z %Y"

    d_fmt="%m/%d/%y"

    t_fmt="%H:%M:%S"

    am_pm="AM";"PM"

    era=""

    era_d_fmt=""

    era_year=""

    t_fmt_ampm="%I:%M:%S %p"

    era_t_fmt=""

    era_d_t_fmt=""

    alt_digits=""
```

If you should find yourself needing to actually do programming related to internationalization or if you have an insatiable curiosity about this, check out some of the references below.

References

1.   IBM International Technical Support Centers, *AIX Version 3.2 for RISC System/ 6000: National Language Support.* Order number GG24-3850-00

2.   IBM Corporation. *AIX Version 3.2 for RISC System/6000: Internationalization of AIX Software—A Programmers' Guide.* Order number SC23-2431-00

3.   X/Open Company Ltd. *Internationalization Guide Version 2.* U.K:. X/Open Company Ltd. ISBN: 1-85912-002-4

4.   Ken Lunde. *Understanding Japanese Information Processing.* Sebastopol, CA: O'Reilly & Associates Inc., 1993. ISBN: 1-56592-043-0

CHAPTER 10

- Unlimited On-line Information

- 1-800-IBM-4FAX—Lots of Information for FREE!

- IBM RS/6000 Welcome Center

- AIX and RS/6000: Resources on the Net

- IBM RS/6000 POWERnet Marketing Support Program

- RS/6000 Technical Support

- AIX News Groups

- RS/6000 Talk Radio

All the Help
You Need

Now that you have your AIX system up and running; have loaded a cool backdrop, window, and icon colors; run a few commands and written a few shell scripts; set up your printer and CD-ROM drive; and backed up your system for the day—you're ready to access help and information from InfoExplorer, the Internet, and multiple IBM resources. So what is and where is all of this help, documentation, and information?

- On-line help and documentation is accessed through InfoExplorer.

  InfoExplorer is a hypertext information retrieval system that enables you to browse 50,000 pages of AIX hardcopy information by topic. InfoExplorer contains information on how to use, manage, and program AIX and AIX software applications.

- Fax information on any IBM product, service, and solutions for specific problems is accessible through 1-800-IBM-4FAX.

  1-800-IBM-4FAX is an automated document retrieval system. You can select documents to be faxed directly to you from a menu including RS/6000, AIX, PowerParallel, personal computers, OS2, AS/400, networking, and IBM education information.

- The RS/6000 Welcome Center, designed to introduce new users to many of the features and capabilities of the RS/6000 product family, contains a massive library of information about RS/6000 systems, helpful AIX setup and configuration utilities, a showcase of IBM and Business Partner solutions optimized specifically for RS/6000 systems and a world-wide directory of RS/6000 service and support offerings.

- The IBM RS/6000 POWERnet Marketing Support Program.

  POWERnet is an RS/6000(TM) marketing and support program to help RS/6000 and other key Internet technology providers develop and maintain the skills to capture the opportunity for RS/6000 Internet and intranet solutions. The POWERnet website is at `http://www.rs6000.ibm.com/solutions/internet/powernet`.

- RS/6000 Technical Support.

  IBM supports AIX and IBM products running on AIX, HP-UX, Solaris, ULTRIX, IRIX or other UNIX operating systems. Direct support from IBM is provided in virtually every country around the globe. To find your way to the many technical support offerings available from IBM for the RS/6000 worldwide, go to `http://service.boulder.ibm.com/rs6000/`.

- The Internet!

  We've included a list (and URL) of IBM resources, sites, and programs available through the Internet. Enjoy!

- AIX News Groups

- RS/6000 Talk Radio

Unlimited On-line Information

InfoExplorer enables you to access the entire AIX library. You can install InfoExplorer on your RS/6000 or you can mount the InfoExplorer CD-ROM. InfoExplorer contains information on how to use, manage, and program the operating system and other applications that run on AIX as well as reference information.

InfoExplorer articles provide conceptual overviews and step-by-step procedures for completing tasks related to a particular topic. InfoExplorer takes you through using, programming, and managing AIX through the use of navigation lists, concept articles, procedure articles, and reference articles, as illustrated in Figure 10–1:

- Navigation lists provide several ways to access information including contents, topic lists, and indexes.

- Concept articles provide background information needed to complete tasks and procedures discussed in procedural and reference articles.

- Procedure articles list the steps necessary for accomplishing a task.

- Reference articles describe commands, calls, subroutines, file formats, and functions. The command reference articles provide diagrams illustrating the command syntax and appropriate flags.

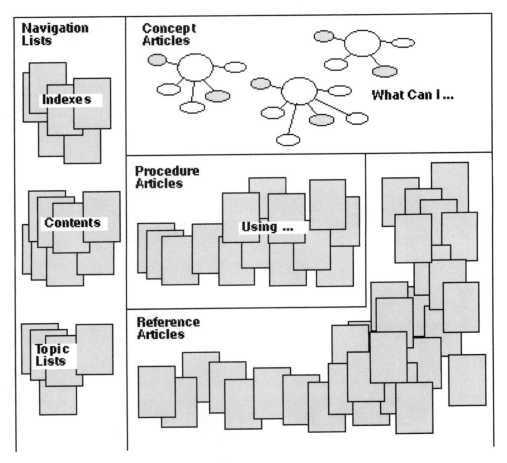

Figure 10–1 How InfoExplorer is Organized (Copied with Permission from IBM)

How Does InfoExplorer Present Information?

To help you quickly find the specific type of information you are interested in, InfoExplorer topics are divided into System Management, Programming, Using, and Problem Solving. When you start InfoExplorer, the Topic & Task Index (Figure 10–2) is activated enabling you to immediately access the most appropriate information. Just click on the topic you are interested in.

A variety of retrieval and navigation tools enable you to find information easily (see Table 10–1).

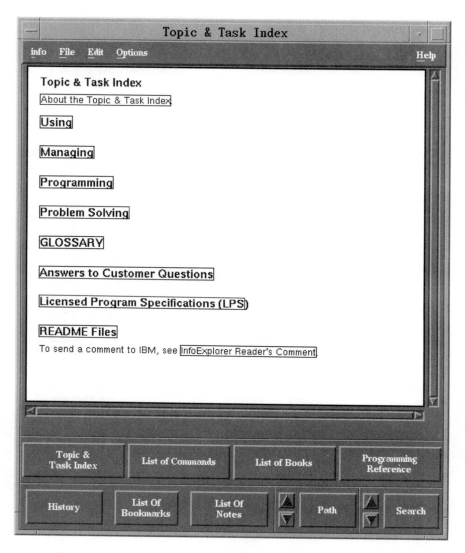

Figure 10–2   InfoExplorer Topic & Task Startup Screen

Table 10–1   InfoExplorer Retrieval Methods (Copied with Permission from IBM)

TASK	RETRIEVAL METHOD
You know what you want to do, but not how to do it.	Topic & Task Index
You want to read about the command you used	List of Commands
You want to read everything about using communications	List of Books
You want to find information about a subject	Search
You want to go back to information you just read	History
You want to mark specific information for review	List of Bookmarks
You want to see only the information you have updated	List of Notes

You can also view information on-line by using the Books list. The Books list enables you to find information using a Contents List, just like you would if reading or referencing a hardcopy book. By selecting the List of Books on the InfoExplorer startup interface and then selecting System Management Guide, you bring up the following Content List for the *AIX System User's Guide: Operating System and Devices* (Figure 10–3).

InfoExplorer Features

InfoExplorer provides several cool features:

- List of Bookmarks

  You can create bookmarks for articles you consult frequently.

- History

  InfoExplorer keeps track of where you've linked to and creates a History file.

- List of Notes

  You can create margin notes in articles to add information, emphasize important tasks, or just doodle. Notes can be private, public, or system level and can be edited and saved.

- Path

  A Path button is provided on the InfoExplorer panel. You can select either the forward or backward arrow. Well, first you select the backward arrow to go back to where you've already visited; then you can select the forward arrow to drive back to where you just backtracked from—WHEW!

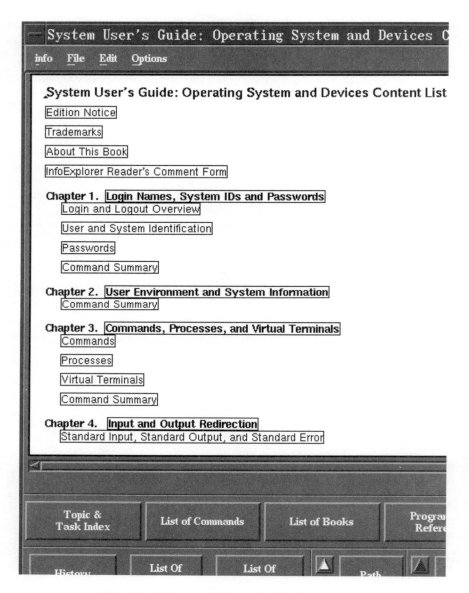

Figure 10–3   On-line Table of Contents

Starting InfoExplorer

To start InfoExplorer from the desktop, move the mouse pointer to the Application Manager icon and click the left mouse button twice. This brings up a window with several application groups, which represent directories. Click on the Information icon and then on the InfoExplorer icon.

You may also start InfoExplorer from an operating system command line in an AIX window. Type the following at the system prompt and press the Enter key:

```
info
```

The Welcome to the InfoExplorer Window Interface displays in the reading window and the Topic & Task Index displays in a navigation window. The welcome information explains how to do basic window operations and how to access InfoExplorer Help, copyrights, and trademarks.

Exiting InfoExplorer

You can stop the InfoExplorer program from any open InfoExplorer window. To exit the InfoExplorer program and save all bookmarks and notes, select the Quit option in the info pull-down menu from any InfoExplorer window. All open windows are closed and the program is exited.

To exit the InfoExplorer program without saving all bookmarks and notes, select **Close** in the navigation window menu located to the left of the title bar. All open windows are closed and the program is exited.

1-800-IBM-4FAX—Lots of Information for FREE!

Tips and solutions for common AIX/6000 problems and questions asked by customers are available for FREE by dialing 1-800-IBM-4FAX. You will be asked to enter document numbers and your fax number—the documents you ordered are then faxed to your fax number. To obtain the faxes outside the U.S., call 415-855-4FAX.

Many faxes are available from this service, from product catalogs to service information. We've included the 12/19/95 list of AIX and RS/6000 faxes list at the end of this section. You can also access the AIX and RS/6000 faxes on the Internet by entering URL `http://aix.boulder.ibm.com/aixsupport`.

For example, an LED C31 during IPL on RS/6000 in AIX 4.1 may be caused by an incorrect console configuration, by a corrupt ODM (Object Data Manager), or by a nonterminal device (such as a modem or printer) plugged into port 1 or 2. If LED C31 is flashing in your front panel window, you would call 1-800-IBM-4FAX and request fax document number 1991 be faxed to you. You would receive the following fax.

Example FAX 1991

To resolve the LED C31, check for a nonterminal device plugged into port 1 or 2. If that is not the problem, you will need to boot up in Service mode and change the console with the `chcons` command as follows:

1. Check for a nonterminal device plugged into serial port 1 or 2. If there is not such a device, go to step 2. If there is one, unplug it or turn it off. Then re-boot the machine with the key in Normal position. You do not need to continue with these steps.

2. Turn the key to the Service position.

3. With BOOTABLE MEDIA OF THE SAME VERSION AND LEVEL AS THE SYSTEM, boot the system.

   The bootable media can be ANY ONE of the following:

   • Bootable cdrom

   • Mksysb

   • Bootable Install Tape

   Follow the prompts to the "Welcome to Base OS" menu.

4. Choose "Start Maintenance Mode for System Recovery" (Option 3). The Next screen would prompt the following Menu "Maintenance."

   Choose "Access a Root Volume Group" (Option 1). At this stage the console would display information about rootvg, and also Display a Menu with 2 Options.

   Choose "Access this volume group and start a shell" (Option 1). If you get errors from the above option, do not continue with the rest of this procedure. Correct the problem causing the error. If you need assistance correcting the problem causing the error, contact your local branch office, your local point of sale, or call 1-800-CALL-AIX (to register for fee-based services).

5. Enter the following command:

   ```
   ODMDIR=/dev/objrepos
   ```

6. Change the system console with the following command. The change will take effect at the next startup of the system.

   If your console is an lft (6091), run the following:

   ```
   chcons -a login=enable /dev/lft/0
   ```

If your console is a tty (ibm3151), run the following:

```
chcons -a login=enable /dev/tty0
```

7. With the key in Normal position, run

```
shutdown -Fr
```

8. If the system does not stop at LED C31 during reboot, you do not need to continue with these instructions. If the system still stops on LED C31 during reboot, repeat steps 2-4 and then follow the following menu. Choose "Start Maintenance Mode for System Recovery" (Option 3). The Next Screen would prompt the following Menu "Maintenance."

Choose "Access a Root Volume Group" (Option 1). At this stage the console would display information about rootvg, and also Display a Menu with 2 Options. Choose "Access this volume group and start a shell before mounting the filesystems" (Option 2).

9. Run the following commands, which will remove much of the system's configuration, saving it to backup directory:

```
mount /dev/hd4 /mnt

mount /dev/hd2 /usr

mkdir /mnt/etc/objrepos/bak

cp /mnt/etc/objrepos/Cu* /mnt/etc/objrepos/bak

cp /etc/objrepos/Cu* /mnt/etc/objrepos

/etc/umount all

exit
```

Determine which disk is the boot disk with the `lslv` command. The boot disk will be shown in the PV1 column of the lslv output:

```
lslv -m hd5
```

Save the clean ODM database to the boot logical volume. ('#' is the number of the fixed disk, determined with the previous command.)

```
savebase -d /dev/hdisk#
```

Continue with step 10.

10. Turn the key to Normal position and run

```
shutdown -Fr
```

11. If LED C31 still occurs when you reboot your system and you need further assistance with this problem, contact your local branch office, your point of sale, or call 1-800-CALL-AIX to register for fee-based services.

Available AIX and RS/6000 Faxes

AIX and RS/6000 faxes currently available include the following (among others):

Fax Number	Document Title
3140	7135 RAIDiant Array—Common Installation Issues
3119	7135 RAIDiant Array—UPDATED Installation Instructions
1829	About AIX Service Hints and Tips from 4FAX
3753	About Sparse Files (AIX 3.2)
4923	AIX 4.1.4 Release
1826	AIX Service Bulletin: Potential Security Exposure
1770	AIX Support Family—Gathering System Crash Information
1762	AIX Support Family—Sending Testcases
2482	Backup/Install—"Tape Not in Backup Format" Error
1293	Backup/Install—AIX 4.1 Installation Tips
2503	Backup/Install—All Files Owned by Root After mksysb
2685	Backup/Install—Backup and Restore ACLs During mksysb
2363	Backup/Install—Installing/Updating with Low Disk Space
1453	Backup/Install—LED 518 or Failed mksysb After Install
2769	Backup/Install—Limitations of mksysb
2443	Backup/Install—Man Pages, Info Don't Work After Install
1456	Backup/Install—Paging Space Problems with mksysb Restoration
2702	Backup/Install—Relative and Absolute Backups
2561	Backup/Install—Restoring 0-Blocksize Tape
1959	Backup/Install—Restoring Multiple Tape Blocks
1294	Booting RS/6000 SP Node Via Manual Node Conditioning
4725	Configuring JetDirect Printer with BOOTP/TFTP Server
2263	Crash Command Information for TTY/Printer Subsystems
2737	Define Restricted Login Device for root
1499	Detection and Correction of Illegal Hard Links
2768	Determining Location and Cause of "core" File
4508	Determining Tape Block Size and Format
2461	Discussion of the Default Values in /etc/security/limits

Fax Number	Document Title
2929	Disk Quota System—Setup and Use
1399	Dynamic Screen Utility (dscreen) Tips
1228	Electronic Fix Distribution for AIX
2609	Error Log Information and TTY Log Identifiers
1895	Fixed Disk—Removing/Replacing a Fixed Disk
3913	HACMP 3.1: Information Needed for Problem Resolution
2483	HACMP/6000 and I/O Pacing
2543	HANFS Helpful Information
1432	HCON—Creating Autolog Script Files
2703	High CPU Percentage for kproc Process 514/516
4925	How cron & at Commands Work
5102	How Manpages Work: Troubleshooting Tips
4510	How to Alter/Restore a Missing .fs.size.file
4618	How to Boot am SP2 Node into Maintenance Mode
4619	How to Install man pages for AIX 4.1
1073	How to Rebuild the Kerberos Database
1957	How to Resolve an X.25 'Device Busy' Condition
2446	How to Set Up sar
4823	How to Setup Hayes Compatible Modem on RISC System/6000
2464	IBM AIX Support Family
1828	Introduction to Reading Dumps
3198	LV Prpblems After Migration fromAIX 3.2 to 4.1.2
3689	LVM—1016 Physical Partitions per Volume Group
3200	LVM—The Logical Volume Control Block
3690	LVM—The Volume Group Descriptor Area
2265	Making a Second Root User
1609	Managing File System Space
1296	Managing The Time Zone Variable
4254	Mirroring the rootvg Volume Group for AIX 4.1
2704	NAMED Configuration Help

Fax Number	Document Title
1400	NetLS—Installing Nodelock and Floating Licenses
1697	NetLS—Planar Board Swapping Procedure
2701	NIS Configuration Tips
1537	Overview of AIX Support
4824	Overview of AIX System Security Audits
1075	Paging Space Tips for AIX 3.2 & 4.1
2770	Performance Tool Vulnerability—Information and Workaround
3199	Preparing Your AIX System for SATAN
2707	Preserve Login Session Information After Accounting
2809	Recovery from "Volume Group Locked" Error Message
2463	Recovery from a Corrupted Boot Logical Volume
4190	Recovery from LED 551, 555, or 557 in AIX 4.1
4825	Recovery From rm* From the Root (/) Directory
2565	Reducing Default Paging Space (hd6) For AIX 3.1—4.1
5101	Reducing File System Size in AIX 4.1
4724	Repairing File Systems with fsck in AIX 4.1
4253	Resetting File Permissions
2564	Resolving TTY "Respawning Too Rapidly" Errors
1715	Service Director Download Instructions
2226	Setting Up an Auditing System to Monitor cron Events
5103	Setting up Man Pages & InfoExplored Using TECHLIB CDROM
1529	SNA Services/6000 Tuning and Performance Tips
1896	Tape Drive Densities and Special Files
2690	TCP/IP Over the X.25 Network Interface (XT)
1301	Tips for Network Communication Failure (Cannot "ping")
4620	Unable to Start Cluster Lock Manager on HACMP
1076	Using bootlist in Maintenance Mode in AIX 4.1
1845	Using iptrace to Track Remote Print Jobs
1760	Using Program Services

Fax Number	Document Title
1470	Using the bootlist Command in Maintenance Mode
1909	UUCP (BNU) Helpful Information
1306	Xstation Problem Solving Hints
2541	Xstations and NIS

IBM RS/6000 Welcome Center

`http://www.rs6000.ibm.com/support/welcome/`

The RS/6000 Welcome Center (Figure 10–10), designed to introduce new users to many of the features and capabilities of the RS/6000 product family, contains a massive library of information about RS/6000 systems, helpful AIX setup and configuration utilities, a showcase of IBM and Business Partner solutions optimized specifically for RS/6000 systems and a world-wide directory of RS/6000 service and support offerings.

As a Web browser based application, the RS/6000 Welcome Center looks and feels like an Internet website. Many of the hyperlinks within each page of information point to HTML-based content and applications available locally on each system. Since many RS/6000 users have access to the World Wide Web network, the Welcome Center also delivers hyperlink access to a massive and growing library of information about the RS/6000 product and solution family on the Internet.

Although unconfirmed, rumors from several RS/6000 customer sites indicate there is also a "highly interactive arcade" hidden within each version of the Welcome Center. Rumored to contain a "lite combat adventure" game, classic boardgames, the legendary "talking head" application, a three-dimensional virtual reality tour of the Acropolis and several other entertainment-oriented titles, this Welcome Center feature, if it really exists, would provide hours of unprecedented entertainment on these mission critical, highly scalable UNIX systems.

The RS/6000 Welcome Center exploits all known features of the Netscape Navigator to provide quick access to a massive library of relevant information and useful applications. Although designed specifically to enhance a new user's first exposure to the RS/6000 product family, the Welcome Center contains a variety of features and content which provide utility beyond the initial setup and configuration of a new RS/6000 system. Eye candy proliferates as shown in Figures 10–4 through 10–6.

Figure 10–4   Welcome Center e-Commerce GIF

The RS/6000 Welcome Center delivers instant hyperlink access to:

- A massive and growing library of information about the RS/6000 product family and the AIX operating system for both end-users and application developers.

- A personal information library which contains useful setup and feature information about each pre-installed application loaded on a new RS/6000 system.

Figure 10–5   Welcome Center Collaboration GIF

- Easy-to-use AIX system set-up and configuration utilities designed to help a user set up and configure his new RS/6000 system in minutes.

- A unique, world-wide RS/6000 Customer Registration Website designed to provide each RS/6000 user with quick access to the RS/6000 Customer Care team.

Figure 10–6   Welcome Center Publishing GIF

- Language support for Japanese, Spanish, Korean, Catalan, Hungarian, Polish, and French
- A showcase of RS/6000 solutions available from IBM, IBM Business Partners and independent AIX Application Developers, and information about a variety of IBM service, support and educational offerings for your new RS/6000 systems.

AIX and RS/6000: Resources on the Net

AIXPort

`http://aixport.sut.ac.jp`

This website is maintained jointly by IBM and the Science University of Tokyo. It provides information on AIX in education and business, Advanced System, Networking, Education, and PTFs. It is available in either English or Japanese.

AIX 4.3 System and Product Libraries (includes 4.3.1 information)

`http://www.austin.ibm.com/doc_link/en_US/a_doc_lib/aixgen/`

This site provides access to AIX System Documentation, including the AIX Version 4.3 Base Documentation and 4.3 Extended Documentation as well as the product documentation for 3270 Host Connection Program 2.1 and 1.3.3 for AIX; AIXLink/X.25 1.1 for AIX; Performance Toolbox Version 1.2 and 2 for AIX; and Ultimedia Services Version 2 for AIX.

IBM Solution Partnership Center

`http://www.spc.ibm.com/`

Go here to test drive an RS/6000!

IBM Solution Developer Program Home Page

`http://www.developer.ibm.com/`

This home page provides information on developer news, events, and assistance available from IBM.

RS/6000 System Expert

`http://systemexpert.services.ibm.com/main.nsf/Country?OpenForm`

Use System Expert as an RS/6000 remote monitoring solution for performance, capacity, configuration, and security of AIX. This "monitor and alert" system constantly monitors RS/6000 systems at customer's main and remote sites.

RS/6000 Mailing Lists

`http://www.rs6000.ibm.com/resource/maillist.html`

This provides a WWW forms based interface to subscribe/unsubscribe to/from various RS/6000 mailing lists and email-based newsletters.

IBM's Java Site

`http://www.ibm.com/Java/`

This is the ultimate resource for Java developers (see Figure 10–7).

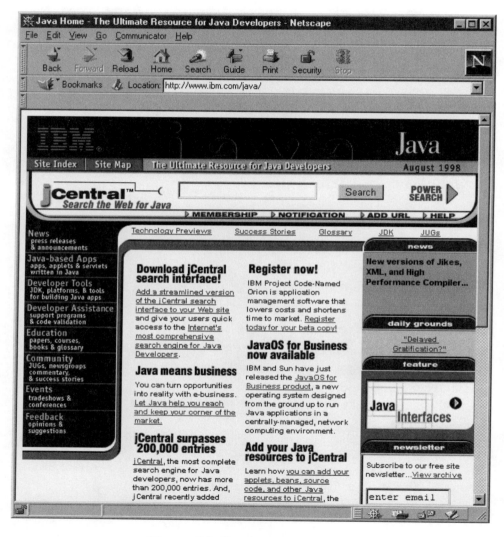

Figure 10–7   Java Home Page

IBM Home Page

`http://www.ibm.com`

This home page offers links to IBM news, lead stories, products offerings, industry solutions, technology and research, and general IBM information. The IBM Home Page is depicted in Figure 10–8.

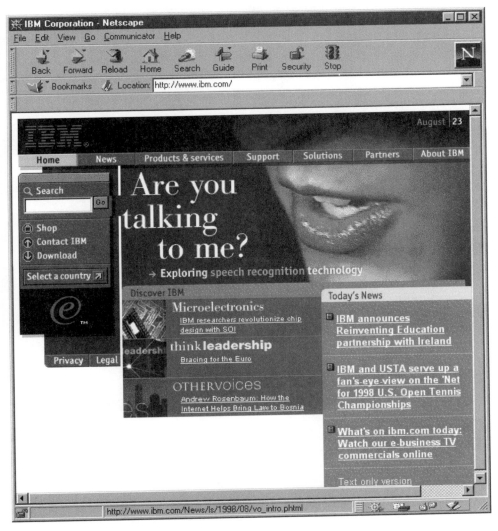

Figure 10–8   IBM Home Page

RS/6000 Web Resources

http://www.rs6000.ibm.com/resource/links.html

Also check out http://www.rs6000.ibm.com/resource/aix_re-source/links.html for AIX-specific resource.

IBM Personal Computers Home Page

http://www.pc.ibm.com

This page links to the IBM Personal Computers desktop, ThinkPad, server, monitor, and options offerings. You can search through and download over 5,000 files for device driver, fixes, reference diskettes, and BIOS upgrades. The latest PC news is also available.

IBM RS/6000 Products and Services

http://www.rs6000.ibm.com

A Comprehensive look at RS/6000 hardware, supported software, services and support, Internet Resources, and current plans/future activities is given here. This home page is shown in Figure 10–9.

IBM RS/6000 Talk Radio—Home Page

http://www.rs6000.ibm.com/talkradio

This page tells you how to participate in RS/6000 Talk Radio—a weekly exchange of information between customers and IBM developers and specialists.

IBM Global Network

http://www.ibm.com/globalnetwork/

This feature links to the IBM Global Network services which include Internet services, network service, information on network outsourcing, e-mail, and electronic data interchange.

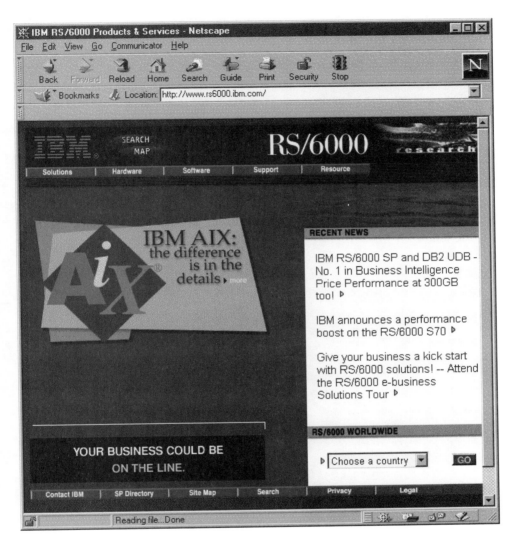

Figure 10–9   RS/6000 Home Page

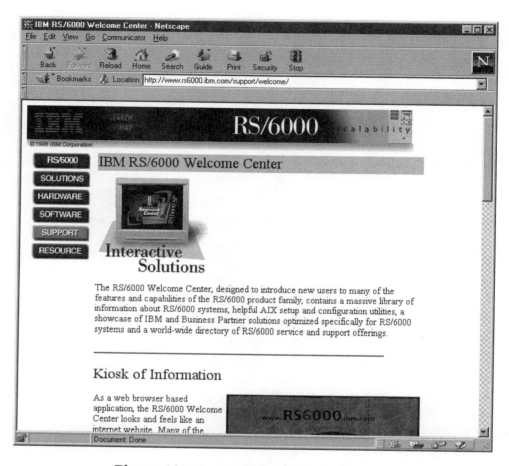

Figure 10–10   RS/6000 Welcome Center

IBM RS/6000 POWERnet Marketing Support Program

POWERnet is an RS/6000 marketing and support program intended for RS/6000 and other key Internet technology providers to develop and maintain the skills to capture the opportunity for RS/6000 Internet and intranet solutions. The POWERnet website is at

```
http://www.rs6000.ibm.com/solutions/internet/powernet
```

Figure 10–11   POWERnet GIF

POWERnet provides infrastructure and support for current and prospective RS/6000 Business Partners interested in investing in the skills needed to sell and implement Internet and intranet solutions on the IBM RS/6000. POWERnet encourages entry into other IBM marketing programs such as the IBM BESTeam, the Lotus(R) Business Partner programs, and non-IBM programs such as the Netscape Solution Expert program (North America), the Netscape International AffiliatePlus program, the Check Point Partner Alliance program (Americas), and the Check Point Partner program. Additionally, for participants who have not yet attained full RS/6000 Internet/intranet skills, the POWERnet program also provides the tools necessary to locate other members to join in a teaming effort to provide total solutions to customers.

Supporting the POWERnet program is the Business Partner Internet Solutions Web Page which provides an index into the IBM Business Partner programs. IBM offers Business Partners many hardware and software products to help increase their revenue by implementing customer solutions. The Web Page will assist Business Partners in following the Internet solution links to products that create individual solutions. This roadmap at

`http://www.internet.ibm.com/partners/roadmap`

provides Business Partners an easy path to find information they need to offer IBM solutions.

RS/6000 Technical Support

IBM supports AIX and IBM products running on AIX, HP-UX, Solaris, ULTRIX, IRIX, or other UNIX operating systems. Direct support from IBM is provided in virtually every country around the globe. To find your way to the many technical support offerings available from IBM for the RS/6000 worldwide, go to `http://service.boulder.ibm.com/rs6000/` (see Figure 10–12).

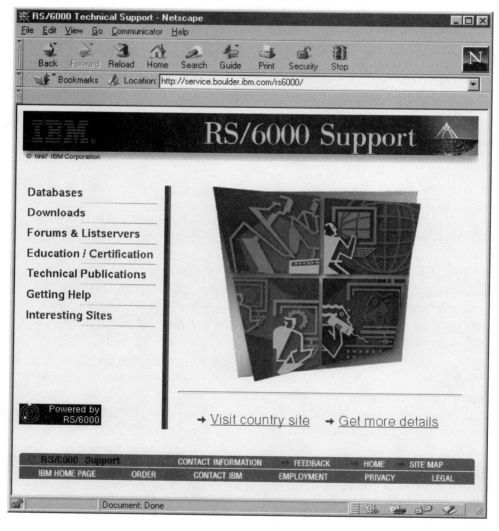

Figure 10–12   RS/6000 Support Page

The "Roadmap to Support" provides users with detailed support information according to their country selection. Services are provided to all Internet users, with or without a support contract. Voice or electronic support for users running on other UNIX systems including HP-UX*, SCO OpenServer*, SINIX*, or Solaris* is also available

Customers with support contracts gain access to the complete knowledge databases as well as electronic incidents submitted directly to the support center and fix order service for tape or CD overnight delivery.

One service available from `http://service.boulder.ibm.com/rs6000/` is access to technical databases. Users will find answers to frequently asked questions and answers to those "not so frequent but ever important" problems. Highlights include:

- Access to the Authorized Problem Analysis Reports database

- A collection of hints, tips, and FAQs for AIX and applications

- Problem solving database (this database of closed items is updated twice each week)

- RS/6000 SP resources (service bulletins, flashes, and FAQs of special interest to SP customers)

- Service reports including quality assurance test results for AIX integration with Pro/ENGINEER, I-DEAS Master Series, and the CATIA environment.

AIX News Groups

comp.unix.aix

This posting contains frequently asked questions (FAQs) and answers about the IBM RS/6000 hardware and AIX. The posting is monitored by `jwarring@aol.net`.

This FAQ is available from: `<ftp://rtfm.mit.edu:/pub/usenet/news.answers/ aix-faq/part1>` `<ftp://mirrrors.aol.com:/pub/rtfm/usenet-by-hierarchy/comp/unix/ aix>` `<http://www.cis.ohio-state.edu:/hypertext/faq/usenet/aix-faq/top.html>`.

All entries are numbered with major and minor subject number (for example, 2.11). If the subject is preceded by an asterisk, that entry has been changed or added since the last posting.

The comp.unix.aix group is for AIX on all IBM platforms—RT, PS/2, 370, RS/6000 and mainframes (ESA based on OSF/1), but the traffic has evolved to discuss predominantly AIX 3.x and the RS/6000. The newsgroups comp.sys.ibm.pc.rt and comp.sys.ibm.ps2.hardware cover the RT, mostly hardware and AOS 4.3, and on PS/2 hardware respectively.

RS/6000 Talk Radio

The RS/6000 Talk Radio show (Figure 10–13) is a weekly 60-minute audio teleconference that allows an exchange of information between AIX customers

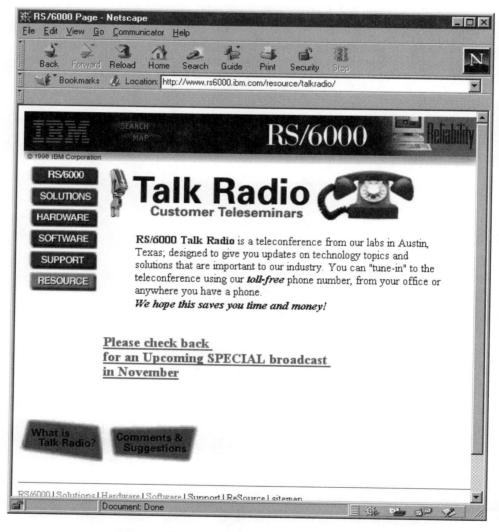

Figure 10–13   Talk Radio Home Page

and IBM developers and specialists. Since it is a toll-free call, you can participate from the comfort of your own office. These lively shows keep you up-to-date on the latest AIX technology. You will receive the toll-free phone number after enrolling, which doesn't cost any money! To enroll, either call 1-800-289-0576 (or 1-913-661-0825), or point your Web browser to `http://www.rs6000.ibm.com/talkradio/`.

Prior shows on audio cassette can be ordered by calling 1-800-222-4260 or 1-513-771-4244. Alternately, you can point your Web browser to `http://www.rs6000.ibm.com/talkradio/tapes.final.html`.

CHAPTER 11

- What Is 64-Bit and Why Should You Care?

- What Is the Year 2000 (AKA Y2K) Issue in General Terms?

- Performance Tools for System Management

- The AIX Development Environment

- Security and System Management

- FixDist—How to Get the Latest Bug Fixes from the Internet

- AIX PitStop—How to Resolve Common AIX Problems

Gathering up the Pieces

I n this chapter we discuss 64-bit AIX performance tools for system management, the development environment, security, file systems, and useful tools to learn more about AIX.

What Is 64-Bit and Why Should You Care?

Promotional material for information processing products ranging from video games to computers to operating systems extol the virtues of 64-bit systems over 32-bit systems, and 32-bit systems over 16-bit systems, etc. Newer and bigger must be better, right? Well, like most things, that really depends on what exactly you're trying to do. For example, a school bus is a great tool to transport 32 school children across town, but it might not be the best choice of vehicles for a single programmer to use to commute to downtown New York City. The best reason to upgrade to a 64-bit computer system is if you need to run an application that requires a 64-bit environment.

So what does a 64-bit system offer? Although the exact details vary from vendor to vendor, it generally provides the ability to perform native computation and manipulation in 64-bit data units. This can yield performance gains in certain cases. Just as it is faster to make one trip with a school bus carrying 64 children than it is to make the same trip twice with a school bus that carries only 32 children, one possible advantage of a 64-bit system over a 32-bit system is that it can move and manipulate large amounts of data faster, as a single instruction could copy, or perform arithmetic on 64 bits at a time rather than just 32 bits.

The real advantage, however, of a 64-bit system is its ability to address more data at the same time (see Table 11–1). Let's try some comparisons. An 8-bit system can directly address 2^8 or 256 bytes of data. A 16-bit system can directly address

2^{16} or 65,536 bytes of data (64 kilobytes). A 32-bit system can directly address 2^{32} or 4,294,967,296 bytes of data (4 gigabytes), and a 64-bit system can directly address 2^{64} or a whopping 18,446,744,073,709,551,616 bytes of data (more than 16 million terabytes). To get a feel for this, let us think about a computer used to process digitized video. Assuming that an image has 640 × 400 pixels times 8 bits of color per pixel, one frame would take 250 kilobytes of memory. So, an 8-bit computer that can directly address only 256 bytes can directly access only 1/1000 of one frame. A 16-bit processor, addressing 64 kilobytes of data, can directly access about one quarter of a frame. A 32-bit processor, with 4 gigabytes of addressable memory, can directly address a respectable 9 minutes of video at 30 frames per second. Our 64-bit process, at 16 million terabytes, however, can directly address over 760,000 YEARS of video. The ability to directly address vast amounts of data is useful when modeling simulations, performing large image processing, or dealing with very large databases.

The 64-bit PowerPC chip that is used in 64-bit RS/6000 systems is designed so that 32-bit instructions are a proper subset of the 64-bit instruction set. In fact, it has the ability to run processes in either 32- or 64-bit mode, and can context switch between any number of 32- or 64-bit processes simultaneously. This is a very good thing, since it means that 64-bit AIX can seamlessly run both 32- and 64-bit programs at the same time. You will be able to continue to use all of your favorite old 32-bit programs as is, while at the same time using that brand new 64-bit program.

What Do I Need to Know to Run 64-Bit Programs and Administer My 64-Bit System?

There's no trick to executing a 64-bit program; you run it just like you would a 32-bit program. However, of course, 64-bit programs can not be run on 32-bit hardware. If you try it, you'll get a message that says, "Cannot run a 64-bit program on a 32-bit machine." The one other thing you need is to be running at least version 4.3.0 of AIX, as earlier versions of AIX do not support 64-bit programs. If

Table 11-1   Computer System Addressability

Number of Addressing Bits	Number of Directly Addressable Bytes	Amount of Directly Addressable Video
8	256 bytes	1/1000 of one frame
16	65,536 bytes	1/4 of one frame
32	4,294,967,296 bytes	9 minutes
64	18,446,744,073,709,551,616 bytes	760,000 YEARS

you have an executable, and you're curious as to whether it is a 32-bit or 64-bit program, you can use the AIX 4.3.0 or later `file` command on that program, and 64-bit programs will be identified as "64-bit AIX executable or object module", 32-bit programs will be identified as, "executable RSystem/6000) or object module".

Administering a 64-bit machine is fairly straightforward also. All you really need to do is to be sure that you install fileset `bos.64bit`, which contains 64-bit support code. After installing, you may need to reboot before 64-bit functionality is enabled. You may wish to know that installing the `bos.64bit` fileset automatically adds an entry to `/etc/inittab` to execute `/etc/methods/cfg64` at boot time. So, if for some reason you wanted to prevent users from running 64-bit programs on a 64-bit system, you could remove this entry from `/etc/inittab`, and reboot, at which point 64-bit programs would no longer run. All you would have to do is reinsert this line, and reboot to re-enable 64-bit program support on your machine.

Large file support allowing single files greater than 2 gigabytes in size is often associated with 64-bit support; however, starting in version AIX 4.2.0, even 32-bit machines support "large files". This can be enabled on both 32- or 64-bit machines by running "smitty crjfs" and selecting "Add a Large File Enabled Journaled File System", to create a filesystem which can hold files larger than 2 gigabytes in size.

What Do I Need to Know to Write 64-Bit Programs?

Well, first it would help to know how to write 32-bit programs. :-) The major difference between a 32-bit and a 64-bit program is that since AIX follows the industry standard LP64 model, longs and pointers are 64 bits (or 8 bytes) long in 64-bit programs, rather than 32 bits or 4 bytes as in traditional 32-bit programs. 64-bit support in AIX was designed to keep the 64-bit environment as similar as possible to the 32-bit environment. In fact, 32- and 64-bit programs coexist quite nicely. 32-bit programs can `fork()` 64-bit programs and vice versa. Inter-process communication (IPC), shared memory, signals, etc., work fine between 32- and 64-bit programs. Porting 32-bit code to 64-bit can be facilitated by using the newly added `-t` option to the `lint` command, which will inform you of certain problems such as 8-byte long pointers being mapped to 4-byte interger values, which would result in data loss or corruption. Properly crafted, there should be no problem using the same source recompiled twice, once for each environment. By invoking the compiler without any special arguments, e.g., `cc`, will compile the program for the 32-bit environment. If you specify the `-q64` argument to the compiler, i.e., `cc -q64`, then a 64-bit executable will be created. Another useful argument to the compiler is -qwarn64, which will instruct the compiler to generate warning messages when attempts are made to store 8-byte data in 4-byte locations. Different code paths within a single program can be supported by using conditional compilation with #ifdef __64BIT__ in your code, as the __64BIT__ macro is turned on only when 64-bit programs are compiled. You could also use dynamic conditionals such as if (sizeof long == 8) to determine if your program is running in 64-bit mode.

AIX compilers, and other programs that create and manipulate executables on AIX 4.3, are all 32-bit programs, so they can run on any machine supported by AIX 4.3. Yet, even though they are 32-bit programs, they "understand", create, and manipulate 64-bit executables on both 32- and 64-bit machines. This means that you can use your 32-bit workstation to compile 64-bit programs by simply using the -q 64 flag when you compile your program with cc. Of course, to run them, you will have to run them on a 64-bit machine. Certain programs, such as dbx, xldb, genld, tprof, gprof, and stripnm will automatically process 64-bit programs, while other programs such as dump, nm, lorder, ranlib, size, and strip will require either an environment variable to be set, or an specific argument to be passed in. Fortunately, this is fairly straightforward; all of these programs share the convention that you can use the argument -X32 to indicate they they should process only 32-bit programs, and the argument -X64 to indicate that they should process only 64-bit programs, -X32_64 to indicate that they can automatically detect and process either 32- or 64-bit programs. Alternatively, you can set the environment variable OBJECT_MODE to 32, 64, or 32_64 to accomplish the same thing. Additionally, when OBJECT_MODE is set to 64, the compiler, linker, loader, lint, etc., will automatically create and manipulate 64-bit programs, rather than the default of 32-bit programs. However, you should note that 32_64 is not a valid OBJECT_MODE setting for compilers, linkers, lint, etc., as they can create only a single type of output, which has to be defined up front.

What Is the Year 2000 (AKA Y2K) Issue in General Terms?

The Year 2000 problem, often labeled Y2K, refers to a variety of date-related problems due largely to programmers, who did not fully consider date processing. Some of the problems are due to programs which were not designed to work correctly past the year 1999, others are due to mistakenly thinking that the year 2000 is not a leap year, and yet others are simply due to overloading data fields. Some consultants and computer industry professionals have nearly predicted the end of civilization as we know it. Others have refused to acknowledge any problem whatsoever. As with most things in life, the actual outcome lies somewhere in between. Let us take a look at some of the problems that have occurred due to improper date processing.

Programs and people often abbreviate the year to two digits rather than four, since that is faster and easier. This works since everyone understands that '98 or '99 really means 1998 and 1999. However, this can be a problem for a literal and incorrectly written computer program. For example, incorrectly programmed credit systems have been known to reject credit cards that expire in the year "00", since "00" represents "1900" to the computer, and is thus considered to be expired.

The most common problem I've seen with UNIX software is that software written to display two-digit years can display strange dates for the year 2000 and beyond. For example, rather than showing 9/14/00 for September 14, 2000, some software will display 9/14/100, or in some cases even truncate the last zero to display 9/14/10. The reason for this is incorrect programmer usage of a year field defined by UNIX standards. More about this shortly.

The leap year problem can also cause inconvenience. If a computer program that allows only "valid" dates to be entered is not aware of a leap year, then it may not be possible to use that program to schedule services such as deliveries on a leap day. This has actually been known to happen!

Some applications have been known to use dates such as 9/9/99 to have a special meaning, such as "this account never expires". Since September 9, 1999, is an actual date, any program which uses that date to indicate anything other than the date itself will have obvious problems.

Interestingly enough, Y2K problems go beyond just computer programs. For instance, personal checks and other paper forms that used to have date lines that included "19__" for convenience, have been reprinted with date lines that are simply blank. Of course, crossing off "19" and writing "20" is much less of an inconvenience than a financial computer program that refuses to permit you to perform a transaction since it is confused about the date. In fact, just about every conceivable kind of date bug can and probably has occurred.

The good news is that date processing bugs are exactly that. They are bugs which can and will be fixed. The trick is identifying and fixing them in an economical fashion, before they actually cause problems.

How Does the Year 2000 Problem Affect AIX Systems?

One AIX, as with any computer system, the Y2K problems can be divided into three distinct categories: hardware, operating system software, and application software. Application software can be further divided into purchased software and software developed in-house. We will discuss each of these in turn.

RS/6000 Hardware.   As of August 28, 1998, IBM has identified six RS/6000 hardware platforms running AIX as requiring firmware upgrades to become Y2K-compliant. If you are using one of the following systems, it would be advisable to contact IBM service or sales for information regarding the fix for your hardware:

- 6015
- 6040
- 6042
- 7020
- 7247
- 7249 (model 851 only)

AIX Operating System Software.   AIX, like most, if not all, UNIX operating systems, stores the date and time in a data structure as the number of elapsed seconds since midnight, January 1, 1970, Greenwich Mean Time (GMT). As of AIX version 4.3, this value is stored in a signed 32-bit variable, which is more capable of storing date and time values only up to January 19, 2038, 03:15:07 GMT, at which point it will overflow unless some action is taken. The fact that dates and times are processed as seconds since the beginning of 1970 is good news since the fundamental data structures and processing of dates and times is done with very little need to treat years specially. This does not, however, mean that AIX and other UNIX operating systems are immune to the Year 2000 problems, since there are UNIX programs and components that do deal with years as two digit dates. The most common Y2K programming error that I've seen is when programmers treat the value `tm.tm_year` as the current two-digit year, in states like `printf("the date is %d/%d/%d",month,day,tm.tm_year)` or even `printf ("the year is 19%d",tm.tm_year)`. Since standards such as XPG and POSIX define this value as the number of years since 1900, the first statement above would work fine until the year 2000, at which point it would start displaying dates such as "9/14/100". The second statement, would be even worse, displaying the same year as "19100". Fortunately, the fix in this case is very simple, as the correct four-digit year can be obtained by adding 1900 to this value, as in `printf("the date is %d/%d/%d",month,day,tm.tm_year+1900)`.

It is important to point out that there are many Unix commands and system files that use only two-digit years. In most of these cases, year values between 70 and 99 refer to the years 1970 through 1999, and values from 00 to 38 refer to the years 2000 through 2038. For example, since the `date` command uses the format `mmddHHMMyy` to change the date, it can be used to change the date of the system to 5:00 PM September 14, 2001, with the command invocation: `date 0914170001`. However, you are out of luck if you want to try to set the year beyond 2038, as this would cause the time variable to overflow. I think it is safe to say, however, that this problem will be resolved before the year 2038.

Since IBM's AIX development organization has found and fixed a number of Y2K date formatting defects, it would be advisable to obtain and install the latest Y2K APAR (set of bug fixes) for any levels of AIX that you are using. A description of the latest APAR levels, and any late breaking Y2K information about AIX can be found at `http://www.software.ibm.com/year2000/papers/aixy2k.html`. IBM has committed to provide Y2K support for AIX 4.3, 4.2, 4.1, and 3.2.5 through January 31, 2001.

Application Software. Regarding Year 2000 problems with application software running on an AIX machine, the best thing to do with software packages provided by a vendor would be to contact that vendor and discuss whether or not that software has Y2K problems, whether or not it should be upgraded, etc. A table of AIX LPP's provided both by IBM and third parties, along with current status can be found from `http://www.ibm.com/IBM/year/2000/`. Applications running on AIX which were written in-house will need to be analyzed on a case-by-case basis. A detailed analysis of how to create Y2K bug-free software is beyond the scope of this book, as there are already fine books written on this subject. However, this analysis would break down into performing formal code reviews searching for date relevant errors in the source code, and actual testing, to determine how well the software functions in the year 2000 and beyond.

How Does One Plan and Cope with Year 2000 Problems on an AIX System?

Initially, it would be worthwhile to review documents such as "AIX, UNIX Operating Systems, and the Year 2000 Issue, An Informational Workbook" (`http://www.software.ibm.com/year2000/papers/aixy2k.html`) and "The Year 2000 and 2-Digit Dates: A Guide for Planning and Implementation" (`http://www.software.ibm.com/year2000/resource.html`, also available in hard copy from 1-800-IBM-4YOU).

The first step is to perform a detailed inventory of all computer hardware, indicating which AIX levels are in use, and all applications in use on these machines, including third party LPP's, third party software, and all software developed in-house. It is important to make sure that this inventory is complete, because, according to Murphy's Law, the single application you miss will be the mission-critical application that will fail without intervention.

Once an inventory has been created, it would be advisable to obtain hardware firmware upgrades for machines identified in the latest "AIX, UNIX Operating Systems and the Year 2000 Issue." Next, it would be advisable to identify and install the latest Y2K APAR's for the AIX levels that you use. The most current source of this information is also the same document.

Once your hardware and AIX operating system have been updated, you will want to be sure that all applications that you use are up-to-date with respect to Y2K issues. This will require contacting the vendors of externally developed software to discuss the availability of patches, new versions, etc. As mentioned above, any software you have developed in-house will likely require both formal code inspection and testing activities. Items which should be taken into consideration include date input and output, date storage, date processing, etc. Naturally, any problems found with code inspection and testing should be fixed. However, there is a class of Y2K problems for which it is worthwhile to consider coping strategies other than actually fixing. For example, the system clock on my PC at home is going to jump back to 1980 the first time I use it in the year 2000 due to a BIOS problem. It is not worth my time, effort, and possibly money to track down and obtain an upgraded BIOS. I am simply going to set the correct year the first time I use it in the year 2000, thus updating the CMOS memory and resolving the problem once and for all. Likewise, suppose that you have an in-house application for which the source code can no longer be found. If you determine that this software creates reports with incorrect dates after the year 2000, e.g., in the format 9/14/100, 9/14/101 rather than 9/14/2000, 9/14/2001, etc., then it may be more cost-effective to simply put up with this unusual, but readable date format than rewrite the entire application.

Performance Tools for System Management

There are a number of questions that you may have about the state of your computer. This section will introduce you to some of the commands in the base operating system that will help you assess the state of your computer.

What is running right now? How much memory is it using?

To answer these questions, use the ps commands (see Table 11–2).

How is memory is being used?

The vmstat command gives a lot of information about the status of a running AIX system. The output from this command falls into five categories: kernel threads, memory, paging, faults, and cpu usage (see Table 11–3).

Table 11–2 Output from `ps ug`

USER	PID	%CPU	%MEM	SZ	RSS	TTY	STAT	STIME	TIME	CMMAND
root	516	98.5	0.0	0	4	-	A	Oct 12	269:15	kproc
trent	13676	1.9	1.0	304	592	pts/3	A	10:30:56	3:14	-ksh
trent	14564	0.0	0.0	132	224	pts/2	A	13:22:47	0:00	ps ug

USER
The name of the user associated with the process.
PID
The "Process ID". It identifies the number of the process running, and can be used as an argument to commands such as kill.
%CPU
The percentage of the CPU used by the process over its lifetime.
%MEM
The percentage of system memory used by the process over its lifetime.
SZ
The virtual size of the process or the total amount of paging space used by the program in kilobytes.
RSS
The resident set size of the process, or the total number of kilobytes of memory used by the program.
TTY
The terminal that is associated with the command. "-" means that there is no terminal associated with the command.
STAT
The current status of the process.
STIME
The time of day that the process started.
TIME
The total CPU time used by the process.
COMMAND
The name of the command that started this process.

How much of the disk is being used?

The `iostat` command can be used to monitor disk activity (see Table 11–4).

How much disk space is being used?

The `df` command shows how much disk space is used and available on each device (see Table 11–5). Disk space is displayed in 512-byte blocks. The Iused value refers to the number or percentage of i-nodes used. Each file takes up a certain number of i-nodes, and when there are no more i-nodes available, it is not possible to create new files even though there may be empty disk space open.

Table 11-3 Output from `vmstat`

kthr		memory		page						faults			cpu			
r	b	avm	fre	re	pi	po	fr	sr	cy	in	sy	cs	us	sy	id	wa
0	0	4189	5533	0	0	0	0	0	0	117	15	19	0	1	98	0

Kernel Threads - r
The number of threads per second placed on the run queue during the observation period.

Kernel Threads - b
The number of threads per second placed on the wait queue during the observation period.

Memory - avm
The number of pages used in memory for paging.

Memory - fre
The number of real memory pages available.

page - re
The number of page reclaims during this period.

page - pi
The number of page-ins per second from paging space during the observation period.

page - po
The number of page-outs per second to paging space during the observation period.

page - fr
The number of pages per second freed during the observation period.

page - sr
The number of pages per second considered for freeing during the observation period.

page - cy
The number of times the paging space was entirely scanned for replacement during the observation period.

faults - in
The number of device interrupts per second during the observation period.

faults - sy
The number of system calls per second during the observation period.

faults - cs
The number of context switches per second during the observation period.

cpu - us
The percentage of CPU time used by the user during the observation period.

cpu - sy
The percentage of CPU time used by the system during the observation period.

cpu - id
The percentage of CPU time that was idle during the observation period.

cpu - wa
The percentage of CPU time that was spent in an I/O wait.

Table 11-4   Output from `iostat -d`

Disks:	% tm_act	Kbps	tps	Kb_read	Kb_wrtn
hdisk0	0.4	1.0	0.1	86557	76426
hdisk1	0.0	0.4	0.0	58031	36
cd0	0.0	0.0	0.0	0	0

% tm_act
Indicates the percentage of the time that the device was in use.

Kbps
Indicates the amount of data that was transferred to/from the device in kilobytes per second.

tps
Indicates the number of transfers per second.

KB_read
The total number of kilobytes read during the observation period.

KB_wrtn
The total number of kilobytes written during the observation period.

What about paging space? How much of that do I have open?

The `lsps` command will show what the size of each disk based paging space is, along with the percentage available for use (see Table 11–6).

How can I increase my paging space?

The `chps` command can be used to increase the size of paging spaces. To increase the size of hd6 in the last example, you could use the following command, which must be run as root, and can be used repeatedly to further increase paging space:

```
$ chps -s'1' hd6
```

Table 11-5   Output from `df`

Filesystem	512-blocks	Free	%Used	Iused	%Iused	Mounted on
/dev/hd4	24576	15184	39%	1313	22%	/
/dev/hd2	983040	21864	98%	31121	26%	/usr
/dev/hd9var	8192	6032	27%	134	14%	/var
/dev/hd3	49152	22912	54%	567	10%	/tmp
/dev/hd1	8192	304	97%	171	17%	/home

Table 11–6   Output from `lsps -a`

Page Space	Physical Volume	Volume Group	Size	%Used	Active	Auto	Type
paging01	hdisk0	rootvg	4MB	82	yes	yes	lv
paging00	hdisk0	rootvg	4MB	82	yes	yes	lv
hd6	hdisk0	rootvg	64MB	13	yes	yes	lv

What about graphical user interfaces (GUIs) to do these kind of things?

Much of this information can be obtained through SMIT via "Performance & Resource Scheduling". Additionally, /usr/bin/X11/xload will show a graphical representation of CPU load. By using the -update option, you can specify exactly how often you want the graph to be updated. By installing the Performance Toolbox for AIX (LPP number 5696-900) you can use "xmperf", a GUI that displays and monitors a variety of statistics including file system activity, and network activity, virtual memory usage.

The AIX Development Environment

This section describes some of the programs and tools that are available to use in the development of software on an AIX platform.

Compilers

Table 11–7 lists some of the compiler LPPs available from IBM.

Table 11–7   Compiler LPPs

LPP Name	Version	Number
C for AIX	3.1	5765-423
C Set++ for AIX	3.1	5765-421
COBOL Set for AIX	1.5	28H2176
XL Fortran for AIX	3.2	5765-176
XL Fortran Runtime Environment for AIX	3.2	5765-526
XL Pascal for AIX	2.1	5765-245
REXX/6000	1.1	5764-057

Source Control (SCCS, CMVC, and RCS)

Source control packages allow teams of programmers to work on the same set of files over a period of time without having to worry about two people changing the same file at the same time. They also allow for a variety of features including version control, change tracking, ability to retrieve an old version, and in some cases provide extensive reporting and security mechanisms.

Two popular source control packages are available on AIX. The Source Code Control System (SCCS) is shipped as part of the base operating system in fileset bos.adt.sccs. SCCS allows basic source management. More information about SCCS can be found in the on-line documentation in InfoExplorer.

Another very powerful source management system available for AIX is Configuration Management Version Control (CMVC) which is based on SCCS. It can be ordered as LPP number 5765-207. CMVC is an extremely powerful system designed to work over a network in a client/server fashion. This allows users on clients to access the server to save, retrieve, and inquire about files. This model allows for extensive security and reporting. CMVC allows users to either use the command line or a powerful Graphical User Interface (GUI). CMVC runs on AIX as well as HP-UX, and SunOS.

Although AIX does not ship the Revision Control System (RCS) as part of the base operating system, RCS is available via anonymous ftp from prep.ai.mit.edu in directory /pub/gnu. The functionality the RCS provides is similar to that found with SCCS.

Programming for Internationalization

As described in the chapter on internationalization, AIX was designed to support a wide variety of countries and natural languages by using the XPG locale model. Programmers can make use of this in their programs by using the following key functions: setlocale(), nl_langinfo(), localeconv(), catopen(), catgets(), catclose(), iconv_open(), iconv(), iconv_close(), mblen(), mbtowc(), wctomb(). Information about these functions is available in InfoExplorer. Other useful references are found in the chapter on internationalization.

Performance Tools for Programmers

AIX provides several tools which can be used by programmers to analyze and assist in increasing program performance. Additional information on the usage of these commands can be found in InfoExplorer.

Prof and gprof are shipped as part of the base operating system in the bos.adt.prof fileset. Both of these tools require recompiling source code to include special routines that profile the program when it is running.

To use `prof`, compile your source code with the –p compiler option (`cc -p test.c`). When you run this program, a file called `mon.out` will be created which contains profiling data describing how much time was spent in each function used in your program, and how many times it was called. Using your program and the `mon.out` data file, `prof` will generate a human readable report containing this performance information.

To use `gprof`, compile your source code with the –pg compiler option (`cc -pg test.c`). When you run this program, a file called `gmon.out` will be created which contains profiling data describing how much time was spent in each function used in your program. Using your program, and `gmon.out` as input, `gprof` command will display a list of how much time was spent in various functions, how many times each was called, along with a call graph that can be used to determine the flow of the program.

`tprof` is shipped in the `perfagent.tools` fileset and can be obtained by ordering the Performance Toolbox LPP (number 5697-900). Unlike `prof` and `gprof`, `tprof` does not require that source code be recompiled. `tprof` can be invoked by simply typing `tprof program_name`, and it will generate a list where the cpu is spending its time. C programs can be recompiled with the –`qlist` compiler option to increase the usefulness of the output.

The dbx debugger

The most popular debugger shipped with AIX is probably `dbx`. It is straightforward to use. It is most useful when used with a program that has been compiled with the –g debugging option turned on, in which it allows stepping through executing code line by line, allowing variable tracking, modification, and so on. It is also of limited use with code that has not been compiled with –g. For instance the `where` subcommand within `dbx` can show a programmer where a core dump was caused. Since this debugger is fairly intuitive, use the help command and experiment!

The adb debugger

Although the `adb` debugger is not as user friendly or sophisticated as `dbx`, it can be used to manipulate memory, set breakpoints, and so on. More information about this debugger can be found in InfoExplorer.

Make

AIX ships a standard version of the `make` command which is often used to automatically generate the necessary commands to compile complex software projects. For more information see either the InfoExplorer documentation on the make command, or the O'Reilly book *Managing Projects with make*.

Imake

Imake is similar to make, and is also a standard part of AIX. It is found in /usr/bin/X11/imake, and is documented in either InfoExplorer or the O'Reilly book on imake.

Security and System Management

AIX provides a number of tools and services that can make security management easier for system administrators. When most people hear the phrase "computer security", they probably think about hackers and computer break-ins. This is, however, only one part of the overall issue of security. The goal of computer security is to protect a computer system and its data from all manor of threats in such a way that the users can count on the software doing what they expect. Threats include things such as unauthorized access, acts of nature that could cause data loss (flood, fire), accidental erasure, malicious users, and so on.

AIX provides individual user accounts, file access control lists (ACL), error and command logging, a trusted computing base, trusted shells, enhanced password rules, extensive auditing capabilities, as well utilities to backup software to protect against data loss (`backup`, `restore`, `tar`, and `pax` commands).

A detailed coverage of security topics is well beyond the coverage of this book, so I would like to initially point out two good books on the subject:

1. IBM, *Elements of Security: AIX 4.1*, (order number GG24-4433-00).

2. Garfinkel, Simson, and Gene Spafford, *Practical Unix Security*, Sebastopol, CA: O'Reilly & Associates, Inc., 1993.

SMIT provides a simple interface to set up effective security. For instance, part of effective security is to use difficult-to-guess passwords, and change them at regular intervals. By selecting "Security & Users" from SMIT's main menu, then "Passwords", then "Change/Show Password Attributes", a system administrator can easily specify how long before a password will expire and must be changed, which words can NOT be used as passwords, and how many characters a password must be.

Some of the useful security related logs that AIX maintains are listed here:

- **/var/adm/wtmp**   Contains a list of who logged on, when they did so, when they logged off, and where they logged in from. This information is viewable with the `last` command:

```
[trent@musashi] /u/trent/ > last | head -5
trent     pts/6                    Sat Oct 14 10:30 still logged in
trent     pts/6                    Fri Oct 13 15:20 - 15:47 (00:27)
trent     ftp     percy.austin.ibm Fri Oct 13 14:07 - 14:07 (00:00)
trent     pts/12 sasaki.austin.ib  Thu Oct 12 23:14 - 23:18 (00:03)
trent     ftp     percy. austin.ibm Thu Oct 12 16:45 - 16:46 (00:00)
```

- **/etc/utmp**   Contains information on each currently active user and processes. For users, such information as user name, terminal, logon date, and total time on are included. This information can be seen with the `who` command:

```
$ who
trent      pts/0     Oct 13 10:08     (musashi.austin.i)
trent      pts/1     Oct 14 14:45     (musashi.austin.i)
```

- **/var/adm/sulog**   Contains a human readable list of all attempts to use the su command. Since this is an ascii file, `cat`, `vi` or any other command can be used to look at it.

```
[trent:root@musashi] / # tail -3 /var/adm/sulog
SU 10/12 10:12 - pts/14 trent-root
SU 10/12 10:13 + pts/14 trent-root
SU 10/14 15:03 + pts/8  trent-root
```

The plus in the fourth column indicates that the `su` command was successful; a minus in the same column indicates that the user provided the wrong password to `su`.

- **/etc/security/failedlogin**   This file contains a list of entries for all login failures. This information can be seen with the `who` command:

```
[trent:root@musashi] /var/adm # who /etc/security/failedlogin
UNKNOWN_    pts/10    Oct 04 19:37     (sitetest.austin.)
root        pts/10    Oct 04 19:40     (sitetest.austin.)
```

AIX's Trusted Computing Base (TCB)

AIX provides software that supports the concept of a trusted computing base, which can be used to ensure that system commands have not been tampered with. The heart of TCB is the `tcbck` command which is used to maintain data pertaining to the trustworthiness of commands and files on the system. Other parts of the trusted computing base include a limited shell called tsh. When used as a login shell, it provides limited functionality so as to limit security risks. See InfoExplorer or *Elements of Security: AIX* (IBM order number GG24-4433) for more information on this topic.

FixDist—How to Get the Latest Bug Fixes from the Internet

FixDist is a free user-friendly program that allows you to easily download the latest bug fixes (called PTFs or APARs by IBM service folks) from the Internet. FixDist also serves as an interface to a database of available fixes so that you can see what kind of bugs are being reported and fixed. In the rare event that you find a bug in AIX, you may be able to find a fix for it, and download it using FixDist. Since FixDist supports both a graphics-based interface in addition to a text-based interface, you will be able to use it in a variety of environments.

In order to use the FixDist tool, you will need to be running at least Version 3.2.4, have your computer connected to the Internet, and of course have sufficient disk space on your system. The FixDist tool may be obtained by getting file `/aix/tools/fixdist/fd.tar.Z` via anonymous ftp from `service.boulder.ibm.com` (IP address 189.17.57.66). Note this example:

```
$ cd /tmp/fixdist
$ ftp service.boulder.ibm.com
Connected to service.boulder.ibm.com.
Name (service.boulder.ibm.com:trent): anonymous
331 Send your complete e-mail address as password.
Password:
ftp> bin
ftp> cd /aix/tools/fixdist
ftp> dir
-rw-rw-r— 1 210       1         3487 Nov 13 09:03 README
-rw-rw-r— 1 210       1       183209 Nov 13 09:03 fd.ANS.tar.Z
-rw-r—r— 1 210        1       342705 Nov 13 09:03 fd.tar.Z
-rw-rw-r— 1 210       1        38001 Nov 13 09:03 fixdist.html
-rw-rw-r— 1 210       1        82021 Nov 13 09:03 fixdist.ps.Z
-rw-rw-r— 1 210       1        39404 Nov 13 09:03 fixdist.txt
ftp> get fd.tar.Z
```

```
ftp> get README
ftp> exit
$
```

In addition to the program (fd.tar.Z), and the README file which explains how to install the program, you may also want to retrieve the documentation file, by getting either the postscript version (fixdist.ps.Z) or the plain text version (fixdist.txt). Since the postscript manual (fixdist.ps.Z) is compressed, you will need to use the uncompress command before you will be able to view or print it.

After you have downloaded FixDist, you can install it by typing in the following as root ("as root" means you need to either log in as the root user, or type suroot and enter the root password):

```
cd /
zcat /tmp/fixdist/fd.tar.Z | tar -xpvf -
```

Now you can run the FixDist command by simply typing in fixdist. When you do, you will see a screen like that in Figure 11–1 after you enter the server, target directory, select the database as 4.1, and press the download button.

At this point, I would recommend reading the FixDist documentation, however, I will explain a few of the features that you can use at this point. If you click on

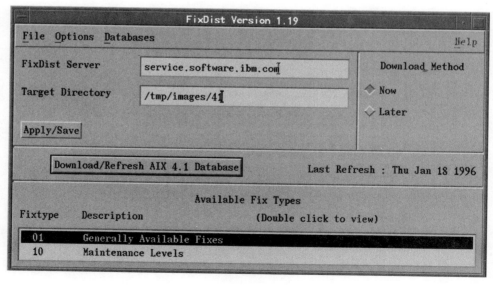

Figure 11–1   FixDist Main Screen

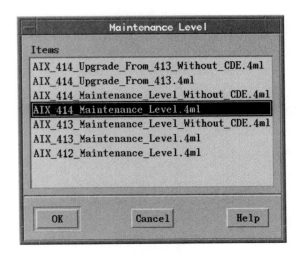

Figure 11–2   FixDist Maintenance Level Screen

Maintenance Level, you will see a window (Figure 11–2) that will allow you to upgrade your machine to a certain level. You can download or view additional information about one of these by clicking on the appropriate line.

You can also select "Generally Available Fixes" from the main menu, to see a screen like the one shown in Figure 11–3. From this menu, you can view lists of either PTFs or APARs. In addition you can search by any text you wish. When you have found either the PTF or the APAR that you wish to download or view

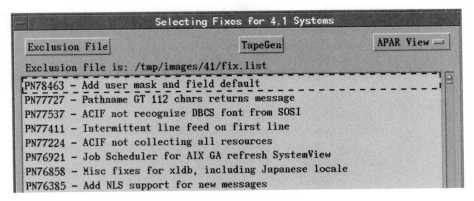

Figure 11–3   FixDist PTF View Screen

more information about, just click on it. See FixDist documentation for further information on installing the fixes after you have downloaded them.

AIX PitStop—How to Resolve Common AIX Problems

PitStop is a free graphics-based tool that is available over the Internet which allows AIX users to perform a variety of service related tasks such as these:

- Service faxes, tips, flashes, and news

- Runs service tools

- Links to Internet Web sites

- Creates a fastpath to the AIX support service center.

To obtain a copy of PitStop, point your web browser to `http://service.boulder.ibm.com/www/support/aix/pitstop`. You will see a page that looks something like the screen in Figure 11–4.

Try the "What is PitStop" and "PitStop—PitStop test drive" options to get a better feel for the package, and when you are ready to download the package select "Get the latest PitStop code" option, and follow the directions on that page to download and install PitStop on your machine. After successful installation, just type "pitstop" to invoke this tool. You should see a tool bar like the one shown in

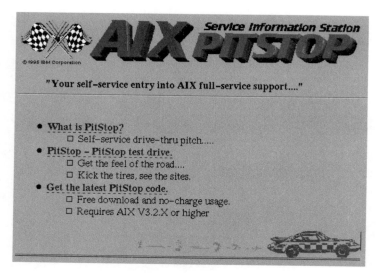

Figure 11–4   PitStop Home Page

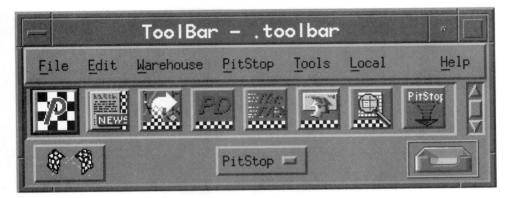

Figure 11–5   PitStop ToolBar

Figure 11–5. Clicking on the icons will bring up the selected HTML page using your Web browser without any need for Internet access since the data was all downloaded. You will find a wealth of interesting and useful information about AIX including, for instance, the AIXpert Certification Program (Figure 11–6).

Figure 11–6   AIXpert Certification Program

CHAPTER 12

- Large Scale Servers

- Enterprise Servers

- Workgroup Servers and/or Workstations

- Hardware-Related Sidebars

Kick Start Your Enterprise: The RS/6000 System Family

Large Scale Servers

At the high end of the RS/6000 family is the SP (Figure 12–1), built using the POWER2 Super Chip and PowerPC processors. The SP system excels at some of the largest and most complex technical and commercial applications (from financial modeling to modeling of the universe). It has the flexibility to function as an application server or data server, or to run combinations of interactive, batch, serial, and parallel jobs concurrently.

Installed in over 3,700 customer locations worldwide, the SP system delivers solutions for some of the most complex, large technical and commercial problems. Customer uses include: mission-critical commercial computing solutions to address data mining and data warehouse applications, on-line transaction processing (OLTP) applications, server consolidation, and collaborative computing comprised of Lotus Notes, Domino Server, Internet, intranet, extranet, and groupware application solutions. Recognized in the industry as a high-capacity and reliable Web server, the SP system is an ideal base for e-business applications. More than 80 companies and organizations worldwide use it to handle their Web sites. Technical computing users, including corporations, universities, and research laboratories use the SP system for leading-edge applications such as seismic analysis, computational fluid dynamics, engineering analysis, and computational chemistry.

The SP's unique multistage packet switch supports high-performance communications between processor nodes and maintains point-to-point communication time independently from the relative position of the nodes. The Switch Router provides the fastest available communication between SP systems and external networks. The single point of administrative control makes system management easier, with less expertise and time required for most tasks.

Figure 12–1   The SP Server

Enterprise Servers

Designed for a broad range of applications serving medium to large companies, RS/6000 Enterprise Servers come in uniprocessor and symmetrical multiprocessor (SMP) models suited for mission-critical commercial, large e-business, numeric-intensive or application development environments.

The **S70 Server** (64-bit SMP) excels in on-line transaction processing (OLTP) applications and supports many popular commercial applications (Figure 12–2). The S70 provides the capacity and scalability for linking mission-critical applications to the corporate intranet for the exploitation of evolving e-business technologies. The S70 system runs both 32- and 64-bit applications concurrently, enabling businesses to manage the evolution of their applications into 64-bit while continuing to support existing 32-bit applications.

Figure 12–2   The S70 Server

The **R50 Server** is a rack-mountable SMP that is very reliable, highly scalable, and readily expandable—qualities that are crucial for today's business and technical environments (Figure 12–3). Designed for placement in a rack enclosure (purchased separately), each R50 server drawer can accommodate up to four dual microprocessor cards, four memory cards, and sixteen Micro Channel adapter cards. And, when enclosed in an R00 System Rack, R50 drawers can be combined with additional storage/media subsystems or other server drawers.

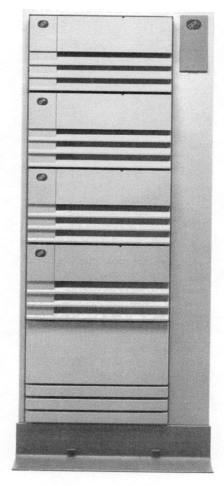

Figure 12–3   The R50 Server

The **J50 PowerPC Server** is a superior mid-range symmetric multiprocessor (SMP) featuring two-, four-, six-, or eight-way processing options and supporting large expandable system memory; reliable operation through continuous fault monitoring and value recovery; and outstanding system availability with hot-swappable disk bays (Figure 12–4).

Figure 12–4   The J50 PowerPC Server

The **595 Deskside Server** (Uniprocessor) is a 135 MHz deskside server based on the POWER2 Super Chip (P2SC) implementation of POWER Architecture (Figure 12–5). It delivers the levels of floating-point and integer power required by the most demanding applications. Its 2.16GB/second memory bandwidth and up to 2GB of memory capacity enable the 595 to process larger, more complex jobs entirely within memory to avoid performance reduction that occurs when relying on disk paging.

Figure 12–5   The 595 Deskside Server

The **H50 PowerPC Enterprise Server** is a one- to four-way SMP that excels as a multiuser application, database, and Internet server (Figure 12–6). It has the connectivity that allows it to participate in many currently installed UNIX and PC networks. The Model H50 has achieved excellent performance benchmark results, capturing industry leadership in decision support performance (TPC-D and 100GB as of 1/26/98) for four-way servers. Relative OLTP (ROLTP) commercial performance is excellent at a value of 32.8, the highest 4-processor configured server in the RS/6000 line-up (equivalent to the Model F50/332 MHz). SPECint95 is also outstanding, the highest of all RS/6000 servers. SPECweb96 results place the Model H50 among the industry leaders (benchmark data from SPEC and LINPACK Performance Benchmarks and TPC-D Published Results).

Figure 12–6   The H50 PowerPC Enterprise Server

The **F50 PowerPC Server** is a one- to four-way SMP that excels as a multiuser application, database, and Internet server (Figure 12–7). The F50 system with the 332 MHz processor has excellent SPECweb96 performance as well, placing the F50 among the industry leaders for four-way SMP systems. As a result of its exceptional performance, expandability and reliability, the Model F50 is well suited as a commercial system for high-demand applications, including mission-critical OLTP and e-business, and collaborative computing, such as Lotus Domino environments.

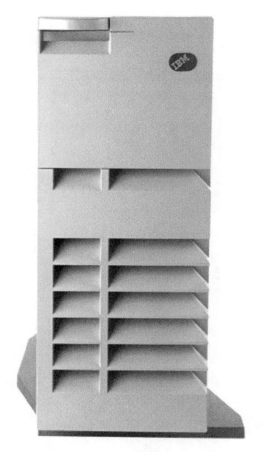

Figure 12–7   The F50 PowerPC Server

The **397 Server** (Uniprocessor) is a high-performance desktop system that runs design, analysis, and simulation applications on the same platform (Figure 12–8). It uses the most sophisticated RISC-based single-chip microprocessor currently produced by IBM which runs at 160 MHz. Supporting 1GB memory capacity with a bandwidth peak of 2.56GB/second, the Model 397 is ideally suited for a variety of scientific and technical applications, including engineering analysis, ECAD, petroleum, chemical, and aerodynamic simulations. This workstation/server has outstanding integer performance and a large memory bandwidth for transaction processing and database applications.

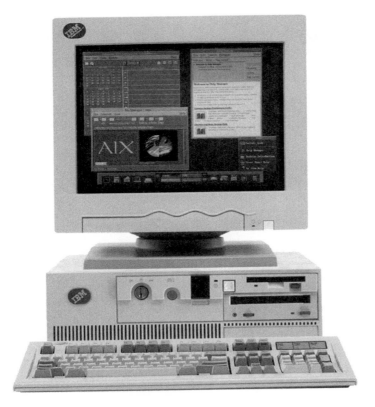

Figure 12–8   The 397 Server

Workgroup Servers and/or Workstations

Included in this group are two 1-2 way SMP Models, 43P-240 and F40, packing expansion and transaction processing performance into an economical package. All RS/6000 Workgroup Servers are designed for collaborative and multi-user environments such as Lotus Notes, Internet/intranet, retail store or bank controller and distributed transaction processing. You can also choose a powerful entry-level workstation ideal for drafting, design and software development, or a POWER2 super-chip processor that handles high-performance graphics and floating-point applications like simulation.

The **F40 PowerPC Server** (SMP) is a deskside one-way or two-way symmetric multiprocessing (SMP) system with the power to run complex commercial, business and engineering applications (Figure 12–9). Designed with reliability, availability, and serviceability (RAS), features typically found in higher-priced sys-

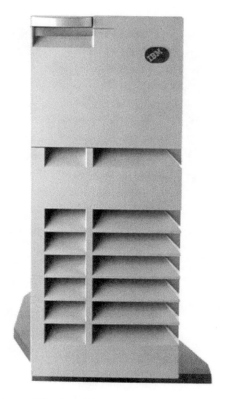

Figure 12–9   The F40 PowerPC Server

tems, such as Error Checking and Correcting (ECC) memory, hot-swappable disks, internal RAID storage, and an internal service processor, the Model F40 can help keep your mission-critical business and technical applications and networks running 24 hours a day, seven days a week. The Model F40 allows the seamless scaling of transaction processing power by adding a second processor to the 233 MHz standard processor. Multiple applications can be balanced between two processors to improve overall throughput.

The **E30 Workgroup Server** (Uniprocessor) is a compact deskside system with growth options for performance, storage, memory, and expansion slots (Figure 12–10). It is designed with the small business or workgroup in mind and is a great choice for environments where a system needs to easily fit into a work area, but where future growth is a must.

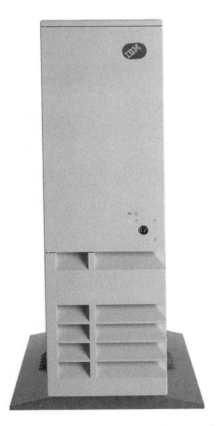

Figure 12–10   The E30 Workgroup Server

The **43P Model 240 Workgroup Server** (SMP) is a desktop one-way or two-way SMP system with an extensive set of connectivity and expansion capabilities (Figure 12–11). Excellent 3D graphics capabilities enhance its end-user appeal. Multiple applications can be balanced between two processors to improve overall throughput. To upgrade from the base 233 MHz microprocessor one-way system to a two-way SMP, you can plug in the second processor card.

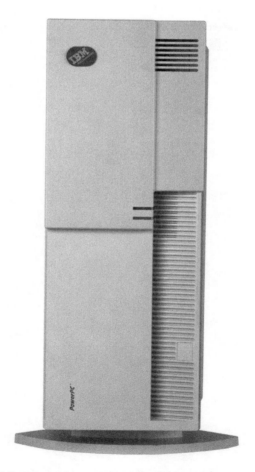

Figure 12–11   The 43P Model 240 Workgroup Server

The **43P Model 140 Workgroup Server** (Uniprocessor) is a desktop system that provides outstanding performance for a graphics workstation or entry-level workgroup server (Figure 12–12). With its graphics capability, the Model 140 is an excellent workstation solution for demanding 2D or high-function 3D applications.

Figure 12–12   The 43P Model 140 Workgroup Server

The **F3L Telecommunications Server** (Uniprocessor) supports demanding applications through the implementation of the 166 or 233 MHz PowerPC microprocessors which deliver high-performance processing coupled with large main memory. Leveraging the design characteristics of the RS/6000, the server integrates storage, industry-common PCI and ISA I/O, PowerPC performance. The F3L mounts in a compact 19-, 21-, or 23-inch telco relay rack that contains all system components. The unit includes two -48 VDC power supplies, and an optional third supply for fault-tolerant power operation.

Hardware-Related Sidebars

IBM Clustering Technology

IBM recently introduced the first packaged *clustered* server, the RS/6000 HA50 (High Availability Cluster Server). *Clustering* technology allows more than one computer to be linked together to provide superior reliability and availability for computer systems that must be available nearly every moment of the day and night. The HA50 couples two 1- to 4-way symmetric multiprocessor (SMP) H50 servers with IBM's High Availability Cluster Multi-Processing (HACMP) software and the AIX operating system to provide a system that will keep a company's business critical applications, data and systems operational and available 7 days a week, 24 hours a day, 365 days a year. The HA50 provides an ideal solution to protect against and recover from unplanned server hardware and application failures, as well as keep servers operational during planned maintenance and upgrades, all with easier systems management. As businesses grow, the HA50 customers can add more processors, memory, disks and H50 servers to the cluster. In addition, the HA50 supports thousands of business and industry applications, including database, on-line transaction processing, enterprise resource planning, collaborative groupware, and network computing.

RS/6000 SP Capable of a Billion Moves Per Second

Nearly one year after its historic victory over chess grand master Garry Kasparov, IBM announced improvements to the RS/6000 SP that deliver five times the performance of Deep Blue. The improvement is the result of IBM's new 332 MHz microprocessor, the fastest chip available to date on the RS/6000 SP. If applied to the system that powered Deep Blue, this processor would increase its calculating power from 200 million to one billion chess moves per second. Applications include e-business, business intelligence, server consolidation, computer-aided design and scientific analysis. And, in February, 1998, the U.S. Department of Energy selected the RS/6000 SP to perform complex computer modeling and simulation to protect the nation's nuclear stockpile. The system will become the world's fastest supercomputer upon completion in the year 2000.

Appendixes

Appendix A
Directory
Commands

mkdir—Makes one or more directories.

SYNOPSIS

mkdir [-mMode] [-p] Directory ...

DESCRIPTION

The mkdir command creates one or more new directories specified by the Directory parameter. You can specify the permissions for the new directories with the -m Mode flag. Using flag -p will create missing intermediate path name directories.

SEE ALSO

See the following commands: chmod, rm, mkdir, rmdir.

cd—Changes the current directory.

SYNOPSIS

cd [directory]

DESCRIPTION

The cd command moves you from your present directory to another. You must have execute (search) permission in the specified directory. If you do not specify a directory, cd moves you to your login directory ($HOME). If the specified directory name is a full path name, it becomes the current directory.

EXAMPLES

1.   To change to your home directory:

    cd

2.   To change to an arbitrary directory:

    cd/etc

This changes the current directory to /etc.

3.   To go down one level of the directory tree:

    cd uucp

If the current directory is /etc and if it contains a subdirectory named uucp, then /etc/uucp becomes the current directory.

4.   To go up one level of the directory tree:

    cd ..

The special filename .. (dot-dot) refers to the directory immediately above the current directory. However, under symbolic links, .. (dot-dot) refers to the parent directory of the symbolic link, not to the directory above the current directory.

rmdir—Removes a directory.

SYNOPSIS

rmdir [-p] directory...

DESCRIPTION

The rmdir command removes a directory from the system. The directory must be empty before you can remove it. Use the ls -a command to see if the directory is empty.

The -p flag removes all directories along the path name specified by the Directory parameter.

EXAMPLE

To empty and remove a directory:

rm mydir/* mydir/.*

rmdir mydir

This removes the contents of mydir, then removes the empty directory.

SEE ALSO

See the following commands: rm and ls.

`mvdir`—Moves (renames) a directory.

SYNOPSIS

```
mvdir directory1 directory2
```

DESCRIPTION

The `mvdir` command renames directories. The `directory1` parameter must name an existing directory. If `directory2` does not exist, `directory1` is moved to `directory2`. If `directory2` exists, `directory1` becomes a subdirectory of `directory2`. `Directory1` and `directory2` may be the names of files. If `directory2` is a filename, it is replaced with `directory1`.

EXAMPLE

To rename or move a directory to another location:

```
mvdir manpages aixbook
```

If `aixbook` does not exist, then this renames the directory `manpages` to `aixbook`. You can also rename a directory with the `mv` command. If a directory named `aixbook` already exists, this moves `manpages` and its contents to `aixbook/manpages`. In other words, `manpages` becomes a subdirectory of `aixbook`.

SEE ALSO

See the following commands: `mkdir` and `mv`.

`ls`—Lists the contents of a directory.

SYNOPSIS

```
ls [-1ACFLNRabcdefgilmnopqrstux] [File...]
```

DESCRIPTION

The `ls` command is the most commonly used command, so it has many options! Try out some of these flags and combinations and find the set that you like the most. The `ls` command displays the contents of each specified directory or file, along with any other information you ask for with the flags. If you do not specify a file or directory, `ls` displays the contents of the current directory. By default, `ls` displays all information in alphabetic order by filename.

There are three main ways to format the output:

- List one entry per line by specifying the -1 or other flags.
- List entries in multiple columns by specifying either the -C or -x flags.
- List entries in a comma-separated series by specifying the -m flag.

The mode displayed with the -e and -l flags are as follows:

d   The entry is a directory.

b   The entry is a block special file.

c   The entry is a character special file.

l   The entry is a symbolic link.

p   The entry is a first-in first-out (FIFO) special file.

s   The entry is a local socket.

-    The entry is an ordinary file.

The next nine characters are divided into three sets of three characters each for owner, group, and other, respectively. The three characters in each set show read, write, and execute permission of the file. Permissions are indicated as follows:

r   Permission to read a file.

w   Permission to edit (write) a file.

x   Permission to search/execute the file.

-    No permission to a file.

When the size of the files in a directory is listed, the ls command displays a total count of blocks, including indirect blocks.

LS FLAGS

-A   Lists all entries except . (dot) and .. (dot-dot).

-a   Lists all entries in the directory, including the entries that begin with a . (dot).

-b   Displays nonprintable characters in an octal (\nnn) notation.

-c   Uses the time of last modification of the inode for either sorting (when used with the -t flag) or for displaying (when used with the -l flag).

-C   Sorts output vertically in a multicolumn format. This is the default method when output is to a terminal.

-d   Displays only the information for the directory named. Directories are treated like files, which is helpful when using the -l flag to get the status of a directory.

-e   Displays the mode (including security information), number of links, owner, group, size (in bytes), time of last modification, and name of each file.

-f   Lists the name in each slot for each directory specified in the directory parameter. The order of the listing is the order in which entries appear in the directory.

-F   Puts a / (slash) after each filename if the file is a directory, an * (asterisk) if the file can be executed, an = (equal sign) if the file is a socket, a | (pipe) sign if the file is a FIFO, and an @ for a symbolic link.

-g   Displays the same information as the -l flag, except the -g flag suppresses display of the owner and symbolic link information.

-i   Displays the i-node number in the first column of the report for each file.

-L   Lists the file or directory contents that the link references.

-l   (Lower case L) Displays the mode, number of links, owner, group, size (in bytes), and time of last modification for each file.

-m   Uses stream output format (a comma-separated series).

-n   Displays the same information as the -l flag, except that the -n flag displays the user and the group ID's instead of the user and group names.

-N   Does not follow symbolic links when determining the status of a file.

-o   Displays the same information as the -l flag, except the -o flag suppresses display of the group and symbolic link information.

-p   Puts a slash after each filename if that file is a directory.

-q   Displays nonprintable characters in filenames as a ? (question mark).

-r   Reverses the order of the sort, giving reverse alphabetic or the oldest first, as appropriate.

-R   Lists all subdirectories recursively.

-s   Gives size in kilobytes (including indirect blocks) for each entry.

-t   Sorts by time of last modification (latest first) instead of by name.

-u   Uses the time of the last access, instead of the time of the last modification, for either sorting (when used with the -t flag) or for displaying (when used with the -l flag).

-x   Sorts output horizontally in a multicolumn format.

-1   Forces output into one-entry-per-line format.

EXAMPLES

1.   To list all files in the current directory:

```
ls -a
```

This lists all files, including . (dot), .. (dot-dot), and other files with names beginning with a dot.

2.   To display detailed information:

`ls -l aixbook toc`

This displays a long listing with detailed information about `aixbook` and `.toc`.

3.   To display detailed information about a directory:

`ls -d -l . aixbook aixbook/manpages`

This displays a long listing for the directories . (dot) and `aixbook`, and for the file `aixbook/manpages`. Without the -d flag, this would list the files in . (dot) and `aixbook` instead of the detailed information about the directories themselves.

4.   To list the files in order of modification time:

`ls -l -t`

This displays a long listing of the files that were modified most recently, followed by the older files.

SEE ALSO

See the following command: `chmod`.

df—Reports information about space on file systems.

SYNOPSIS

`df [-P] | [-IMitv] [-k] [-s] [filesystem ...] [file ...]`

DESCRIPTION

The `df` command writes to standard output information about total space and available space on the specified file systems. `filesystem` can be the name of the device on which the file system resides or the directory on which it is mounted. If you specify file, then `df` will provide information about the filesystem file is located in. If you do not specify either file or filesystem, `df` provides information on all mounted file systems. File system statistics are displayed in units of 512-byte blocks by default.

FLAGS

-i   Displays the number of free and used i-nodes for the file system; this output is the default when the specified file system is mounted.

-I   Displays information on the total number of blocks, the used space, the free space, the percentage of used space, and the mount point for the file system.

-k   Displays statistics in units of 1024-byte blocks.

-M   Displays the mount point information for the file system in the second column.

-P   Displays information on the file system in POSIX portable format. When the -P flag is specified, the header line appears similar to:

Filesystem 512-blocks Used Available Capacity Mounted on

If the -k flag is specified in addition to the -P flag, the column heading 512-blocks is replaced by the heading 1024-blocks. File system statistics are displayed on one line in the following order:

FileSystem, TotalSpace, UsedSpace, FreeSpace, UsedPercentage, MountPoint

-s   Gets file system statistics from the VFS specific file system helper instead of the statfs system call.

-t   Includes figures for total allocated space in the output.

-v   Displays all information for the specified file system.

EXAMPLE

To list information about all file systems:

```
df
```

Appendix B
File Manipulation
Commands

cp—Copies files.

SYNOPSIS

```
cp [-fhip] [-r|-R] [- -] SourceFile target
cp [-fhip] [-r|-R] [- -] src1 ... srcN directory
```

DESCRIPTION

The cp (copy) command copies a source file or the files in a source directory to a target file or directory. If your output is to a directory, then the files are copied to that directory with the same filename.

FLAGS

-f   Specifies removal of the destination file if it cannot be opened for write.

-h   Forces the cp command to copy symbolic links.

-I   Prompts for confirmation before overwriting any existing files.

-p   Preserves the modification times and modes of the source file for the copy.

-r   Copies each subtree rooted at the source file (recursive copy). Special files are created as regular files.

-R   Copies each subtree rooted at the source file (recursive copy). Special files are recreated as special files.

- -   Indicates that the arguments following this flag are to be interpreted as file-names.

EXAMPLES

1. To make another copy of a file in the current directory:

```
cp book.txt book.bak
```

This copies `book.txt` to `book.bak`. If the file `book.bak` does not already exist, then `cp` creates it. If it does exist, then `cp` replaces it with a copy of `book.txt`.

2. To copy a file to another directory:

```
cp jones /u/trent/authors
```

This copies `jones` to `/u/trent/authors/jones`.

3. To copy all the files in a directory to a new directory:

```
cp /u/trent/authors/* /u/trent/team
```

This copies the files and directories in the directory `authors` to the directory `team`.

4. To copy a directory, its files, and its subdirectories to another directory:

```
cp -r /u/trent/authors /u/trent/team
```

This copies the directory `clients`, its files, its subdirectories, and the files in the subdirectories to the directory `customers`.

SEE ALSO

See the following command: `mv`.

mv—Moves and renames files.

SYNOPSIS

```
mv [-i | -f] [- -] src target
mv [-i | -f] [- -] src1 ... srcN TargetDirectory
```

DESCRIPTION

The `mv` command moves files and directories from one directory to another, or renames a file or directory. When you move a directory into an existing directory, the directory and its contents are added under the existing directory. When you use the `mv` command to rename a file or directory, the TargetDirectory parameter can specify either a new filename or a new directory path name.

FLAGS

-f   Does not prompt before overwriting an existing file.

-I   Prompts before moving a file or directory that would overwrite an existing file.

- -   Specifies that the following parameters are filenames.

EXAMPLES

1.   To rename a file:

      `mv manpgs manpages`

      This renames `manpgs` to `manpages`.

2.   To rename a directory:

      `mv book aixbook`

      This renames `book` to `aixbook`.

3.   To move a file to another directory, keeping the same name:

      `mv manpages aixbook`

      This moves `chap3` to `aixbook/chap3`.

4.   To move several files into another directory:

      `mv manpages overview aixbook`

      This moves `manpages` to `aixbook/manpages` and `overview` to `aixbook/overview`.

SEE ALSO

See the following command: `mvdir`.

rm—Removes files or directories.

SYNOPSIS

`rm [-firRe] [- -] File ...`

DESCRIPTION

The `rm` command removes the specified files from a directory.

FLAGS

-e   Displays a message after each file is deleted.

-f   Does not prompt before removing a write-protected file.

-i   Prompts you before deleting each file. When you use the -i and -r flags together, the `rm` command also prompts before deleting directories.

-r   Causes recursive removal of directories and their contents when the File parameter is a directory. This flag is equivalent to the -R flag.

-R   Causes recursive removal of directories and their contents when the File parameter is a directory. This flag is equivalent to the -r flag.

EXAMPLES

1.   To delete a file:

```
rm myfile
```

2.   To delete a file silently:

```
rm -f core
```

This removes core without asking any questions or displaying any error messages.

3.   To delete files one by one with prompting:

```
rm -i mydir/*
```

This interactively asks you if you want to remove each file. After each filename is displayed, enter y to delete the file, or press Enter to keep it.

4.   To delete a directory tree with prompting:

```
rm -ir aixbook
```

SEE ALSO

See the following command: `rmdir`

ln—Links files.

SYNOPSIS

```
ln [-fs] src [target]
ln [-fs] src1 ... srcN directory
```

DESCRIPTION

The `ln` command links the source file to the target file. If you are linking a file to a new name, you can specify only one file. If you are linking to a directory, you can list more than one file.

FLAGS

-f   Causes ln to overwrite existing files without displaying an error message.

-s   Creates a symbolic link to a file or directory.

EXAMPLES

1.   To create another name (also called an alias) for a file:

```
ln chap1 overview
```

This links chap1 to the new name overview. Now chap1 and overview are two filenames that refer to the same file. Any changes made to one also appears in the other.

2.   To create a symbolic link:

```
ln -s chap1 my_chap1
```

SEE ALSO

See the following commands: rm, mv, and cp.

cat—Concatenates or displays files.

SYNOPSIS

```
cat [-urSsq] [-n[b]] [-v[te]] [-|file ...]
```

DESCRIPTION

The cat command reads each file in sequence and writes it to standard output. If you do not specify file, or if you specify - (minus) instead of a file, cat reads from standard input.

FLAGS

-b   Omits line numbers from blank lines, when specified with the -n flag.

-e   Displays a $ (dollar sign) at the end of each line, when specified with the -v flag.

-n   Displays output lines preceded by line numbers, numbered sequentially from 1.

-q   Does not display a message if the cat command cannot find an input file. This flag is identical to the -s flag.

-r   Replaces multiple consecutive empty lines with one empty line. This flag is identical to the -S flag.

-s   Does not display a message if the `cat` command cannot find an input file. This flag is identical to the -q flag.

-S   Replaces multiple consecutive empty lines with one empty line. This flag is identical to the -r flag.

-t   Displays tab characters as ^I if specified with the -v flag.

-u   Does not buffer output.

-v   Displays nonprinting characters as visible characters.

-     Allows standard input to the `cat` command.

EXAMPLES

1.   To display a single file:

```
cat notes
```

2.   To concatenate several files:

```
cat file1 file2 file3 >files
```

This creates a filenamed `files` that is a copy of `file1` followed by `file2` and `file3`.

3.   To append one file to the end of another:

```
cat file4 >>files
```

This appends a copy of `file4` to the end of `files`. The ">>" is shell I/O redirection to append data to the end of `files`.

SEE ALSO

See the following command: pg.

pg—Formats files to the work station.

SYNOPSIS

```
pg [-number][-p string][-cefns][+line][+/pattern/][file...]
```

DESCRIPTION

The `pg` command reads files and writes them to standard output, one screen at a time. If you specify file as - (minus) or run `pg` without arguments, `pg` reads standard input. Each screen is followed by a prompt. If you press the Enter key, another page is displayed. The `pg` command lets you back up to review a prior page. In the text below <number> simply means a number you type. Pattern generally refers to a string to search for.

SUBCOMMANDS

When `pg` pauses and issues its prompt, you can issue a subcommand. Some of these subcommands change the display to a particular place in the file, some search for specific patterns in the text, and others change the environment in which `pg` works.

The following commands display a selected place in the file:

`page`	Displays the specified page.
`+<number>`	Displays the page <number> pages after the current page.
`-<number>`	Displays the page <number> pages before the current page.
`l`	Scrolls the display one line forward.
`<number>l`	Displays a screen with the specified line number at the top.
`+<number>l`	Scrolls the display <number> lines forward.
`-<number>l`	Scrolls the display <number> lines backward.
`d`	Scrolls half a screen forward. Pressing `Ctrl-D` also does this.
`-d`	Scrolls half a screen backward. Pressing `-Ctrl-D` also does this.
`Ctrl-L`	Displays the current page again. A single period also does this.
`$`	Displays the last page in the file.

The following commands search for text patterns in the text:

`[<number>]/pattern/`	Searches for the <number>th occurrence of pattern. The default for <number> is 1.
`<number>?pattern?`	
`<number>^pattern^`	Searches backward for the <number>th occurrence of pattern. The default for <number> is 1.

After searching, `pg` normally displays the line found at the top of the screen. You can change this by adding m or b to the search command to leave the line found in the middle or at the bottom of the window with all succeeding subcommands. Use the suffix t to return to displaying the line with the pattern to the top of the screen.

You can change the `pg` environment with the following subcommands:

`[<number>]n`	Begins examining the <number>th next file in the command line. The default <number> is 1.
`[<number>]p`	Begins examining the <number>th previous file on the command line. The default <number> is 1.

`[<number>]w`	Displays another window of text. If <number> is present, sets the window size to <number>.
`s file`	Saves the input in file. Only the current file being examined is saved.
`h`	Displays an abbreviated summary of available subcommands.
`q or Q`	Quits pg.
`!<shell-cmd>`	Runs the specified shell command

FLAGS

`-c`	Moves the cursor to the home position and clears the screen before each page.
`-e`	Does not pause at the end of each file.
`-f`	Does not split lines. Normally, pg splits lines longer than the screen width.
`-n`	Stops processing when a pg command letter is entered. Normally, commands must end with a new-line character.
`-p string`	Uses string as the prompt. If the string contains a %d, the %d is replaced by the current page number in the prompt. The default prompt is : (colon).
`-s`	Highlights all messages and prompts.
`+<linenum>`	Starts at <linenum>.
`-<number>`	Specifies the number of lines in the window.
`+/pattern/`	Starts at the first line that contains pattern.

SEE ALSO

See the following commands: cat and grep.

chmod—Changes permission codes.

SYNOPSIS

```
chmod [-Rfh]{u|g|o|a ...}{+|-|=}{r|w|x|X|s|t ...} File ...
chmod [-Rfh] OctalNumber File ...
```

DESCRIPTION

The chmod command modifies the read, write, execute (file), or search (directory) permission codes of specified files or directories. You can use either symbolic or absolute mode (octal) to specify the desired permission settings.

FLAGS

-f   Suppresses all error reporting except invalid permissions and usage statements.

-h   Suppresses a mode change for the file or directory pointed to by the encountered symbolic link.

-R   Descends directories recursively. The -R flag changes the file mode bits of each directory and of all files specified.

SYMBOLIC MODE

When you use the symbolic mode to specify permission codes, the first set of flags selects the permission field, as follows:

u   User (owner)

g   Group

o   All others

a   User, group, and all others (same effect as ugo). This is the default permission field.

The second set of flags selects whether permissions are to be taken away, added, or set exactly as specified:

-      Removes specified permissions.

+   Adds specified permissions.

=   Clears the selected permission field and sets it to the code specified.

The third set of flags of the chmod command selects the permissions as follows:

r   Read permission.

w   Write permission.

x   Execute permission for files; search permission for directories.

X   Execute permission for files if the current (unmodified) mode bits have at least one of the user, group, or other execute bits set; otherwise, the X flag is ignored.

s   SetUser-ID or set Group-ID permission. This permission bit sets the effective User-ID or Group-ID to that of the file whenever the file is run.

t   For directories, indicates that only file owners can link or unlink files in the specified directory. For files, sets the save-text attribute.

ABSOLUTE MODE (specify mode with octal numbers)

4000   Sets User-ID on execution.

2000   Sets Group-ID on execution.

1000   Sets the link permission to directories or sets the save-text attribute for files.

0400   Permits read by owner.

0200   Permits write by owner.

0100   Permits execute or search by owner.

0040   Permits read by group.

0020   Permits write by group.

0010   Permits execute or search by group.

0004   Permits read by others.

0002   Permits write by others.

0001   Permits execute or search by others.

EXAMPLES

1.   To add a type of permission to several files:

```
chmod g+w chap1 chap2
```

This adds write permission for group members to the files chap1 and chap2.

2.   To make several permission changes at once:

```
chmod go-w+x mydir
```

This denies group members and others the permission to create or delete files in mydir ("go-w"). It allows them to search mydir or use it in a path name ("go+x"). This is equivalent to the command sequence:

```
chmod g-w mydir
chmod o-w mydir
chmod g+x mydir
chmod o+x mydir
```

3.   To use the absolute mode form of the chmod command:

```
chmod 644 text
```

This sets read and write permission for the owner, and it sets read-only mode for the group and others.

SEE ALSO

See the following command: `ls`.

cmp—Compares two files.

SYNOPSIS

```
cmp [ -l ] [ -s ] file1 file2
```

DESCRIPTION

The `cmp` command compares file1 and file2 and writes the results to standard output. If you specify a - (minus) for file1, `cmp` reads standard input. Under default conditions, `cmp` displays nothing if the files are the same. If they differ, `cmp` displays the byte and line number at which the first difference occurs. Normally, you use `cmp` to compare nontext files and the `diff` command to compare text files.

FLAGS

-l   Displays, for each difference, the byte number in decimal and the differing bytes in octal.

-s   Returns only an exit value. (0 indicates identical files; 1 indicates different files; 2 indicates inaccessible files or a missing argument.)

EXAMPLE

1.   To determine whether two files are identical:

```
cmp prog.o.bak prog.o
```

This compares `prog.o.bak` and `prog.o`. If the files are identical, then a message is not displayed. If the files differ, then the location of the first difference is displayed.

SEE ALSO

See the following command: `diff`.

diff—Compares text files.

SYNOPSIS

```
diff [-bcitw][[-C Lines|-D String|-e|-f|-n]|[-h]] File1 File2
diff [-bcilrstw][[-C Lines|-e|-f|-n]|[-h]][-S File] Directory1
Directory2
```

DESCRIPTION

The `diff` command compares `file1` and `file2` and writes to standard output information about what changes must be made to bring them into agreement. If you specify a - (minus) for `file1` or `file2`, `diff` reads standard input. If `file1` is a directory, then `diff` uses a file in that directory with the name `file2`. If `file2` is a directory, then `diff` uses a file in that directory with the name `file1`.

The normal output contains lines of these three forms:

Lines Affected in file 1	Action	Lines Affected in file 2
num1	a	num2[,num3]
num1[,num2]	d	num3
num1[,num2]	c	num3[,num4]

These lines resemble `ed` subcommands to convert `file1` into `file2`. The numbers before the action letters pertain to `file1`; those after pertain to `file2`. Thus, by exchanging a for d and reading backward, you can also tell how to convert `file2` into `file1`. As in `ed`, identical pairs (where num1 = num2) are abbreviated as a single number.

Following each of these lines, `diff` displays all lines affected in the first file preceded by a <, then all lines affected in the second file preceded by a >.

An exit value of 0 indicates no differences, 1 indicates differences found, and 2 indicates an error.

FLAGS

-b   Ignores leading spaces and tab characters and considers other strings of spaces to compare as equal.

-C Lines   Produces a `diff` command comparison with a number of lines of context equal to the value specified by the Lines variable. The -C flag modifies the output slightly. The output begins with identification of the files involved and their creation dates. Each change is separated by a line with a dozen * (asterisks). The lines removed from File1 are marked with a - (minus sign) and those added to File2 are marked with a + (plus sign). Lines changed from one file to the other are marked in both files with an ! (exclamation point).

-c	Produces a `diff` command comparison with three lines of context. The -c flag modifies the output slightly. The output begins with identification of the files involved and their creation dates. Each change is separated by a line with a dozen * (asterisks). The lines removed from File1 are marked with a – (minus sign) and those added to File2 are marked with a + (plus sign). Lines changed from one file to the other are marked in both files with an ! (exclamation point).
-D [String]	Causes the `diff` command to create a merged version of File1 and File2 on the standard output. The C preprocessor controls are included so that a compilation of the result without defining String is equivalent to compiling File1, while defining String yields File2.
-e	Produces output in a form suitable for use with the ed editor to convert File1 to File2.
-f	Produces output in a form not suitable for use with the ed editor, showing the modifications necessary to convert File1 to File2 in the reverse order of that produced under the -e flag.
-h	Performs an alternate comparison which may be faster if the changed sections are short and well-separated.
-i	Ignores the case of letters.
-l	Long output format. Each result from the `diff` command text file comparison is piped through the `pr` command for pagination. Other differences are remembered and summarized after all text file differences are reported.
-n	Produces output similar to that of the -e flag, but in the opposite order and with a count of changed lines on each insert or delete command. This is the form used by the revision control system (RCS).
-r	Causes application of the `diff` command recursively to common subdirectories encountered.
-s	Reports files that are the same and otherwise not mentioned.
-S [File]	Ignores files whose names collate before the file specified by the File variable when comparing directories.

-t   Expands tabs in output lines. Normal output or the -c flag output adds characters to the front of each line, which may affect indentation of the original source lines and make the output listing difficult to interpret. This flag preserves the original source's indentation.

-w   Ignores all spaces and tab characters.

EXAMPLES

1. To compare two files:

    ```
    diff chap1.bak chap1
    ```

2. To compare two files, ignoring differences in the amount of white space:

    ```
    diff -w prog.c.bak prog.c
    ```

SEE ALSO

See the following command: cmp.

grep—Searches a file for a pattern.

SYNOPSIS

```
grep [-E|-F] [-c|-l|-q] [-insvxbhwy] [-p[parasep]] -e
  pattern_list... [-f pattern_file...] [file...]

grep [-E|-F] [-c|-l|-q] [-insvxbhwy] [-p[parasep]]
  [-e pattern_list...] -f pattern_file... [file...]

grep [-E|-F] [-c|-l|-q] [-insvxbhwy] [-p[parasep]] pattern_list
  [file...]
```

DESCRIPTION

This command is one of our favorites! Don't get overwhelmed with the number of options and some of the syntax. The power of this command is the ability to search through a bunch of files for a character string.

Commands of the grep family search input files for lines matching a pattern. Normally, they copy each line found to standard output. Three versions of the grep command permit you to express the matching pattern in varying levels of complexity:

grep   Searches for patterns which are basic regular expressions.

egrep   Searches for patterns which are extended regular expressions.

fgrep   Searches for patterns that are fixed strings.

All versions of `grep` display the name of the file containing the matched line if you specify more than one filename. Characters with special meaning to the shell ("$ * [| ^ ( ) \") must be quoted when they appear in patterns. When the pattern is not a simple string, you usually must enclose the entire pattern in single quotation marks.

FLAGS

-b	Precedes each line by the block number on which it was found.
-c	Displays only a count of matching lines.
-E	Treats each pattern specified as an extended regular expression (ERE). The `grep` command with the -E flag is almost the same as the `egrep` command.
-e PatternList	Specifies one or more search patterns. This works like a simple pattern but is useful when the pattern begins with a - (minus). Patterns should be separated by a new-line character. (Hint, enclose the pattern list in single or double quotes.)
-F	Treats each specified pattern as a string instead of a regular expression. The `grep` command with the -F flag is almost the same as the `fgrep` command.
-f PatternFile	Specifies a file containing search patterns.
-h	Suppresses filename output when multiple files are specified.
-i	Ignores the case (uppercase or lowercase) of letters when making comparisons.
-l	Lists just the names of files (once) which contain matching lines.
-n	Precedes each line with the relative line number in the file.
-p[Separator]	Displays the entire paragraph containing matched lines. Paragraphs are delimited by either the Separator Pattern or by a blank line if a Separater isn't specified.
-q	Suppresses all writing to standard output, regardless of matching lines. Exits with a zero status if a pattern is found.
-s	Suppresses error messages ordinarily written for nonexistent or unreadable files.
-v	Displays all lines not matching the specified pattern.
-w	Does a word search.

-x   Displays lines that match the specified pattern exactly with no additional characters.

-y   Ignores the case of letters when making comparisons.

EXAMPLES

1.   To search several files for a simple string of characters:

```
grep "strcpy" *.c
```

This searches for the string `strcpy` in all files in the current directory with names ending in `.c`

2.   To count the number of lines that match a pattern:

```
grep -c "AIX" preface
```

This displays the number of lines in `preface` that contains the string `AIX`.

3.   To display the names of files that contain a pattern:

```
grep -l "strcpy" *.c
```

This searches the files in the current directory that end with `.c` and displays the names of those files that contain the string `strcpy`.

cut—Writes out selected fields from each line of a file.

SYNOPSIS

```
cut {-b<list>[-n]|-c<list>|-f<list>[-d<char>][-s]} file ...
```

DESCRIPTION

The `cut` command cuts out columns from a table or cuts out fields from each line of a file and writes these columns or fields to standard output. If you do not specify a file, `cut` reads standard input.

You must specify either the -b, -c, or -f flag. The list parameter is a comma, blank, or hyphen separated list of integer numbers (in increasing order). The hyphen separator indicates ranges. Some sample lists are "1,4,7"; "1-3,8"; "-5,10" (short for "1-5,10"); and "3-" (short for third through last field).

FLAGS

-b List   Specifies byte positions.

-c List   Specifies character positions. For example, if you specify -c 1-40, the `cut` command writes out the first 40 characters in each line of the file.

-d Character	Uses the character specified by the Character variable as the field delimiter when you specify the -f flag.
-f List	Specifies a list of fields assumed to be separated in the file by a delimiter character, which is by default the tab character. For example, if you specify -f 1,7, the `cut` command writes out only the first and seventh fields of each line. If a line contains no field delimiters, the `cut` command passes them through intact (useful for table subheadings), unless you specify the -s flag.
-n	Suppresses splitting of multibyte characters. Only characters which are completely contained in the style list specified by the -f parameter will be displayed.
-s	Suppresses lines that do not contain delimiter characters. Use only with the -f flag.

EXAMPLE

1. To display several fields of each line of a file:

```
cut -f1,5 -d: /etc/passwd
```

This displays the login name and full user name fields of the system password file. These are the first and fifth fields ("-f1,5") separated by colons ("-d:"). So, if the `/etc/passwd` file looks like this:

```
sys:*:3:3::/usr/src:
adm:*:4:4:System Administrator:/var/adm:/bin/sh
Cannon:*:200:200:Casey Cannon:/home/pierre:/bin/ksh
bentti:*:202:200:Davin Bentti:/home/joan:/bin/sh
```

then `cut` produces:

```
sys:
adm:System Administrator
Cannon:Casey Cannon
bentti:Davin Bentti
```

join—Joins data fields of two files.

SYNOPSIS

```
join [-a FileNumber|-v FileNumber][-e String][-o List]
[-t Character][-1 Field][-2 Field] File1 File2
```

DESCRIPTION

The `join` command reads the files specified by the `File1` and `File2` parameters, joins lines in the files according to the flags, and writes the results to standard output. The `File1` and `File2` parameters must be text files. Both `File1` and `File2` must be sorted on the field that they are being joined by before invoking the `join` command.

One line appears in the output for each identical join field appearing in both files. The join field is the field in the input files examined by the `join` command to determine what will be included in the output. The output line consists of the `join` field, the rest of the line from the file specified by the `File1` parameter, and the rest of the line from the file specified by the `File2` parameter. Specify standard input in place of either the `File1` or `File2` parameter by substituting a - (dash) as the filename.

Fields are normally separated by one or more space, tab character, or new-line characters.

FLAGS

-1 Field	Joins the two files using the field number specified by the Field variable in the `File1` input file.
-2 Field	Joins the two files using the field number specified by the Field variable in the `File2` input file.
-a FileNumber	Produces an output line for each line in the file specified by the FileNumber variable whose `join` fields do not match any line in the other input file. The output lines are produced in addition to the default output. The value of the FileNumber variable must be either 1 or 2, corresponding to the files specified by the `File1` and `File2` parameters, respectively.
-e String	Replaces empty output fields with the string specified by the String variable.
-o List	Constructs an output line to comprise the fields specified in the List variable.

One of the following forms applies to the List variable:

FileNumber.Field	Where FileNumber is a file number and Field is a decimal-integer field number. Separate multiple fields with a , (comma) or space characters with quotation marks around the multiple fields.

0 (zero)	Represents the join field. The -o 0 flag essentially selects the union of the join fields.
-t Character	Uses the character specified by the Character parameter as the field separator character in the input and the output. Every appearance of the character in a line is significant. The default separator is a space.
-v FileNumber	Produces an output line for each line in the file specified by the FileNumber variable whose join fields do not match any line in the other input file. Default output is not produced. The value of the FileNumber variable must be either 1 or 2, corresponding to the files specified by File1 and File2 parameters, respectively.

SEE ALSO

See the following commands: sort and cut.

sort—Sorts or merges files.

SYNOPSIS

```
sort [ -Abcdfimnru] [-o OutFile ] [ -t Character ]
[ -T Directory ] [ -y [ Kilobytes ] ] [ -z RecordSize ] ...
[ -k KeyDefinition ] ... [ File ... ]
```

DESCRIPTION

Sort is a useful command. It's easy to sort a file by name or number so that you can get information out of all that data! If the descriptions are too much for you, just go straight to the examples.

The sort command sorts lines in the files specified by the File parameter and writes the result to standard output. If the File parameter specifies more than one file, the sort command concatenates the files and sorts them as one file. A - (minus sign) in place of a filename specifies standard input. If you do not specify any filenames, the command sorts standard input. An output file can be specified with the -o flag.

SORT KEYS

A sort key is a portion of an input line that is specified by a field number and a column number. Fields are parts of input lines that are separated by field separators. The default field separator is a sequence of one or more consecutive space or tab characters. A different field separator can be specified using the -t flag.

When using sort keys, the `sort` command first sorts all lines on the contents of the first sort key. Next, all the lines whose first sort keys are equal are sorted upon the contents of the second sort key, and so on. Sort keys are numbered according to the order they appear on the command line. If two lines sort equally on all sort keys, the entire lines are then compared based upon the collation order in the current locale.

When numbering columns within fields, the blank characters in a default field separator are counted as part of the following field. Leading blanks are not counted as part of the first field, and field separator characters specified by the -t flag are not counted as parts of fields. Leading blank characters can be ignored using the -b flag.

Sort keys can be defined using the following -k flag:

Sort Key Definition Using the -k Flag. The -k KeyDefinition flag uses the following form:

```
-k [ FStart [ .CStart ] ] [ Modifier ] [ , [ FEnd [ .CEnd ] ]
[ Modifier ] ]
```

The sort key includes all characters beginning with the field specified by the FStart variable and the column specified by the CStart variable and ending with the field specified by the FEnd variable and the column specified by the CEnd variable. If Fend is not specified, the last character of the line is assumed. If CEnd is not specified, the last character in the FEnd field is assumed. Any field or column number in the KeyDefinition variable may be omitted. The default values are as follows:

FStart   Beginning of the line

CStart   First column in the field

FEnd   End of the line

CEnd   Last column of the field

The value of the Modifier variable can be one or more of the letters b, d, f, i, n, or r. The modifiers apply only to the field definition they are attached to and have the same effect as the flag of the same letter. The modifier letter b applies only to the end of the field definition to which it is attached. For example,

-k 3.2b,3r

specifies a sort key beginning in the second non-blank column of the third field and extending to the end of the third field, with the sort on this key to be done in reverse collation order. If the FStart variable and the CStart variable fall beyond the end of the line or after the FEnd variable and the CEnd variable, then the sort key is ignored.

FLAGS

-A   Sorts on a byte-by-byte basis using ASCII collation order instead of collation in the current locale. This is the fastest way to sort.

-b   Ignores leading spaces and tabs to find the first or last column of a field.

-c   Checks that input is sorted according to the ordering rules specified in the flags.

-d   Sorts using dictionary order. Only letters, digits, and spaces are considered in comparisons.

-f   Changes all lowercase letters to uppercase before comparison.

-i   Ignores all nonprinting characters during comparisons.

-k KeyDefinition   Specifies a sort key. The format of the KeyDefinition option is:

[FStart][.CStart][Modifier][,[FEnd][.CEnd][Modifier]]

The sort key includes all characters beginning with the field specified by the FStart variable and the column specified by the CStart variable and ending with the field specified by the FEnd variable and the column specified by the CEnd variable. The value of the Modifier variable can be b, d, f, i, n, or r. The modifiers are equivalent to the flags of the same letter.

-m   Merges multiple input files only; the input is assumed to be already sorted.

-n   Sorts numeric fields by arithmetic value.

-o OutFile   Directs output to the file specified by the OutFile parameter instead of standard output. The value of the OutFile parameter can be the same as the File parameter.

-r   Reverses the order of the specified sort.

-t Character   Specifies Character as the single field separator character.

-u   Suppresses all but the first line in each set of lines that sort equally according to the sort keys and options.

-T Directory   Places all temporary files that are created into the directory specified by the Directory parameter.

-y[Kilobytes] Starts the `sort` command using the number of kilobytes of memory specified by the Kilobytes parameter and adds more as needed.

-z RecordSize Prevents abnormal termination if any of the lines being sorted are longer than the default buffer size. RecordSize must designate a value in bytes equal to or greater than the longest line to be merged.

EXAMPLES

1. To perform a simple sort in the file `fruits`:

```
sort fruits
```

This displays the contents of `fruits` sorted in ascending lexicographic order. This means that the characters in each column are compared one by one, including spaces, digits, and special characters. For instance, if `fruits` contains the text:

banana

orange

Persimmon

apple

%%banana

apple

ORANGE

then `sort` displays in the Clocale:

%%banana

ORANGE

Persimmon

apple

banana

orange

This order follows from the fact that in the ASCII collating sequence, "%" (percent sign) precedes the uppercase letters, which precede the lowercase letters.

2.   To sort in dictionary order:

`sort` -d fruits

This sorts and displays the contents of "fruits", comparing only letters, digits, and blanks. If "fruits" is the same as in Example 1, then sort displays:

ORANGE

Persimmon

apple

%%banana

banana

orange

The "-d" flag tells sort to ignore the "%" character because it is not a letter, digit, or blank. This puts "%%banana" next to "banana".

3.   To group lines that contain uppercase and special characters with similar lowercase lines:

`sort` -d -f fruits

This ignores special characters ("-d") and differences in case ("-f"). Given the "fruits" of Example 1, this displays:

apple

%%banana

banana

ORANGE

orange

Persimmon

4.   To sort as in Example 3 and remove duplicate lines:

`sort` -d -f -u fruits

The "-u" flag tells sort to remove duplicate lines, making each line of the file unique. This displays:

apple

%%banana

orange

Persimmon

Note that not only was the duplicate "apple" removed, but "banana" and "ORANGE" as well. These were removed because the "-d" told sort to treat "%%banana" as if it were "banana", and the "-f" told it to treat "ORANGE" as "orange". Thus, `sort` considered "%%banana" to be a duplicate of "banana" and "ORANGE" a duplicate of "orange". Note: There is no way to predict which duplicate lines `sort -u` will keep and which it will remove.

SEE ALSO

See the following commands: `join` and `uniq`.

Appendix C
Backup
Commands

compress—Compress and expand data.

SYNOPSIS

```
compress [ -f ] [ -v ] [ -c ] [ -b bits ] [ name ... ]
uncompress [ -f ] [ -v ] [ -c ] [ name ... ]
zcat [ name ... ]
```

DESCRIPTION

The command compress reduces the size of the named files using adaptive Lempel-Ziv coding. Whenever possible, each file is replaced by one with the extension .Z, while keeping the same ownership modes, access, and modification times. If no files are specified, the standard input is compressed to the standard output. Compressed files can be restored to their original form using command uncompress or zcat.

The -f option will force compression. If -f is not given, the user is prompted as to whether an existing name.Z file should be overwritten.

The -c ("cat") option makes compress/uncompress write to the standard output; no files are changed. The behavior of zcat is similar to that of uncompress -c.

The amount of compression obtained depends on the size of the input, the number of bits per code, and the distribution of common substrings. Typically, text such as source code or English is reduced by 50-60%. The -v option displays the percentage reduction of each file.

cpio—Copies files into and out of archive storage and directories.

SYNOPSIS

```
cpio -o[-acv][-BCvalue]

cpio -i[cdmrtuvfsSb6] [-BCvalue] [ patterns ... ]

cpio -p[adlmuv] directory
```

DESCRIPTION

The CPIO-O command reads file path names from standard input and copies these files to standard output along with path names and status information.

The CPIO-I command reads from standard input an archive file created by the cpio -o command and copies from it the files with names that match pattern. These files are copied into the current directory tree. You may list more than one pattern, using the filename notation described in the section on file globbing. Note, however, that in this application the special characters "*" (asterisk), "?" (question mark), and [" . . . "] (ellipse) also match the "/" (slash) in path names. The default pattern is "*" (select all files in the current directory).

The CPIO -P command reads file path names from standard input and copies these files into the named directory. The specified directory must already exist. If these path names include directory names and if these directories do not already exist, you must use the d flag to cause the directory to be created.

FLAGS

All flags must be listed together, without any blanks between them. Not all of the following flags can be used with each of the -o, -i, and -p flags.

a   Resets the access times of copied files to the current time.

b   Swaps both bytes and halfwords.

B   Performs block input/output, 512 bytes to a record.

c   Writes header information in ASCII character form.

Cvalue   Performs block input/output, value * 512 bytes to a record.

d   Creates directories as needed.

f   Copies all files except those matching pattern.

l   Links files rather than copies them, whenever possible.

m   Retains previous file modification time.

r   Renames files interactively.

s   Swaps bytes.

S   Swaps halfwords.

t   Creates a table of contents. This does not copy any files.

u   Copies unconditionally.

v   Lists filenames.

6   Processes an old file (one written in UNIX Sixth Edition format).

EXAMPLES

1. To copy files onto diskette:

```
cpio -ov <filenames >/dev/rfd0
```

This copies the files with path names that are listed in the file `filenames` onto the diskette. The v flag causes `cpio` to display the name of each file as it is copied. This command is useful for making backup copies of files. The diskette must already be formatted, but it should not contain a file system or be mounted.

2. To copy files in the current directory onto diskette:

```
ls *.c | cpio -ov >/dev/rfd0
```

This copies all the files in the current directory whose names end with `.c`.

3. To copy the current directory and all subdirectories onto diskette:

```
find . -print | cpio -ov >/dev/rfd0
```

This saves the directory tree that starts with the current directory (.) and includes all of its subdirectories and files. A faster way to do this is:

```
find . -cpio /dev/rfd0 -print
```

4. To list the files that have been saved onto a diskette with `cpio`:

```
cpio -itv </dev/rfd0
```

This displays the table of contents of the data previously saved onto `/dev/rfd0` in `cpio` format.

5. To copy the files previously saved with `cpio` from a diskette:

```
cpio -idmv </dev/rfd0
```

This copies the files previously saved onto `/dev/rfd0` by `cpio` back into the file system. The d flag allows `cpio` to create the appropriate directories as needed. The m flag maintains the last modification time that was in effect when the files were saved. The v flag causes `cpio` to display the name of each file as it is copied.

6. To copy selected files from diskette:

```
cpio -i "*.txt" </dev/rfd0
```

This copies the files that end with .txt from diskette. Note that the pattern must be enclosed in quotation marks to prevent the shell from treating the * as a pattern-matching character.

SEE ALSO

See the following command: ln.

tar—Manipulates archives.

SYNOPSIS

```
tar [-c -r -t -u -x] [-BFdhilmopsvw] [-number] [-ffile] [-bblocks]
[-Sfeet] [-Sfeet@density] [-Sblocksb] [-LinputList] [-Nblocks]
[-Cdirectory] [file directory]...
```

DESCRIPTION

The tar command writes files to or retrieves files from an archival storage medium. The tar command looks for archives on the default device (usually tape), unless you specify another device with the -f flag. Filenames must not be longer than 100 bytes and must not contain blanks.

FLAGS

You must supply one of the following five function flags to control the actions of tar:

-c Creates a new archive and writes the file at the beginning of the archive.

-r Writes the file at the end of the archive. This option will not work on tape devices.

-t Lists the files in the order in which they appear in the archive.

-u Adds files to the end of the archive only if not in the archive already or if they have been modified since written to the archive. This option will not work on a tape device.

-x Extracts a file from the archive. If you specify a directory, tar extracts all files in that directory from the archive. If you do not specify a file or a directory, tar extracts all of the files from the archive.

-B Forces blocking to 20 blocks per record.

OPTIONAL FLAGS

-bblocks	Specifies the number of 512-byte blocks per record. The default is 16, which is appropriate for tape records.
	The block size is determined automatically when tapes are read (function flags -x or -t). When archives are updated with the -u and -r functions, the existing record size is used. The `tar` command writes archives using the specified blocks value only when creating new archives with the -c flag.
-C directory	Causes `tar` to change to the specified directory. This flag must appear after all others and may be repeated and interspersed with filenames.
-d	Makes separate entries for directories, blocks and character special files, and FIFOs. Normally, `tar` will not archive these files.
-F	Checks file type before archiving. SCCS, RCS, files named core, eirs, a, out, and files ending in .O are not archived.
-ffile	Uses file as the archive to be read or written. When this flag is not specified, `tar` uses the default filename /dev/rmto. If the file specified is "-" (minus), `tar` writes to standard output or reads from standard input.
-h	Forces `tar` to follow symbolic links. Normally `tar` does not do this.
-i	Ignores header check sum errors.
-Linput list	Writes the files listed in the input list file to the archive. The input list should contain one filename per line. These files are not treated recursively.
-l	Writes error messages to standard output if `tar` cannot resolve all of the links to the files archived.
-m	Uses the time of extraction as the modification time. The default is to preserve the modification time of the files.
-O	Provides backwards compatibility with older non-AIX versions of `tar`.
-N	Blocks uses the specified number of blocks when creating or reading an archive.
-P	Restores fields to original modes, ignoring present umask.
-S	Tries to create symbolic link if `tar` is unsuccessful using regular link.

-S	<blocks>b
-S	feet

-S feet @density Specifies the number of 512-byte blocks per volume (first format), independent of the tape blocking factor. You can also specify the size of the tape in feet by using the second form, and tar assumes a default density. The third form allows you to specify both tape length and density. Feet are assumed to be 11 inches long to be conservative.

-v Lists the name of each file as it is processed. With the -t flag, -v gives more information about each entry.

-w Displays the action to be taken followed by the filename, then waits for user confirmation.

-<number> Uses /dev/rmt<number> instead of the default. For example, -1 is the same as -f/dev/rmt1.

EXAMPLES

1. To write chap1 and chap2 to a new archive on the default tape drive:

```
tar -c chap1 chap2
```

2. To display the names of the files in the disk archive file book.tar on the current directory:

```
tar -vtf book.tar
```

backup—Backs up files and files systems.

SYNPOSIS

```
backup -i [ -b Number ] [ -p [ -e RegularExpression ] ]
[ -f Device ] [ -l Number ] [ -o ] [ -q ] [ -v ]
backup [ [ -Level ] [ -b Number ] [ -c ] [ -f Device ] [ -u ] ]
[ FileSystem ] | [ -w | -W ]
```

DESCRIPTION

The backup command creates copies of your files on a backup medium, such as a magnetic tape or diskette. The copies are in one of the two backup formats:

- Specific files backed up by name using the -i flag.
- Entire file system backed up by i-node using the Level and FileSystem parameters.

If you issue the backup command without any parameters, it defaults to a level 9 i-node backup of the root file system to the /dev/rfd0 device.

A single backup can span multiple volumes.

FLAGS

-b Number	For backups by name, specifies the number of 512-byte blocks; for backups by i-node, specifies the number of 1024-byte blocks to write in a single output operation. When the backup command writes to tape devices, the default value is 100 for backups by name and 32 for backups by i-node.
-c	Specifies that the tape is a cartridge, not a nine-track.
-e RegularExpression	Specifies that the files with names matching the regular expression are not to be packed.
-f Device	Specifies the output device. To send output to standard output, specify a - (minus sign).
-i	Specifies that files be read from standard input and archived by filename.
-l Number	Limits the total number of blocks to use on the diskette device.
-o	Creates a Version 2-compatible backup by name.
-p	Specifies that the files be packed, or compressed, before they are archived. Only files of less than 24MB are packed.
-q	Indicates that the removable medium is ready to use. When you specify the -q flag, the backup command proceeds without prompting you to prepare the backup medium and press the Enter key to continue.
-u	Updates the /etc/dumpdates file with the raw device name of the file system and the time, date, and level of the backup.
-v	Causes the backup command to display additional information about the backup.
-w	Currently disabled. If the -w flag is specified, no other flags are applied.

-W   Displays, for each file system in the /etc/dumpdates file,
                        the most recent backup date and level. If the -W option is
                        specified, no other flags are applied.

-Level   Specifies the backup level (0 to 9). The default level is 9.

EXAMPLES

1. To backup all the files and subdirectories in the /home directory using full
   pathnames, enter:

```
find /home -print | backup -i -f /dev/rmt0
```

The -i flag specifies that files will be read from standard input and archived
by filename. The `find` command generates a list of all the files in the
/home directory. The files in this list are full path names. The -f flag directs
the `backup` command to write the files to the /dev/rmt0 tape device.

2. To backup the / (root) file system, enter:

```
backup -0 -u -f /dev/rmt0 /
```

The 0 level specifies that all the files in the / (root) file system be backed up.
The -u flag causes the `backup` command to update the /etc/dumpdates
file for this backup.

3. To run the `backup` command using the System Management Interface Tool
   (SMIT), enter:

```
smit backup
```

SEE ALSO

See the following command: `restore`.

restore—Copies back files created by the `backup` command

SYNOPSIS

```
restore -x [ dMvq ] [ -b Blocks ] [ -f Device ] [ -s SeekBackup ]
[ -X Number ] [ File ... ]
restore -T [ qv ] [ -b Blocks ] [ -f Device ] [ -s SeekBackup ]
restore -r [ Bqvy ] [ -b Blocks ] [ -f Device ] [ -s SeekBackup ]
restore -R [ Bvy ] [ -b Blocks ] [ -f Device ] [ -s SeekBackup ]
restore -i [ hmqvy ] [ -b Blocks ] [ -f Device ] [ -s SeekBackup ]
restore -x [ Bhmqvy ] [ -b Blocks ] [ -f Device ]
[ -s SeekBackup ] [ File ... ]
```

```
restore -t | -T [ Bhqvy ] [ -b Blocks ] [ -f Device ]
[ -s SeekBackup ] [ File ... ]
```

DESCRIPTION

The restore command reads archives created by the backup command and extracts the files stored on them.

The diskette device, /dev/rfd0, is the default media for the restore command.

Use either the -x, -r, -R, or -i flag to restore archived files.

Use either the -T or -t flag to list archived files.

File-System Archives.   File-system archives are also known as i-node archives due to the method used to archive the files. A file-system name is specified with the backup command, and all files within that file system are archived.

FileName Archives.   Filename archives are created by specifying a list of filenames to archive to the backup command.

FLAGS

-B	Specifies that the archive should be read from standard input. The archive is assumed to be in file-system format.
-b Blocks	Specifies the number of 512-byte blocks to read in a single input operation. The default value for the Blocks parameter is 100.
-d	Indicates that, if the File parameter is a directory, all files in that directory should be restored.
-fDevice	Specifies the input device. To receive input from standard input, specify a - (minus sign).
-h	Restores only the actual directory, not the files contained in it.
-i	Allows you to interactively restore selected files from a file-system archive. The subcommands for the -i flag are:

	cd Directory	Changes the current directory to the specified directory.
	add [File]	Specifies that the File parameter is added to the list of files to extract.

`delete` [File]	Specifies that the File parameter is to be removed from the list of files to be extracted.
`ls` [Directory]	Displays the directories and files contained within the Directory parameter.
`extract`	Restores all the directories and files on the extraction list.
`pwd`	Displays the full path name of the current directory.
`verbose`	Causes the `ls` subcommand to display additional information about each file and directory.
`setmodes`	Sets the owner, mode, and time for all directories added to the extraction list.
`quit`	Causes restore to exit immediately without doing any more processing.
`help`	Displays a summary of the subcommands.
-M	Sets the access and modification times of restored files to the time of restoration.
-m	Renames restored files to the file's i-node number as it exists on the archive.
-q	Specifies that the first volume is ready to use and that the `restore` command should not prompt you to mount the volume and hit `Enter`.
-r	Restores all files in a file-system archive.
-R	Requests a specific volume of a multiple-volume, file-system archive.
-s SeekBackup	Specifies the backup to seek and restore on a multiple-backup tape archive.
-t	Displays information about the backup archive.
-T	Displays information about the backup archive. Identical to -t flag for file-system format archives.
-v	Displays additional information when restoring.

-x   Restores individually named files specified by the File parameter. If the File parameter is not specified, all the archive members are restored. If the File parameter is specified, then those members will be restored.

-X VolumeNumber   Begins restoring from the specified volume of a multiple-volume, filename backup.

-y   Continues restoring when tape errors are encountered.

EXAMPLES

1. To list the names of files in either a filename or file-system archive on the diskette device /dev/rfd0, enter:

```
restore -T
```

The archive is read from the /dev/rfd0 default restore device. The names of all the files and directories contained in the archive are displayed.

2. To restore a specific file, enter:

```
restore -xvf backupdata myfile
```

This command extracts the file `myfile` into the current directory from the archive backupdata. The -v flag displays additional information during the extraction.

3. To restore an entire file-system archive, enter:

```
restore -rvf /dev/rmt0
```

This command restores the entire file system archived on the tape device, /dev/rmt0, into the current directory. This example assumes you are in the root directory of the file system to be restored.

SEE ALSO

See the following command: `backup`.

Appendix D
Miscellaneous
Commands

crontab—Submits a schedule of commands to cron.

SYNOPSIS

```
crontab [ -e | -l | -r | -v | File ]
```

DESCRIPTION

The crontab command submits, edits, lists, or removes cron jobs. A cron job is a command run by the cron daemon at regularly scheduled intervals, all as specified via crontab file entries configured with the crontab command. The cron daemon mails you any command output or errors. If you specify a cron job incorrectly in your crontab file, the cron daemon does not run the job.

THE CRONTAB FILE ENTRY FORMAT

A crontab file contains entries for each cron job. Entries are separated by new-line characters. Each crontab file entry contains six fields separated by spaces or tabs in the following form:

```
minute  hour  day_of_month  month  weekday command
```

These fields accept the following values:

minute	0 through 59
hour	0 through 23
day_of_month	1 through 31
month	1 through 12

weekday   0 through 6 for Sunday through Saturday

command   a shell command

You must specify a value for each field. Except for the command field, these fields can contain the following:

- A number in the specified range. To run a command in July, specify 7 in the month field.

- Two numbers separated by a dash to indicate an inclusive range. To run a cron job on Monday through Friday, place 1-5 in the weekday field.

- A list of numbers separated by commas. To run a command on the first and 15th day of a month, you would specify 1,15 in the day_of_month field.

- An * (asterisk), meaning all allowed values. To run a job every hour, specify an asterisk in the hour field.

FLAGS

-e   Edits a copy of your crontab file or starts an editing session if you don't already have a crontab file. When editing is complete, the entry is installed as your crontab file.

-l   Lists your crontab file.

-r   Removes your crontab file from the crontab directory.

-v   Lists the status of your cron jobs.

EXAMPLES

1.   To have the cron deamon use a file called myjobs, enter the following:

    crontab myjobs

2.   To write the time to the console every hour on the hour, enter:

    0 * * * * echo The hour is 'date' . >/dev/console

3.   **To run the** calendar command at 7:30 a.m. every Monday, Wednesday, and Friday, enter:

    30 7 * * 1,3,5 /usr/bin/calendar

4.   To define text for the standard input to a command, enter:

    30 17 15-31 12 5 /usr/bin/wall%HAPPY HOLIDAY!%Have a
    nice weekend.

The text following the % (percent sign) defines the standard input to the `wall` command as follows to be displayed at 5:30 PM every Friday between December 15 and December 31:

```
HAPPY HOLIDAY!
Have a nice weekend.
```

FILES

`/var/spool/cron/crontabs`	Contains all user `crontab` files.
`/var/adm/cron/cron.allow`	Specifies a list of users allowed to use the `crontab` command.
`/var/adm/cron/cron.deny`	Specifies a list of users not allowed to use the `crontab` command.

Appendix E
Connectivity
Commands

rcp **Command**

PURPOSE

Copies (transfers) files between a local and a remote host or between two remote hosts.

SYNTAX

```
rcp [-p] { {User@Host:File | Host:File | File } { User@Host:File |
Host:File | File | User@Host:Directory | Host:Directory |
Directory } | [-r] { User@Host:Directory | Host:Directory |
Directory } { User@Host:Directory | Host:Directory | Directory } }
```

DESCRIPTION

The /usr/bin/rcp command is used to copy one or more files between the local host and a remote host, between two remote hosts, or between files at the same remote host.

Remote destination files and directories require a specified Host: parameter. If a remote host name is not specified for either the source or the destination, the rcp command is equivalent to the cp command. Local file and directory names do not require a Host: parameter.

If a Host is not prefixed by a User@ parameter, the local user name is used at the remote host. If the path for a file or directory on a remote host is not specified or is not fully qualified, the path is interpreted as beginning at the home directory for the remote user account.

Permissions. The user name entered for the remote host determines the file access privileges the `rcp` command uses at that host. Additionally, the user name given to a destination host determines the ownership and access modes of the resulting destination file or files. The remote host allows access if one of the following conditions is satisfied:

- The local host is included in the `remote host /etc/hosts.equiv` file and the remote user is not the root user.

- The local host and user name is included in a `$HOME/.rhosts` file on the remote user account.

For security reasons, any `$HOME/.rhosts` file must be owned by either the remote user or root user and should allow write access only by the owner.

FLAGS

-p   Preserves the modification times and modes of the source files in the copies sent to the destination only if the user has root authority or is the owner of the destination. Without this flag, the `umask` command at the destination modifies the mode of the destination file, and the modification time of the destination file is set to the time the file is received.

-r   Recursively copies, for directories only, each file and subdirectory in the source directory into the destination directory.

PARAMETERS

Host:File
Specifies the host name (Host) and filename (File) of the remote destination file, separated by a : (colon).

User@Host:File
Specifies the user name (User@) that the `rcp` command uses to set ownership of the transferred file, the host name (Host), and filename (File) of the remote destination file. The user name entered for the remote host determines the file access privileges the `rcp` command uses at that host.

File
Specifies the filename of the local destination file.

Host:Directory
Specifies the host name (Host) and directory name (Directory) of the remote destination directory.

User@Host:Directory
Specifies the user name (User@) the `rcp` command uses to set ownership of the transferred file, the host name (Host), and directory name (Directory) of the remote

destination directory. The user name entered for the remote host determines the file access privileges the `rcp` command uses at that host.

Directory

The directory name of the local destination directory. The name of the local host is named in the file `/etc/hosts.equiv` at `remotehost:` for example, `rcp myfile remotehost:/home/carolynj/boo`

rexec Command

PURPOSE

Executes commands one at a time on a remote host.

SYNTAX

```
rexec [ -d | -n ] Host Command
```

DESCRIPTION

The `/usr/bin/rexec` command executes a command on the specified remote host. The `rexec` command provides an automatic login feature by checking for a $HOME/ .netrc file that contains the user name and password to use at the remote host.

FLAGS

-d   Enables socket-level debugging.

-n   Prevents automatic login. With the -n flag specified, the `rexec` command prompts for a user name and password to use at the remote host, rather than searching for a $HOME/.netrc file.

PARAMETERS

Command   Specifies the command, including any flags or parameters, to be executed on the remote host.

Host   Specifies in alphanumeric form the name of the host where the command is to be executed.

EXAMPLE

To execute the who command on a remote host, enter:

```
rexec musashi who
```

The output from the who command is now displayed on the local system.

If you do not have a valid entry in the $HOME/.netrc file for the remote host, you will be prompted for your login ID and password.

rexecd Daemon

PURPOSE

Provides the server function for the rexec command.

SYNTAX

/usr/sbin/rexecd [-s]

DESCRIPTION

The /usr/sbin/rexecd daemon is the server (background process) for the rexec command. This daemon processes commands issued by a foreign host and returns the output of those commands to that foreign host. The rexecd daemon sends and receives data over a Transmission Control Protocol/Internet Protocol (TCP/IP) connection.

The rexecd daemon is normally started by the inetd daemon. It can also be controlled from the command line, using SRC commands.

Changes to the rexecd daemon can be made using the System Management Interface Tool (SMIT) or System Resource Controller (SRC), by editing the /etc/inetd.conf or /etc/services file. Entering rexecd at the command line is not recommended.The rexecd daemon is started by default when it is uncommented in the /etc/inetd.conf file.

The inetd daemon gets its information from the /etc/inetd.conf file and the /etc/ services file. After changing the /etc/inetd.conf file, run the refresh -s inetd or kill -1 InetdPID command to inform the inetd daemon of the changes to its configuration file.

Service Request Protocol. When the rexecd daemon receives a request, it initiates the following protocol:

1. The server reads characters from the socket up to a null () byte and interprets the resulting string as an ASCII number (decimal).

2. If the number received is nonzero, the rexecd daemon interprets it as the port number of a secondary stream to be used for standard error output. The rexecd daemon then creates a second connection to the specified port on the client machine.

3. The `rexecd` daemon retrieves a null-terminated user name of up to 16 characters on the initial socket.

`rlogin` **Command**

PURPOSE

Remote logins, connects a local host with a remote host.

SYNTAX

```
rlogin RemoteHost [ -e Character ] [ -8 ] [ -l User ]
```

DESCRIPTION

The `/usr/bin/rlogin` command logs into a specified remote host and connects your local terminal to the remote host. The remote terminal type is the same as that given in the TERM local environment variable. The `Ctrl-S` and `Ctrl-Q` key sequences stop and start the flow of information.

Remote Command Execution. When using the `rlogin` command, you can create a link to your path using a host name as the link name. For example: ln -s `/usr/bin/rsh HostName`.

Entering the host name specified by the HostName parameter with a command at the prompt, automatically uses the `rsh` command to remotely execute the command specified on the command line of the remote host specified by the HostName parameter.

Entering the host name specified by the HostName parameter without an argument (command) at the prompt, automatically uses the `rlogin` command to log in to the remote host specified by the HostName parameter.

FLAGS

-e Character   Changes the escape character. Substitute the character you choose for Character. The default characters the tilde (~).

-l User   Changes the remote user name to the one you specify. Otherwise, your local user name is used at the remote host.

-8   Allows an 8-bit data path at all times.

SECURITY

The remote host allows access only if one or both of the following conditions is satisfied:

- The local host is included in the `remote /etc/hosts.equiv` file, the local user is not the root user, and the -l User flag is not specified.

- The local host and user name is included in the `$HOME/.rhosts` file in the remote user account.

For security reasons, any `$HOME/.rhosts` file must be owned by either the remote user or root and should allow write access only by the owner.

SRC Daemon

PURPOSE

Controls background daemons.

DESCRIPTION

The System Resource Controller (SRC) is used normally during system initialization to bring up background processes (daemons) such as `telnetd` and `inetd`.

COMMANDS

`startsrc`   starts a subsystem, group of subsystems, or a subserver

`stopsrc`   stop a subsystem, group of subsystems, or a subserver

`lssrc`   display start states which returns process name, ID, and state (active or inactive)

EXAMPLES

1.   To start `telnetd` daemon, enter `startsrc -t telnet`

2.   To force `stop telnet`, enter `stopsrc -f -t -telnet`

`talk` Command

PURPOSE

Converse with another user across the network.

SYNTAX

```
talk { User@Host | Host!User | Host.User | Host:User } [ Tty ]
[ Pty ]
```

DESCRIPTION

The `/usr/bin/talk` command allows two users on the same host or on different hosts to have an interactive conversation. The `talk` command opens both a send window and a receive window on each user's display. Each user is then able to type into the send window while the `talk` command displays what the other user is typing.

To initiate a conversation, a local user executes the `talk` command and specifies a remote user's login ID. If the remote user is on a remote host, the name of the host must also be specified in one of the following ways:

User@Host Host!User Host.User Host:User

When using full domain names, the only valid form for specifying the user and host is User@Host.

When the local user initiates the conversation, a message is sent to the remote user, inviting a conversation. If the local user also specifies tty, the invitation message is sent only to the specified terminal. Otherwise, the invitation is sent to the remote user's login terminal.

To have the conversation, the remote user also has to execute the `talk` command from any terminal and specify the local user's account name and host name, if appropriate. When the remote user accepts the invitation, the `talk` command displays two windows on each user's terminal. One window displays what is typed by the local user; the other window displays what is typed by the remote user. To end the conversation, either user can press the `Interrupt` (`Ctrl-C`) key sequence and the connection is closed.

To disallow `talk` command invitations, the remote user can issue the `mesg n` command.

`talkd` **Daemon**

PURPOSE

Provides the server function for the `talk` command.

SYNTAX

```
/usr/sbin/talkd [ -s ]
```

DESCRIPTION

Note: The `talkd` daemon is normally started by the `inetd` daemon. It can also be controlled from the command line, using SRC commands.

The `/usr/sbin/talkd` daemon is the server that notifies a user (the recipient) that another user (the caller) wants to initiate a conversation. The daemon sets up the conversation if the recipient accepts the invitation. The caller initiates the conversation by executing the `talk` command specifying the recipient. The recipient accepts the invitation by executing the `talk` command specifying the caller.

Changes to all the `ftp` daemons can be made using the System Management Interface Tool (SMIT) or System Resource Controller (SRC), or by editing the `/etc/inetd.conf` or `/etc/services` file. Entering `talkd` at the command line is not recommended. The `talkd` daemon is started by default when it is uncommented in the `/etc/inetd.conf` file. After changing the `/etc/inetd.conf` or `/etc/services` file, run the `refresh -s inetd` or `kill -1 InetdPID` command to inform the `inetd` daemon of the changes to its configuration file.

Debugging messages are sent to the `syslogd` daemon.

FLAGS

-s   Turns on socket-level debugging.

`telnet, tn, or tn3270` **Command**

PURPOSE

Connects the local host with a remote host, using the Telnet interface.

SYNTAX

```
{ telnet | tn | tn3270 } [ -d ] [ -n TraceFile ]
[ -e TerminalType ] [ Host [ Port ] ]
```

DESCRIPTION

The `telnet` command, which is also referred to as the `tn` or `tn3270` command, operates in two different modes: command mode and input mode.

Command Mode.   When the `telnet` command is issued without arguments, it enters command mode, as indicated by the `telnet>`, `tn>`, or the `tn3270>` prompt. A user can also enter command mode from input mode by pressing Ctrl-] for the `telnet` command, `Ctrl-T` for the `tn` command, or `Ctrl-C` for the `tn3270` command. In command mode, subcommands can be entered to manage the remote system. Some of these subcommands return you to the remote session upon completion. For those subcommands that do not, pressing the Enter key returns you to the remote session.

If the client and the server negotiate to use a 3270 data stream, the keyboard mapping is determined by the following precedence:

$HOME/.3270keys   Specifies the user's 3270 keyboard mapping when the `tn` or `telnet` command is invoked. If you are using a color display, you can also change this file to customize the colors for 3270 displays.

/etc/map3270   Specifies the user's 3270 keyboard mapping when the `tn3270` command is invoked. The `/etc/map3270` file defines keyboard mapping and colors for the `tn3270` command.

/etc/3270.keys   Specifies the base 3270 keyboard mapping for use with limited function terminals.

Environment Variables.   The following environment variables can be used with the `telnet` command:

EMULATE   Overrides terminal-type negotiation in the same way as the -e flag. If the value of the EMULATE environment variable is defined as vt100 or 3270, the `telnet` command emulates a DEC VT100 terminal or 3270 terminal, respectively.

TNESC   Specifies an alternate TELNET escape character, other than the default, `Ctrl-]` for the `telnet` command, Ctrl-T for the `tn` command, or `Ctrl-C` for the `tn3270` command. To change the telnet escape sequence, set TNESC to the octal value of the character you want to use. Then export TNESC. For example, set TNESC to 35 to change the TELNET escape sequence to Ctrl-].

MAP3270   Specifies an alternate file that contains the user's 3270 keyboard mapping. The MAP3270 variable must contain the full path name to the alternate file. Create the alternate file using the same format as the default `/etc/map3270` file.

FLAGS

-d   Turns debugging mode on.

-e TerminalType   Overrides terminal-type negotiation. Possible values are vt100, 3270, or none.

-n TraceFile   Records network trace information in the file specified by the TraceFile variable.

telnetd **Daemon**

PURPOSE

Provides the server function for the TELNET protocol.

SYNTAX

`/usr/sbin/telnetd [ -n ] [ -s ]`

DESCRIPTION

Note: The `telnetd` daemon is normally started by the `inetd` daemon. It can also be controlled from the command line, using SRC commands.

The `/usr/sbin/telnetd` daemon is a server that supports the Defense Advanced Research Product Agency (DARPA) standard Telnet Protocol (TELNET).

Changes to the `telnetd` daemon can be made using the System Management Interface Tool (SMIT) or System Resource Controller (SRC), by editing the `/etc/inetd.conf` or `/etc/services` file. Entering `telnetd` at the command line is not recommended. The `telnetd` daemon is started by default when it is uncommented in the `/etc/inetd.conf` file.

The `inetd` daemon get its information from the `/etc/inetd.conf` file and the `/etc/ services` file. After changing the `/etc/inetd.conf` or `/etc/ser-vices` file, run the `refresh -s inetd` or `kill -1 InetdPID` command to inform the `inetd` daemon of the changes to its configuration file. Since the `telnetd` daemon allows the sending and receiving of 8-bit ASCII, NLS is supported.

The `telnetd` daemon supports the following TELNET options:

* Binary
* Echo/no echo
* Support SAK
* Suppress go ahead
* Timing mark
* Negotiate About Window Size (NAWS)

The `telnetd` daemon also recognizes the following options for the remote client:

* Binary
* Suppress go ahead

- Echo/no echo
- Terminal type

FLAGS

-n   Disables transport-level keep-alive messages. Messages are enabled by default.

-s   Turns on socket-level debugging.

`tftp` or `utftp` **Command**

PURPOSE

Transfers files between hosts using the Trivial File Transfer Protocol (TFTP).

SYNTAX

```
{tftp | utftp} {-g | -o | -p | -r | -w } LocalName HostPort
RemoteName [netascii | image]
```

DESCRIPTION

The `/usr/bin/tftp` and `utftp` commands transfer files between hosts using the Trivial File Transfer Protocol (TFTP). Since TFTP is a minimal file transfer protocol, the `tftp` and `utftp` commands do not provide all of the features of the `ftp` command.

The remote host must have a `tftpd` daemon started by its `inetd` daemon and have an account defined that limits the access of the `tftpd` daemon.

Maximum Time-out Value.   The user can pick the maximum time-out value, but the initial time-out value for the first block is hardcoded. The user cannot pick the maximum time-out value for the server; the server times out after six retries with a maximum time-out value of 64 seconds.

Access Control.   The `/etc/tftpaccess.ctl` file is searched for lines that start with allow: or deny:. Other lines are ignored. If the file doesn't exist, access is allowed. The entries in the `/etc/tftpaccess.ctl` file must be absolute path names.

The `/etc/tftpaccess.ctl` file should be write-only by the root user and must be readable by all groups and others (that is, owned by root with permissions of 644). For more information, refer to the sample `tftpaccess.ctl` file, which resides in the `/usr/ samples/tcpip` directory. Further information and example configurations for Xstations, Diskless clients, and restricted entry can be found in the `/usr/samples/tcpip/tftpaccess.ctl` file.

The `tftp` and `utftp` commands and subcommands have two forms: interactive form and command-line form.

Interactive Form. In the interactive form, the `tftp` and `utftp` commands are issued alone or with a Host parameter that specifies the default host to use for file transfers during this session. If you choose, you can also specify with the Port parameter which the `tftp` or `utftp` connection should use. When you enter the interactive form of either of these commands, the `tftp>` prompt is displayed.

When transferring data to a remote host, the transferred data is placed in the directory specified by the RemoteName parameter. The remote name must be a fully specified filename, and the remote file must both exist and have write permission set for others.

Command-Line Form. The command-line forms of the `tftp` and `utftp` commands are equivalent, except that the `utftp` command does not overwrite a local file. The `tftp` command can overwrite a file, but prompts the user before doing so. Because it is not interactive, the command line form of the `utftp` command can be more useful than the `tftp` command in a pipe.

Subcommands

Subcommands Used in the Interactive Form. Once the `tftp>` prompt is displayed, the following subcommands can be issued:

? [Subcommand]	Displays help information. If a Subcommand parameter is specified, only information about that subcommand is displayed.
ascii	Synonym for the mode ascii subcommand.
binary	Synonym for the mode binary subcommand. This subcommand is used in the interactive mode.
connect Host [Port]	Sets the remote host, and optionally the port, for file transfers.
get RemoteFile [LocalFile]	or get RemoteFile RemoteFile RemoteFile [RemoteFile . . .]

Gets a file or set of files from the remote host to the local host. Each of the RemoteFile parameters can be specified in one of the following two ways:

- As a file (File) that exists on the remote host if a default host has already been specified.

- As a host file (Host:File), where Host is the remote host and `File` is the name of the file to copy to the local system. If this form of the parameter is used, the last host specified becomes the default host for later transfers in this tftp session.

mode Type	Sets the type (Type) of transfer mode to either ascii or binary. A transfer mode of ascii is the default.
put LocalFile [RemoteFile]	or put LocalFile LocalFile LocalFile [LocalFile . . .]
RemoteDirectory	Puts a file or set of files from the local host onto the remote host. The RemoteDirectory and RemoteFile parameters can be specified in one of the following two ways:

- As a file or directory that exists on the remote host if a default host has already been specified.

- With Host:RemoteFile parameter, where Host is the remote host and `RemoteFile` is the name of the file or directory on the remote system. If this form of the parameter is used, the last host specified becomes the default host for later transfers in this `tftp` session.

In either case, the remote file or directory name must be a fully specified path name, even if the local and remote directories have the same name.

quit	Exits the `tftp` session. An End-Of-File key sequence also exits the program.
status	Shows the current status of the `tftp` program, including, for example, the current transfer mode (ascii or binary), connection status, and time-out value.
timeout Value	Sets the total transmission time out to the number of seconds specified by the Value parameter.
trace	Turns packet tracing on or off.
verbose	Turns verbose mode, which displays additional information during file transfer, on or off.

Subcommands Used in the Command Line Form

-w or -p   Writes (or puts) local data, specified by the LocalName parameter, to the file specified by the RemoteName parameter on the remote host specified by the Host parameter. If the LocalName parameter is a filename, the `tftp` command transfers the specified local file. If the LocalName parameter is specified as a - (dash), the `tftp` command transfers data from local standard input to the remote host.

`-r` or `-g` or `-o`   Reads (or gets) remote data from the file specified by the RemoteName parameter at the remote host specified by the Host parameter and writes it to the file specified by the LocalName parameter. If the LocalName parameter is a filename, the `tftp` command writes the data to the specified local file. For the -r and -g actions, the `tftp` command prompts for verification before overwriting an existing local file. For the -o action, the `tftp` command overwrites an existing local file without prompting. If the LocalName parameter is specified as a - (dash), the `tftp` command writes the data to local standard output.

Since the `tftp -g` and `tftp -r` commands prompt before overwriting an existing local file, it may be impractical to use the `tftp` command in a pipe. The `utftp` command performs the same `-r` and `-g` actions as the `tftp` command, but simply stops before overwriting a local file. Thus, the `utftp` command may be more appropriate for use in a pipe.

For both of the following modes of file transfer, the RemoteName parameter is the name of a file that has write permission set for others.

The mode of transfer is one of the following:

netascii   Transfers the data as 7-bit ASCII characters in 8-bit transfer bytes. This is the default.

image   Transfers the data as 8-bit binary data bytes in 8-bit transfer bytes, with no conversion. image transfer can be more efficient than netascii transfer when transferring between two hosts. It is recommended that netascii be used when transferring ASCII files from a workstation to a different type of host.

`ftp` **Command**

PURPOSE

Transfers files between a local and a remote host.

SYNTAX

```
ftp [ -d ] [ -g ] [ -i ] [ -n ] [ -v ] [ HostName [ Port ] ]
```

DESCRIPTION

The `ftp` command uses the File Transfer Protocol (FTP) to transfer files between the local host and a remote host or between two remote hosts.

The FTP protocol allows data transfer between hosts that use dissimilar file systems. Although the protocol provides a high degree of flexibility in transferring data, it does not attempt to preserve file attributes (such as the protection mode or modification times of a file) that are specific to a particular file system.

If you are transferring files between systems and need to preserve file attributes or recursively copy subdirectories, use the `rcp` command.

Issuing Subcommands.   At the `ftp>` prompt, you can enter subcommands to perform tasks such as listing remote directories, changing the current local and remote directory, transferring multiple files in a single request, creating and removing directories, and escaping to the local shell to perform shell commands. See the "Subcommands" section for a description of each subcommand.

If you execute the `ftp` command and do not specify the HostName parameter for a remote host, the `ftp` command immediately displays the `ftp>` prompt and waits for an `ftp` subcommand. To connect to a remote host, execute the open subcommand. When the `ftp` command connects to the remote host, the `ftp` command then prompts for the login name and password before displaying the `ftp>` prompt again.

The command interpreter handles filename parameters according to the following rules:

- If a - (hyphen) is specified for the parameter, standard input (stdin) is used for read operations and standard output (stdout) is used for write operations.

- If the preceding check does not apply and filename expansion is enabled (see the -g flag or the glob subcommand), the interpreter expands the filename according to the rules of the C shell. When globbing is enabled and a pattern-matching character is used in a subcommand that expects a single filename, results may be different than expected.

Note: The `ftp` command interpreter does not support pipes. It also does not necessarily support all multibyte-character filenames.

To end an `ftp` session when you are running interactively, use the `quit` or `bye` subcommand or the End of File (`Ctrl-D`) key sequence at the `ftp>` prompt. To end a file transfer before it has completed, press the Interrupt key (`ctrl-c`) sequence.

Security and Automatic Login. If you execute the ftp command and specify the host name (HostName) of a remote host, the ftp command tries to establish a connection to the specified host. If the ftp command connects successfully, the ftp command searches for a local $HOME/.netrc file in your current directory or home directory. If the file exists, the ftp command searches the file for an entry for the remote host. If the $HOME/.netrc file or automatic login entry does not exist or if your system has been secured with the securetcpip command, the ftp command prompts the user for a user name and password.

If the ftp command finds a $HOME/.netrc automatic login entry for the specified host, the ftp command attempts to use the information in that entry to log in to the remote host.

The HostName parameter is the name of the host machine to which files are transferred. The optional Port parameter specifies the ID of the port through which to transmit. (The /etc/services file specifies the default port.)

FLAGS

-d   Sends debugging information about ftp command operations to the syslogd daemon. If you specify the -d flag, you must edit the /etc/syslog.conf file and add one of the following entries:

user.info FileName

or

user.debug FileName

Note: The syslogd daemon debug level includes info level messages.

If you do not edit the /etc/syslog.conf file, no messages are produced. After changing the /etc/syslog.conf file, run the refresh -s syslogd or kill -1 SyslogdPID command to inform the syslogd daemon of the changes to its configuration file. For more information about debug levels, refer to the /etc/syslog.conf file and the debug subcommand.

-g   Disables the expansion of metacharacters in filenames. Interpreting metacharacters can be referred to as expanding (sometimes called globbing) a filename. See the glob subcommand.

-i   Turns off interactive prompting during multiple file transfers. See the prompt, mget, mput, and mdelete subcommands for descriptions of prompting during multiple file transfers.

-n   Prevents an automatic login on the initial connection. Otherwise, the ftp command searches for a $HOME/.netrc entry that describes the login and initialization process for the remote host. See the user subcommand.

-v   Displays all the responses from the remote server and provides data trans-
      fer statistics. This display mode is the default when the output of the `ftp`
      command is to a terminal, such as the console or a display.

FTP Subcommands.   The following `ftp` subcommands can be entered at the
`ftp>` prompt. Use double quotes (" ") to specify parameters that include blank
characters.

![Command [Parameters]]   Invokes an interactive shell on the local host. An
   optional command, with one or more optional parameters, can be given with
   the `shell` command.

$Macro [Parameters]   Executes the specified macro, previously defined with the
   `macdef` subcommand. Parameters are not expanded.

?[Subcommand]   Displays a help message describing the subcommand. If you
   do not specify a Subcommand parameter, the `ftp` command displays a list of
   known subcommands.

account [Password]   Sends a supplemental password that a remote host may require before granting access to its resources. If the password is not supplied
   with the command, the user is prompted for the password.

append LocalFile [RemoteFile]   Appends a local file to a file on the remote
   host. If the remote filename is not specified, the local filename is used, altered
   by any setting made with the `ntrans` subcommand or the `nmap` subcommand. The `append` subcommand uses the current values for `form`, `mode`,
   `struct`, and `type` subcommands while appending the file.

ascii   Synonym for the type `ascii` subcommand.

bell   Sounds a bell after the completion of each file transfer.

binary   Synonym for the `type binary` subcommand.

block   Synonym for the `mode block` subcommand.

bye   Ends the file-transfer session and exits the `ftp` command. Same as the
   `quit` subcommand.

carriage-control   Synonym for the form `carriage-control` subcommand.

case   Sets a toggle for the case of filenames. When the `case` subcommand is On,
   the `ftp` command changes remote filenames displayed in all capital letters
   from uppercase to lowercase when writing them in the local directory. The default is Off (so the `ftp` command writes uppercase remote filenames in uppercase in the local directory).

cd RemoteDirectory   Changes the working directory on the remote host to
   the specified directory.

cdup Changes the working directory on the remote host to the parent of the current directory.

close Ends the file-transfer session, but does not exit the `ftp` command. Defined macros are erased. Same as the `disconnect` subcommand.

copylocal Toggles local copy. copylocal defaults to Off. An effort is made by `ftp` to make sure you do not zero out a file by `ftp`'ing it to itself (same hostname, same pathname). Turning copylocal ON bypasses this check.

cr Strips the carriage-return character from a carriage-return and line-feed sequence when receiving records during ASCII-type file transfers. (The `ftp` command terminates each ASCII-type record with a carriage-return and line feed during file transfers.)

Records on non-AIX remote hosts can have single line feeds embedded in records. To distinguish these embedded line feeds from record delimiters, set the `cr` subcommand to Off. The `cr` subcommand toggles between On and Off.

delete RemoteFile Deletes the specified remote file.

debug [0 | 1] Toggles debug record keeping On and Off. Specify debug or debug 1 to print each command sent to the remote host and save the restart control file. Specify debug again, or debug 0, to stop the debug record keeping. The `Ctrl-C` key sequence also saves the restart control file.

dir [RemoteDirectory] [LocalFile] Writes a listing of the contents of the specified remote directory (RemoteDirectory) to the specified local file (LocalFile). If the RemoteDirectory parameter is not specified, the `dir` subcommand lists the contents of the current remote directory. If the LocalFile parameter is not specified or is a - (hyphen), the `dir` subcommand displays the listing on the local terminal.

disconnect Ends the file-transfer session but does not exit the `ftp` command. Defined macros are erased. Same as the `close` subcommand.

ebcdic Synonym for the type `ebcdic` subcommand.

exp_cmd Toggles between conventional and experimental protocol commands. The default is off.

file Synonym for the `struct file` subcommand.

form [carriage-control | non-print | telnet] Specifies the form of the file transfer. The `form` subcommand modifies the `type` subcommand to send the file transfer in the indicated form. Valid arguments are carriage-control, non-print, and telnet.

carriage-control Sets the form of the file transfer to carriage-control.

non-print Sets the form of the file transfer to non-print.

telnet   Sets the form of the file transfer to Telnet. Telnet is a Transmission Control Protocol/Internet Protocol (TCP/IP) protocol that opens connections to a system.

get RemoteFile [LocalFile]   Copies the remote file to the local host. If the LocalFile parameter is not specified, the remote filename is used locally and is altered by any settings made by the `case`, `ntrans`, and `nmap` subcommands. The `ftp` command uses the current settings for the `type`, `form`, `mode`, and `struct` subcommands while transferring the file.

glob   Toggles filename expansion (globbing) for the `mdelete`, `mget`, and `mput` subcommands. If globbing is disabled, filename parameters for these subcommands are not expanded. When globbing is enabled and a pattern-matching character is used in a subcommand that expects a single filename, results may be different than expected.

To preview the expansion of a directory name, use the `mls` subcommand:

```
mls RemoteFile
```

To transfer an entire directory subtree of files, transfer a `tar` archive of the subtree in binary form, rather than using the `mget` or `mput` subcommand.

hash   Toggles hash sign (#) printing. When the `hash` subcommand is on, the `ftp` command displays one hash sign for each data block (1024 bytes) transferred.

help [Subcommand]   Displays help information. See the `?` subcommand.

image   Synonym for the `type image` subcommand.

lcd [Directory]   Changes the working directory on the local host. If you do not specify a directory, the `ftp` command uses your home directory.

local M   Synonym for the `type local M` subcommand.

ls [RemoteDirectory] [LocalFile]   Writes an abbreviated file listing of a remote directory to a local file. If the RemoteDirectory parameter is not specified, the `ftp` command lists the current remote directory. If the LocalFile parameter is not specified or is a - (hyphen), the `ftp` command displays the listing on the local terminal.

macdef Macro   Defines a subcommand macro. Subsequent lines up to a null line (two consecutive line feeds) are saved as the text of the macro. Up to 16 macros, containing at most 4096 characters for all macros, can be defined. Macros remain defined until either redefined or a `close` subcommand is executed.

The $ (dollar sign) and (backslash) are special characters in ftp macros. A $ symbol followed by one or more numbers is replaced by the corresponding macro parameter on the invocation line (see the $ subcommand). A $ symbol followed by the letter i indicates that the macro is to loop, with the $i character combination being replaced by consecutive parameters on each pass.

The first macro parameter is used on the first pass, the second parameter is used on the second pass, and so on. A symbol prevents special treatment of the next character. Use the symbol to turn off the special meanings of the $ and /. (backslash period) symbols.

mdelete RemoteFiles   Expands the files specified by the RemoteFiles parameter at the remote host and deletes the remote files.

mdir [RemoteDirectories LocalFile]   Expands the directories specified by the RemoteDirectories parameter at the remote host and writes a listing of the contents of those directories to the file specified in the LocalFile parameter. If the RemoteDirectories parameter contains a pattern-matching character, the mdir subcommand prompts for a local file if none is specified. If the RemoteDirectories parameter is a list of remote directories separated by blanks, the last argument in the list must be either a local filename or a - (hyphen).

If the LocalFile parameter is - (hyphen), the mdir subcommand displays the listing on the local terminal. If interactive prompting is On (see the prompt subcommand), the ftp command prompts the user to verify that the last parameter is a local file and not a remote directory.

mget RemoteFiles   Expands the RemoteFiles parameter at the remote host and copies the indicated remote files to the current directory on the local host. See the glob subcommand for more information on filename expansion. The remote filenames are used locally and are altered by any settings made by the case, ntrans, and nmap subcommands. The ftp command uses the current settings for the form, mode, struct, and type subcommands while transferring the files.

mkdir [RemoteDirectory]   Creates the directory specified in the RemoteDirectory parameter on the remote host.

mls [RemoteDirectories LocalFile]   Expands the directories specified in the RemoteDirectories parameter at the remote host and writes an abbreviated file listing of the indicated remote directories to a local file. If the RemoteDirectories parameter contains a pattern-matching character, the mls subcommand prompts for a local file if none is specified. If the RemoteDirectories parameter is a list of remote directories separated by blanks, the last argument in the list must be either a local filename or a - (hyphen).

If the LocalFile parameter is - (hyphen), the `mls` subcommand displays the listing on the local terminal. If interactive prompting is on (see the prompt subcommand), the `ftp` command prompts the user to verify that the last parameter is a local file and not a remote directory.

mode [stream | block]   Sets file-transfer mode. If an argument is not supplied, the default is stream.

    block   Sets the file-transfer mode to block.

    stream   Sets the file-transfer mode to stream.

modtime   Shows the last modification time of the specified file on the remote machine. If the `ftp` command is not connected to a host prior to execution, the modtime subcommand terminates with an error message. The `ftp` command ignores parameter beyond the first parameter. If the FileName parameter is not specified, the `ftp` command prompts for a filename. If no filename is given, the `ftp` command sends a usage message to standard output and terminates the subcommand.

If the name specified by the FileName parameter exists on the remote host, and the name specifies a file, then the `ftp` command sends a message containing the last modification time of the file to standard output and terminates the subcommand. If FileName specifies a directory, the `ftp` command sends an error message to standard output and terminates the subcommand. Note: The `modtime` subcommand interprets metacharacters when allowed.

mput [LocalFiles]   Expands the files specified in the LocalFiles parameter at the local host and copies the indicated local files to the remote host. See the `glob` subcommand for more information on filename expansion. The local file-names are used at the remote host and are altered by any settings made by the `ntrans` and `nmap` subcommands. The `ftp` command uses the current settings for the `type`, `form`, `mode`, and `struct` subcommands while transferring the files.

nlist [RemoteDirectory][LocalFile]   Writes a listing of the contents of the specified remote directory (RemoteDirectory) to the specified local file (LocalFile). If the RemoteDirectory parameter is not specified, the `nlist` subcommand lists the contents of the current remote directory. If the LocalFile parameter is not specified or is a - (hyphen), the `nlist` subcommand displays the listing on the local terminal.

nmap [InPattern OutPattern]　　Turns the filename mapping mechanism On or Off. If no parameters are specified, filename mapping is turned Off. If parameters are specified, source filenames are mapped for the `mget` and `mput` subcommands and for the `get` and `put` subcommands when the destination filename is not specified. This subcommand is useful when the local and remote hosts use different file naming conventions or practices. Mapping follows the pattern set by the InPattern and OutPattern parameters.

The InPattern parameter specifies the template for incoming filenames, which may have already been processed according to the case and ntrans settings. The template variables $1 through $9 can be included in the InPattern parameter. All characters in the InPattern parameter other than the $ (dollar sign) and the \$ (backslash, dollar sign) define the values of the template variables. For example, if the InPattern parameter is $1.$2 and the remote filename is `my-data.dat`, the value of $1 is `mydata` and the value of $2 is `dat`.

The OutPattern parameter determines the resulting filename. The variables $1 through $9 are replaced by their values as derived from the InPattern parameter, and the variable $0 is replaced by the original filename. Additionally, the sequence [Sequence1,Sequence2] is replaced by the value of Sequence1, if Sequence1 is not null; otherwise, it is replaced by the value of Sequence2. For example, the subcommand:

```
nmap $1.$2.$3 [$1,$2].[$2,file]
```

would yield `myfile.data` from `myfile.data` or `myfile.data.old`, `myfile.file` from `myfile`, and `myfile.myfile` from `.myfile`. Use the \ (backslash) symbol to prevent the special meanings of the $ (dollar sign), [(left bracket),] (right bracket), and , (comma) in the OutPattern parameter.

non-print　　Synonym for the form `non-print` subcommand.

ntrans [InCharacters [OutCharacters]]　　Turns the filename character translation mechanism On and Off. If no parameters are specified, character translation is turned off. If parameters are specified, characters in source filenames are translated for `mget` and `mput` subcommands and for `get` and `put` subcommands when the destination filename is not specified.

This subcommand is useful when the local and remote hosts use different file naming conventions or practices. Character translation follows the pattern set by the InCharacters and OutCharacters parameter. Characters in a source filename matching characters in the InCharacters parameter are replaced by the corresponding characters in the OutCharacters parameter.

If the string specified by the InCharacters parameter is longer than the string specified by the OutCharacters parameter, the characters in the InCharacters parameter are deleted if they have no corresponding character in the OutCharacters parameter.

open HostName [Port]   Establishes a connection to the FTP server at the host specified by the HostName parameter. If the optional port number is specified, the `ftp` command attempts to connect to a server at that port. If the automatic login feature is set (that is, the -n flag was not specified on the command line), the `ftp` command attempts to log in the user to the FTP server.

You must also have a `$HOME/.netrc` file with the correct information in it and the correct permissions set. The `.netrc` file must be in your home directory.

prompt   Toggles interactive prompting. If interactive prompting is on (the default), the `ftp` command prompts for verification before retrieving, sending, or deleting multiple files during the `mget`, `mput`, and `mdelete` subcommands. Otherwise, the `ftp` command acts accordingly on all files specified.

proxy [Subcommand]   Executes an `ftp` command on a secondary control connection. This subcommand allows the `ftp` command to connect simultaneously to two remote FTP servers for transferring files between the two servers. The first `proxy` subcommand should be an open subcommand to establish the secondary control connection. Enter the `proxy ?` subcommand to see the other `ftp` subcommands that are executable on the secondary connection.

The following subcommands behave differently when prefaced by the `proxy` subcommand:

- The `open` subcommand does not define new macros during the automatic login process.
- The `close` subcommand does not erase existing macro definitions.
- The `get` and `mget` subcommands transfer files from the host on the primary connection to the host on the secondary connection.
- The `put`, `mput`, and `append` subcommands transfer files from the host on the secondary connection to the host on the primary connection.
- The `restart` subcommand can be handled by the proxy command.
- The `status` subcommand displays accurate information.

File transfers require that the FTP server on the secondary connection must support the PASV (passive) instruction.

put LocalFile [RemoteFile]   Stores a local file on the remote host. If you do not specify the RemoteFile parameter, the `ftp` command uses the local filename to name the remote file, and the remote filename is altered by any settings made by the `ntrans` and `nmap` subcommands. The `ftp` command uses the current settings for the `type`, `form`, `mode`, and `struct` subcommands while transferring the files.

pwd   Displays the name of the current directory on the remote host.

quit   Closes the connection and exits the `ftp` command. Same as the `bye` subcommand.

quote String   Sends the string specified by the String parameter verbatim to the remote host. Execute the `remotehelp` or `quote help` subcommand to display a list of valid values for the String parameter. Note: "Quoting" commands that involve data transfers can produce unpredictable results.

record   Synonym for the `struct record` subcommand.

recv RemoteFile [LocalFile]   Copies the remote file to the local host. Same as the `get` subcommand.

reinitialize   Reinitializes an `ftp` session by flushing all I/O and allowing transfers to complete. Resets all defaults as if a user had just started an `ftp` session without logging in to a remote host.

remotehelp [Subcommand]   Requests help from the remote `ftp` server.

rename FromName ToName   Renames a file on the remote host.

reset   Clears the reply queue. This subcommand resynchronizes the command parsing.

restart get | put | append   Restarts a file transfer at the point where the last checkpoint was made. To run successfully, the subcommand must be the same as the aborted subcommand, including structure, type, and form. Valid arguments are `get`, `put`, and `append`.

rmdir RemoteDirectory   Removes the remote directory specified by the RemoteDirectory parameter at the remote host.

runique (ReceiveUnique)   Toggles the facility for creating unique filenames for local destination files during `get` and `mget` subcommands. If this facility is Off (the default), the `ftp` command overwrites local files. Otherwise, if a local file has the same name as that specified for a local destination file, the `ftp` command modifies the specified name of the local destination file.

send LocalFile [RemoteFile]   Stores a local file on the remote host. Same as the `put` subcommand.

sendport   Toggles the use of FTP PORT instructions. By default, the `ftp` command uses a PORT instruction when establishing a connection for each data transfer. When the use of PORT instructions is disabled, the `ftp` command does not use PORT instructions for data transfers. The PORT instruction is useful when dealing with FTP servers that ignore PORT instructions while incorrectly indicating the instructions have been accepted.

site Args   Displays or sets the idle time-out period, displays or sets the file-creation `umask`, or changes the permissions of a file, using the `chmod` command. Possible values for the Args parameter are `umask` and `chmod`.

size   RemoteFile Displays the size, in bytes, of the remote file specified by the RemoteFile parameter.

status   Displays the current status of the `ftp` command as well as the status of the subcommands.

stream   Synonym for the mode stream subcommand.

struct [file | record]   Sets the data transfer structure type. Valid arguments are file and record.

file   Sets the data-transfer structure type to file.

record   Sets the data-transfer structure type to record.

sunique (Send/Store Unique)   Toggles the facility for creating unique filenames for remote destination files during put and mput subcommands. If this facility is off (the default), the `ftp` command overwrites remote files. Otherwise, if a remote file has the same name as that specified for a remote destination file, the remote FTP server modifies the name of the remote destination file. Note that the remote server must support the STOU instruction.

system   Shows the type of operating system running on the remote machine.

telnet   Synonym for the form `telnet` subcommand.

tenex   Synonym for the type `tenex` subcommand.

trace   Toggles packet tracing.

type [ascii | binary | ebcdic | image | local M | tenex]   Sets the file-transfer type. Valid arguments are ascii, binary, ebcdic, image, local M, and tenex. If an argument is not specified, the current type is printed. The default type is ascii; the binary type can be more efficient than ascii.

ascii   Sets the file-transfer type to network ASCII. This type is the default. File transfer may be more efficient with binary-image transfer. See the binary argument for further information.

binary   Sets the file-transfer type to binary image. This type can be more efficient than an ASCII transfer.

ebcdic   Sets the file-transfer type to EBCDIC.

image   Sets the file-transfer type to binary image. This type can be more efficient than an ASCII transfer.

local M   Sets the file-transfer type to local. The M parameter defines the decimal number of bits per machine word. This parameter does not have a default.

tenex   Sets the file-transfer type to that needed for TENEX machines.

user User [Password] [Account]   Identifies the local user (User) to the remote FTP server. If the Password or Account parameter is not specified and the remote server requires it, the ftp command prompts for the password or account locally. If the Account parameter is required, the ftp command sends it to the remote server after the remote login process completes. Note: Unless automatic login is disabled by specifying the -n flag on the command line, the ftp command sends the User, Password, and Account parameters automatically for the initial connection to the remote server. You also need a .netrc file in your home directory in order to issue an automatic login.

verbose   Toggles verbose mode. When the verbose mode is on (the default), the ftp command displays all responses from the remote FTP server. Additionally, the ftp command displays statistics on all file transfers when the transfers complete.

ftpd **Daemon**

PURPOSE

Provides the server function for the Internet FTP protocol.

SYNTAX

Note: The ftpd daemon is normally started by the inetd daemon. It can also be controlled from the command line, using SRC commands.

```
/usr/sbin/ftpd [ -d ] [ -k ] [ -l ] [ -t TimeOut ]
[ -T MaxTimeOut ] [ -s ] [ -u OctalVal ]
```

DESCRIPTION

The /usr/sbin/ftpd daemon is the DARPA Internet File Transfer Protocol (FTP) server process. The ftpd daemon uses the Transmission Control Protocol (TCP) to listen at the port specified with the ftp command service specification in the /etc/ services file.

Changes to the `ftpd` daemon can be made using the System Management Interface Tool (SMIT) or System Resource Controller (SRC), by editing the `/etc/inetd.conf` or `/etc/services` file. Entering `ftp` at the command line is not recommended. The `ftpd` daemon is started by default when it is uncommented in the `/etc/inetd.conf` file.

The `inetd` daemon gets its information from the `/etc/inetd.conf` file and the `/etc/ services` file. If you change the `/etc/inetd.conf` or `/etc/services` file, run the `refresh -s inetd` or `kill -1 InetdPID` command to inform the `inetd` daemon of the changes to its configuration files.

The `ftpd` daemon expands filenames according to the conventions of the `csh` command. This command allows you to use such metacharacters as the * (asterisk), the ? (question mark), [ ] (left and right brackets), { } (left and right braces), and the ~ (tilde).

Before the `ftpd` daemon can transfer files for a client process, it must authenticate the client process. The `ftpd` daemon authenticates client processes according to these rules:

- The user must have a password in the password database, `/etc/security/passwd`. (If the user's password is not null, the client process must provide that password.)

- The user name must not appear in the `/etc/ftpusers` file.

- The user's login shell must appear in the shells attribute of the `/etc/security/ login.cfg` file.

- If the user name is anonymous or `ftp`, an anonymous FTP account must be defined in the password file. In this case, the client process is allowed to login using any password. By convention, the password is the name of the client host. The `ftpd` daemon takes special measures to restrict access by the client process to the anonymous account.

File Transfer Protocol Subtree Guidelines.   When handling an anonymous FTP user, the server performs the `chroot` command in the home directory of the FTP user account. For greater security, implement the following rules when you construct the FTP subtree:

    `~ftp`   Make the home directory owned by root and mode r-xr-xr-x (555).

    `~ftp/bin`   Make this directory owned by the root user and unwritable by anyone. The `ls` program must be present in this directory to support the `list` command. This program should have mode 111.

~ftp/etc   Make this directory owned by the root user and unwritable by anyone.

~ftp/pub   Make this directory mode 777 and owned by ftp. Users should then place files that are to be accessible through the anonymous account in this directory.

Note: The shell script /usr/samples/tcpip/anon.ftp uses the above rules to set up the anonymous ftp account for you.

The server must run as the root user to create sockets with privileged port numbers. The server maintains an effective user ID of the logged-in user, reverting to the root user only when binding addresses to sockets.

FLAGS

-l   Sends logging information about ftpd daemon operations to the syslogd daemon. If you specify the -l flag, you must edit the /etc/syslog.conf file and add the following entry:

daemon.info FileName

If you do not edit the /etc/syslog.conf file, no messages are produced. After changing the /etc/syslog.conf file, run the refresh -s syslogd command or kill -1 SyslogdPID command to inform the syslogd daemon of the changes to its configuration file. For more information about debug levels, refer to the /etc/syslog.conf file.

-t   TimeOut logs out inactive sessions after the number of seconds specified by the TimeOut variable. The default limit is 15 minutes (900 seconds).

-T   MaxTimeOut logs out inactive client sessions after a maximum number of seconds specified by the MaxTimeOut variable. The default limit is 2 hours (7200 seconds).

-s   Turns on socket-level debugging.

-u   OctalVal Sets the ftpd daemon's umask. The OctalVal variable must be specified as an octal value to define the umask. The default umask is an octal value of 027, which results in file permissions of rw-r———.

Index